Praise for Getting High

'A beautiful meditation on flight, memory and meaning in a world still struggling to come to terms with the loss of the Most High'

Simon Critchley, author of BOWIE and MEMORY THEATRE, Hans Jonas Professor of Philosophy, The New School, New York

—

'A fascinating book, using personal history and cultural archeology to provide a revelatory insight: that our various forms of "getting high" are ultimately about the same thing'

Andrew Smith, author of MOONDUST and TOTALLY WIRED

—

'The ability to craft a such beautifully coherent story out of so many disparate worlds is a truly rare gift. *Getting High* is Brewin at his best'

Tad Delay, author of GOD IS UNCONSCIOUS

—

'Grounds the vertiginous story of how we accomplished the super-human heights that killed God within a moving personal narrative. Honest, accessible and compelling.'

Katharine Moody, author of RADICAL THEOLOGY

—

'Mr Toad's wild ride is nothing compared to this journey through psychedelia, space and consciousness. Every twist offers up new thoughts about how to live beyond the ache for transcendence, where real life begins.'

Barry Taylor, Brehm Centre for the Arts, Los Angeles

Getting High

High

**A Savage Journey to the Heart
of the Dream of Flight**

Getting High

High

A Savage Journey to the Heart of the Dream of Flight

Kester Brewin

@kesterbrewin | kesterbrewin.com

First published 2016

Copyright © 2016 by Kester Brewin

Vaux Publishing
5 Fitzroy Gardens
London
SE19 2NP

vaux.net/books

ISBN 978 0 9935628 0 8

Cover image © NASA

For my father, and my son
For my mother, and my daughter

but mostly, for

Mike and Becca

who flew from the same nest,
but with so much more style

[I might be wrong]

Contents

'Before lighting out, before this hop to the Moon and outward bound, we had better look into some of this'
- Saul Bellow, Mr Sammler's Planet

We are all born flightless, every one.

Despite great longing, despite the fact that the majority—me included—would choose flight as our superpower, after so many thousands of years each of us still drops into the world smooth-skinned and featherless.

From that moment on the ground suckles us to itself. Gravity calcifies in our bones and we do not like it, so our fathers make us laugh by swinging us into the air.

When we grow heavy they let us down and we turn instead to gods to lift us, only later understanding that if we are going to be able to fly we will have to forge our wings for ourselves.

This is the story of our yearning for transcendence.

This is a story of ecstasy, religion, and technology.

This is also my story.

Simon Peter and the Fall of Simon Magus
Benozzo Gozzoli, Florence, 1460s

1. Lift Off

In 1978 I was 6 years old, living in a land of flat caps and deep coal mines. I'd never set foot in an airport, let alone been on an actual aeroplane; the tower of the village church—so squat now I look back at photographs—was not only the highest place I'd ever been, but pretty much the highest place I could imagine. That was about to change.

For my birthday that year Mum and Dad took me and some friends into Sheffield, some 15 miles away, to see a matinee of *Star Wars*. Nobody used the word 'blockbuster' then. All I knew was that the queue was so monstrously long when we arrived that I was sure that we wouldn't get in. The snakes twisted in my stomach and I sealed my lips to stop the worries getting out. I had started to have to do that quite a lot. It was becoming clear that there was something not right with my older sister, and my brother—the eldest—was being bullied at school. He'd become withdrawn and unhappy, finding best release in goading and taunting me. Only later I found out that he'd been persecuted because of our Dad's job. He was vicar of the church and though a strong man, this line of work apparently made him weak and feline. Other people's dads sweated underground in the local mines or wrestled animals on the surrounding farms. They didn't wear dresses.

My Mum wore dresses. Dad was out a lot in the evenings, and sometimes she popped out too to see a neighbour, and that made my stomach twist more because even though I was only 6 the whole playground hummed with talk about women in nearby towns going missing and then being found dead, their clothes all torn by a man they called the Ripper.

Unable to put any of this into words, a nagging sense that my parents had enough to be coping with, I did what I thought Jesus would do and swallowed down my thoughts, sending them back, gradually turning my young guts to lead.

I needn't have worried; the cinema queue did begin to move and miraculously we all snaked inside, past the glass booth that spat our tickets out of a steel desk and on into the huge screen. The lights went down and the orchestra struck up and the words scrolled and faded to the blackness of space as the largest, most awesome spaceship floated into the frame and thundered slowly through it. As the vast propulsion engines finally emerged in a blinding burst of light I was completely blown away.

3

No planes flew over my house. I couldn't have told you if there was an airport within 100 miles, but that afternoon at the cinema I became gripped by flight. I was a boy filling up with worries, a child with a foreboding sense that there were multiple strands in my life beginning to tie me down, but as Luke Skywalker lifted away from the wreckage of his bombed-out home and off into space I was gifted a new hope, a force I secured as a concealed weapon, one that I believed someday, at some time, would be my salvation.

—

Lifting us above our lives, flight changes us. But flying is strange. It is unnatural, and because of this, though we think we understand the ways in which we have been transformed, the new perspectives it offers often come accompanied by shock. When we leave the ground we are disturbed, and when we land again, though we might not quite know the precise dimensions, we do so altered.

It was a subtly different lad who walked out of that Yorkshire cinema.

Once Luke had been thrust into the above he could never return to his old life, just as once a man named Harvey Kling had flown to Japan, he could never return to the comfortable vision of the United States that he'd lifted away from. His story is worth telling.

In the Spring of 1970, just as the wildness of the 60s climbed over into the uneasy decade of the years to come, Kling, an American man remarkable only for his thorough ordinariness, eased his comfortable slacks out of his airline seat, hung his sensibly-organised bag from his shoulder and took his wife by the elbow as they made the short walk to the cabin door. They had just landed in Osaka, going to visit *Expo '70*.

Flight perhaps still seemed miraculous to a man like him. He was a good Christian of course, but he was sure Jesus wouldn't mind him saying that climbing aboard an airliner in America and stepping out into Japan just a few hours later sure felt like something from the Acts of the Apostles.

At the vast exhibition complex, Kling and his wife had to stop regularly as local Japanese shook their hands and wanted autographs simply because they were Americans. With its racing cars, a life-sized reproduction of the Apollo 11 landing site, and a large piece of actual Moon rock, the American stand was where they—and everyone else—headed. The queues were huge, but they finally turned the last corner, and here they were.

"There was the American flag," he later wrote, "the first one we had witnessed in quite some time. What a feeling!" But what was this? Who were those men? In an instant his joy curdled, like a White Russian gone wrong. "Up on the platform near the entrance were three hippies, heavily bearded, unclean, in mod clothes, singing rock music."[1]

He jostled his way through the turbulence to confront these louts and stop them ruining the spectacle. But as one of them brushed their long locks over their shoulder, he explained to Kling that they were part of the Expo, 'Telling it like it is about modern America.'

Kling spluttered and fumed and marched back to his hotel, drafting a ballistic missive to Richard Nixon himself.

"Believe me, Mr. President, you are not 'telling it like it is' for if you know anything about America you know that these people do not exemplify or represent us as we are."

A White House post clerk opened the letter and passed it to his supervisor, who thought America's reputation in Japan a serious matter and passed it on up again to the Head of Communications. He huffed and wondered how the hell was he meant to know who these goons were, and shoved it over to the organisers of the American pavilion. There, Eugene Rosenfeld, the assistant director of the United States Information Agency, wrote back to Mr Kling, the letter hitting his Denver doormat like a hydrogen bomb, brutally shattering his idea of what his nation was—and should be—in the process.

"We believe you would like to know about these 'hippies' in the photo you sent us. They are: Mike Rivers, a graduate engineer in electronics who works for the U.S. Navy; Andy Wallace, a graduate in English literature of George Washington University [who] lectures on American songs and American folklore; Jonathan Eberhart, a graduate of Harvard University who is the Aero Space editor for Science Magazine."

Flying to the Land of the Rising Sun, a man was forced finally to confront the fact that the sun had apparently set on the kind of nation he thought he lived in. The upright and honourable place that had bravely conquered space turned out to have been aided in doing so by a bunch of scruffy hippies who looked as if they probably smoked pot.

As Harvey sat reading the letter, head in hands at his desk, he could be forgiven for wondering aloud what in Christ's name had happened.

10 years before, as the brown tweed of the 1950s was ripped away to reveal the bare flesh of a brand new decade, all of this would have been unthinkable. 10 years before, *no one*—let alone any American—had ever been into space. 10 years before the idea that men with long hair and beards could be ambassadors for American progress would have been absurd.

In the blink of an eye the country he'd known had gone. As to *where* it had gone, his excitement at taking a jet to Japan now came back to haunt him: in all manner of ways—aeronautically, pharmacologically, spiritually and technologically—the generations beneath his own had lifted away. America had got high.

He may have flown at 30,000 feet, but these young guns seem to have blasted as high as the ascended Christ himself and, as far as he could surmise, this sudden ability to look down and gaze on things from god's own perspective had messed with their minds.

Getting high had sent shockwaves through their sense of what it was to be human. Beards and long hair. God dammit, may be flying to the Moon hadn't been such a great idea after all. He blamed the liberals on both coasts. This kind of nonsense didn't play in Middle America, not in the church he went to, where sin was still sin and men had short hair and flowery blouses were for ladies, and young people didn't get above their station.

—

I'm sat at my desk thinking about Kling. When I'd first unearthed his story I'd laughed at the outrage and confusion rising from his sensible shoes into his practical trousers and up through his sober-coloured shirt. Now, buffeted by a crisis in my own life, I knew something of what he'd been through and none of it was a laughing matter.

Born in 1972, just after his fateful visit to Japan, I too had missed the thundering lift-off of the 60s. Like him, its turbulence had only hit me afterwards, echoes of it sounding all through my young life, the bright colours of it still glowing, the alluring taste and smell of it lingering, complex and bittersweet.

Brought up surrounded by religion, like Kling I'd sent indignant missives to a Higher Authority who never replied in person, and I too was now being forced to accept that the world wasn't ordered how I'd seen it.

Without quite knowing why, through the prism of this decade I loved, I'd recently begun to write about flight. The more I delved into world of the 60s the more there came creeping an understanding of how shaken my own life had been by the quest to get high. With a Klingian sense of shock I realised that I'd begun a history of altitude because, subconsciously, I hadn't been able to process my own desperate, life-long attempts to leave the ground, hadn't dealt with the vast echoing spaces of the empty hangars of my heart.

In a tiny rented flat, sitting staring at my computer screen, I finally have to admit it: I'm not flying, I'm falling. When I'd been able to focus only on the screen in front of me I could pretend it was all clear skies, but with a wider view suddenly torn open, my life is revealed as an angry mess, my wings strafed, my fuselage damaged, my engines spluttering and smoking.

I turn a notebook over, a scribbled page of dates and arrows. Condensed like this I can understand Kling's trauma. In the long history of things the move into the above happened phenomenally quickly. If we compressed the story of modern humans into that wonderful Moon-landing day of July 20th, 1969, we'd have spent every moment of it until less than two minutes to midnight almost permanently rooted to the earth, unable to lift ourselves off the ground further than the low ceiling of a bedroom. Any departures were short and unremarkable: the world high jump record still stands at around 2.5m, not even double my height, a trajectory composing less than 1.5 seconds of flight. It wouldn't have been until around 20 seconds before midnight that Kling's parents would have heard about the Wright brothers demonstrating the first heavier-than-air flying machine, and only at 4 seconds to midnight would mankind have first risen in thunder aboard a rocket ship, piercing space, the sky no longer the limit.

That we'd made it there at all was remarkable enough, but what had these high achievements *meant*? This was the question that fascinated me.

Through this long history it was clear that there had always been a fervent desperation to touch the above. The unknown was the jet engine of desire: because we had to wait so long to achieve flight, this one thing that we could not do we filled with great mystery and meaning. We became convinced that 'up there' contained the part of us that was missing, the part that meant that, without it, we were destined always to be inadequate and fall short. Achieving altitude became less a challenge of ingenuity than a means of fulfilling a spiritual quest: the unknown above became about the unknown within.

I knew this was true for me. Having been infected by *Star Wars* I had to wait until my mid-teens before my own inaugural flight, and this enduring physical grounding seemed inextricably connected to the writhing undergrowth of unknowns that lashed my early childhood and had left me stumbling and tripping for decades to come.

When I did finally lift away the myths I had loaded onto this event were so large that it couldn't possibly bear them. Just as for Skywalker, just as for Kling, flight brought rupture for me too. So when I flick through notebooks and sources, what keeps grabbing me is not simply the history of our quest for altitude, but what happens to us once we achieve it. What happens when flying ends up tearing down the world we thought we knew and extinguishing the sun we thought would always sustain us?

Scattered around my desk are the raw nuggets I've mined about the deep and ancient stories where this had taken place, stories from the Renaissance to the Enlightenment through World Wars and on into the 60s and beyond. Yet now, to my horror, I'm faced with the fact that if I'm ever going to understand how I'd ended up on such a fucked-up trajectory myself, I'm going to have to go back to my own Dark Ages, back to *Star Wars*, to the black-box data of my own early childhood and the things that fuelled my attempts to fly from it ever since.

—

Psychogeology: like the fist-sized piece of Moon rock that had awed the crowds in Japan, ancient grey-white stones formed my own past too, hewn, shaped and piled into the small hilltop church, 12th century in its oldest parts, a huge spire added later with a full peal of bells.

It stands in the centre of the village, our house a large, draughty vicarage abutting the graveyard. Down below the surrounding lawn, through the lychgate, terraced cottages huddle from the A57 trunk road that sends lorries shuddering into Sheffield, or off over the Pennines to Manchester and Liverpool.

I remember the sweet shop and the farms, primary school a short walk, the deep cut of the railway line further along through the scrub. My first school trip: a class walk down to The Leeds Arms, to see how a pub is run, all smoke and the sweet sticky smell of beer as we gather inside and go down to the cellar. We went back and started one ourselves—The One Inn—and later had another class outing to see my friend's singing dog. There's a photo of me from the local paper, smiling, holding a young piglet. We'd moved on from pubs and started a project looking at how the farm worked just next door to the school.

There was greater beauty on the hills further on, but we didn't go there often. This was ordinary Yorkshire. Modest people, Klings one and all, labouring at what they could in the week, a climb up to church for some still on Sundays.

It was here in this ancient place of worship that I was initiated into the story that we told about ourselves, one recounted in this same place for over 800 years, that we had been created 'a little lower than the angels,' but 'with all the animals under our feet.' This was a confusing idea for a boy already struggling to understand the tectonic fissures that were straining his family's foundations. This was my Dad's first time being in charge of his own parish and the workload was relentless, the resistance to his attempts to enliven the church enormous. Just before we'd moved to the village from central Sheffield his father had died very suddenly, and now that we were here there was grief for this loss, and my grandmother distraught and all of this accentuated by the sadness my mum felt for the loss of her friends back in the city. The vicarage was so large that my brother and sister and I were frightened. We held onto my mum's skirts as she tried to build a home while Dad was off doing God's work building a kingdom far off, above in heaven.

We joined him on Sundays. Dressed in hopelessly large choir robes, fidgeting in the pew, fighting an urge to lash out at something, I felt a great deal less than angelic. A longing look out of the leaded windows showed plenty of creatures enjoying their Sunday morning more than I was, flying and swooping in the treetops.

After church I sometimes opened the narrow wooden door in the narthex and twisted myself up the spiral stone steps to a perfectly square room above where long ringers' ropes dangled, a ladder rising higher still through a wooden trapdoor into the bell tower. It was like being shrunk down and placed inside a wooden clock, everywhere stuffed with mechanisms that threatened to break from their stillness and turn in loud ratchets to deafen you with hammer strikes.

Edging around the eight bronze beasts that turned over and woke on each hour, through slatted openings I could peer at the village laid out below like the model railway I had at home, wondering at the men who had built this high, who had laboured all those hundreds of years ago to mark this special place, ascending fragile scaffolds, hauling huge stones to this hilltop site, risking so much with so little protection to raise this temple so far off the ground.

They had done what had been done for thousands of years before them. Stretching back to Babel and beyond, we have always built up towards the sky as far as our technologies have allowed us. With piled rocks and wooden poles we have poked at the underbelly of the above, doing so from whatever hills and mountains offered the best head start.

The high places—churches, temples, totems—were built as places where we focused our human struggles and negotiated the boundaries of our existence. They were where we willed fertility and grieved death, where we prayed for protection from enemies and willed the gods to lift their curses. They were places where we reached up, and thus stood as symbols of our frustration that we couldn't ourselves rise up, couldn't escape the painful reality of our fragile, vulnerable existence on the ground.

Paradoxically, accompanying this was a holy fear of height. In *Mountains of the Mind*, Robert Macfarlane notes how early travellers being led over the Alps would do so blindfolded to prevent them being terrified. 'It was obvious from the nausea, dizziness and headaches they experienced that there was a bad fit between height and human body.'[2] The first to make it to the Himalayas were surprised to find that locals weren't keen to help them ascend. To do so would have been sacrilegious.

High spires and mountain temples: there is a mixture of worship and exasperation in these sacred sites. Reaching for the heavens, we simultaneously jump in frustration. Why, having given us so much, didn't you also give us wings? If we were stewards of all of creation, why did so much of it remain out of reach? Why must our soles remain shackled to the surface?

These same frustrations played out each Sunday in Yorkshire. In church Dad would tell again the story of our higher status and then afterwards, as we gathered round a roasted bird, one of the millions of flies from the neighbouring pig farm would lift off from the kitchen wall, achieving altitudes utterly out of reach, buzzing, hovering above us. Out of his vestments, Dad would climb on his chair, rolled up paper in hand, cursing, defeated, just the latest in a line of conscious, intelligent apes stretching back millions of years who'd jumped, flapped hands at these damned bluebottles, unable to get to them, thinking: how can that which is so superior in mind be so limited in flesh?

—

When I got home from the cinema I slipped on a new pair of trainers that I'd been given for my birthday. I thought they were awesome. They had a *sponge wedge* in the heel. These shoes would lift me off the ground. We didn't have money, or a spaceship, but the vicarage had the largest garden in the village. With an early Beatles record playing in the background I opened the back door. The heady smells of the warm evening hit me, the mown grass from the lawn and the pig shit from the farm over the fence, Mum's rose-beds all topped with manure that was kept piled next to the vegetable patch she and Dad toiled over to keep us fed. I opened that door and stepped out, truly believing that with my sponge wedge trainers tightly laced to my mercurial feet I would jump up and fly, up and away from my the growing anxiety, up and away from the pits and the filth and worries about the Ripper.

Flight: a twin-engined word carrying ideas of escape, fleeing the place of pain and lifting away into the air. To fly is to flee. It is to move along an axis that confounds any obstacle put in front of us. This is different to running away; we get high when absconding along the horizontal is not enough.

Hemmed in on all sides, Superman, Spiderman, the Jedi Knights— all of them surprise their enemies with a vertical move into the air. When you can't run away, you have to move upwards. You have to get high.

I later saw the same reading Peter Pan. The story opened in an enormous house, with Wendy in a place of great anxiety. She was in the nether-land of childhood, needing to cross over to maturity, but didn't know how. Her siblings were helpless and her parents absent and she—along with the family's dog—had been left in charge. Unable to see any way out of the suffocating Edwardian life that lay ahead of her, she took the unageing, undying Pan's hand and simply lifted away.

Haven't we all dreamt of being able to do that?

When I was 3 I'd been playing a superheroes game with a friend, and while our mums had drunk tea and dunked digestives in the kitchen below, I'd given this girl a mighty shove at the top of the flight of stairs—actually sent her flying—and broken both of her legs.

Despite this inauspicious track record, returning from *Star Wars* I leapt from the door and ran and leapt again, Billy Elliott long before Billy Elliott, springing and leaping all over that garden, hands in the air reaching up, arms like an X-Wing, thumbs firing lasers, all of me desperate for flight.

Seeing with each tiring breath that the emerging stars above were no closer, nor the ground below any further away, in that hilltop garden next to the church I eventually sank, lay back on the cooling lawn in resignation, looking at the spire stretching above me, annoyed at the rooks in the trees and the birds settling on the eaves of the barn, realising that the force was not yet strong enough, that I was stuck here for now.

I got up after a while to return to the house, leaving a little piece of my infancy behind flattened on the grass. I wasn't Luke Skywalker, I wasn't going to be able to fly, but though I could barely sense it, I was having to steel myself for a great battle against a dark force that was gathering. Like Luke taking Ben Kenobi's hand, his home destroyed, when the time came I would have to be ready for flight, by whatever means presented itself.

—

Wednesday 18th February

I am in hospital for the second time with Anorexia Nervosa.

I'm sure I will never ever forget for as long as I live how terribly, terribly unhappy I am.

I also feel very, very, very lonely for my Mummy and Daddy are only allowed to come and see me every other day, and I just cannot bear spending another whole day without them.

This was what had been coming. Over the next year, like a vast black hawk, the wings of this illness spread over us, its talons pinning us to the ground, separated, terrified.

The nurses are very kind to me, but I feel terribly frightened. I pray and pray all day every day in my mind that I won't have to stay here as long as last time, which was about 10 weeks and I'm really, really sure I will never forget how terribly happy I will be on my journey home with Mummy. I feel too unhappy, lonely and frightened to explain it to you.

When my sister wrote this, already into her second admission for a chronic eating disorder, she was just 10 years old.

My own daughter is around the same age that my sister was then. It seems impossible that, before this diary, she had already been hospitalised once before—and that after a long period during which the local GP had scoffed and sent my parents away, saying it couldn't possibly be anorexia, she was far too young.

She was. She was far too young. Far too young to understand or process the psychic storm that had somehow decided to conduct itself through her tiny body.

It ripped at us all, but my sister had somehow channelled its ire most powerfully. Too young to avoid capture, she'd then embarked on the most drastic escape plan of all, one that she documented in surgical detail over the pages of a notebook from the Victoria and Albert Museum. Lightening by the day, shedding ounce by dangerous ounce, she would shrink her self so completely that she could slip her chains, turn herself into a skin-taut frame that might glide up on the breeze and disappear like a cracked autumn leaf.

This was the blow that shattered me. This was the force that sent me flying.

Reading it now, each sentence of the diary comes at me like an electric shock. It turned up just a few months ago in a box my sister had been given during a clear out of my parents' loft. With prescience and insight so typical of her, she'd photocopied it and sent it over to me with a note explaining that she thought I might find it useful, given what I was writing about. I've been her brother too long to ask how—having told not a soul about the project I was embarking on—she knew that I had actually been hunting through these same shadowed corners of my mental attic, trying to remember details of these violently interrupted, locust-ravaged years.

From Sheffield Children's Hospital, she was moved to Shirle Hill, an adolescent psychiatric facility that I can only recall as one of the most unnerving and unkind places I have ever been to. She was under the care of one Doctor Thorpe, whose idea of treating a frightened, traumatised 10 year old was to berate her for being a naughty girl who shouldn't be so bloody-minded, who would be punished unless she ate.

I think fat people look ugly too—his writing next to one of her entries—but *sometimes* *they are very nice people. Is there anything else you want to tell me?*

I understand now: she was writing it all for him. Telling him in no uncertain terms how lonely she was and how much she missed and loved her parents, with whom she was blissfully happy.

We were blisteringly unhappy. We had been visited by a terrible evil. It stuck to us, ripped us from one another, the force of it creating a rupture so large neither my small arms nor hers could reach across to find anyone to hold us. My Mum missed her friends, my father was working all hours while grieving his father and struggling with a bereft and constantly weeping mother. We were all in the dark, lonely, frightened by the things that had befallen us, each of us straining, doing anything we could to get out from under it. To fly. To flee. To lift away.

I don't want to see the doctor for he frightens me such a terrible lot. I'm going to go home sometime and I'll never ever come back again, I hate it all so much!

To her credit, she did manage this, and did come home. But she found us living in ruins. The bullying my brother suffered had continued and, while away on a Scout camp, as the leaders laughed and looked on, some of the same boys had put him through a mock crucifixion.

Where we'd once laughed and watched Dad swat flies, as my sister had worsened the kitchen became a minefield we all edged to each mealtime, the one-time heart of our home now a frightening, wire-strung and loaded table, detonation a risk with any tiny move.

I wanted to go ballistic.

I couldn't.

—

Hoping a change of geography would help, in 1981 we moved south to Buckinghamshire, to a beautiful, oak-panelled vicarage in Aylesbury, a gravelled bow drive and ornamental front garden. It was to be a fresh start for all of us. An old investment surprisingly came good and my brother was thrust off to boarding school near Bath where, to the relief of my parents, he expanded like Popeye on spinach, no one there or since thinking of messing with him.

In contrast, as if keeping the scales balanced, my sister worsened.

Saturday 23rd January

8am - glass of milk

12:30 - a pear

7:00 - pack of crisps

The milk perhaps has no less food value but to me it seemed less because it was a nice idea to think I hadn't had anything to eat.

There were hushed conversations and screaming arguments, the pleading for her to finish the diminishing portions on her plate, my brother away and the rest of us sat in the breakfast room off the kitchen, dad to the right, mum to the left, her opposite, me trapped by the window, staring at my empty plate and the curved knife on the cheeseboard.

She was admitted to Stoke Mandeville hospital, a sprawling maze of low buildings that felt more like an RAF airfield than a place to get well. I was thrilled and then frightened at Jimmy Saville creeping round the ward in his shell suit, coming over when I was visiting my sister and giving her an Easter egg.[3] I'd written to him a few years before wanting to be a train driver, and was now petrified that he might dig out the letter and reply and offer to fix this for me.

I wasn't old enough to understand any of what was going on. All I did know was that I was frightened to see Mum and Dad desperate with worry, tied up with journeys to hospitals and meetings with doctors who appeared to have no idea what to do. Weeks and months this went on, me walking myself up to my new school and letting myself in at the end of the day, through the side gate, in the back door, down the long hall past Dad's study, up past the heavy, turned balusters and the smell of wax polish and into my room. Lego. Model trains. Famous Five books. Sneaking down to the larder to prise open the old cake tin and smuggle up a Penguin.

The more she starved in hospital, the more the house became starved of oxygen, quiet and cold until she came back on short visits, when it would blow up until it burst.

In the midst, through these mists, once she'd finished her endless morning exercises she'd come down the stairs and we'd play badminton in the garden and she'd make me curl up with laughter with the characters she made up. 'Make way! Make way!' her top lip curled into her gums, 'Make way for Guthrum the King!'

9 o'clock: got my lunch ready and set off to the stables and ran round the yard looking at all the horses and saying hello to everyone. I then groomed Cinderella and when she was done had my lunch, tacked her up and got changed. Then we all went out for a ride.

There were good times. I sift my memories and find so much to be fond of. But then, oozing off the page come the unrepeatable passages, reminders of the arguments, the screaming matches, the endless late-night walks she took with my dad to burn off calories she simply didn't have; the biting, the hitting, the rough handling, the pinning down, the getting her back in the car to return her to the ward, the sound of the car on the long, bowed gravel drive, me pulling the blankets over my head, desperate for heat.

Grand and elegant, Edwardian sinks in each room, the house had a suite of electric bells that once summoned servants. They now hung in silence for more glamorous days to return.

For our part, we could hardly afford to heat it, let alone pay others to tend fires and cook. Each Sunday we would drive up into the woods to gather what fuel we could glean, piling sodden branches into the boot of the car to be dried in the garage and sawn into logs. On the coldest mornings I would wake with my breath steaming above me, ice clinging to the insides of my bedroom window, the water frozen in the plug hole. Each evening, after the church committee meetings held in the posh lounge, dad would heave a shovel into the grate of the open fire and tentatively carry the coals through into our living room, heaping them onto the low embers where we'd gather and kneel by the burning offering. An altar to heat, smoke rising, working its way up through the dark chimney to freedom above.

—

Why did we look up for answers? Why did we build upwards when we found ourselves at the limits of our experience?

Back in Yorkshire, descending from our hilltop vicarage and church, following the brook, after Sunday lunch we had often walked out to Anston Stones, designated a site of Special Scientific Interest because of the limestone gorges and ancient woodlands.

The stone was good, and had been mined to rebuild the Houses of Parliament after the fire of 1834. Deep down in the dank cut near to the railway was Dead Man's Cave. Stinking of piss and graffitied by older local kids, it had been excavated in the 60s and found to be a shelter for hunters 12,000 years ago, the debris of animal bones scattered in the dirt.

I hardly had language, almost no knowledge. All families have skeletons, and here were mine. Lying in my bed listening to my sister being taken away, in my barely-evolved mind it was in dark primeval places that I processed the pain. Starlight. Open fires. Troubled dreams. Aeons ago my ancestors climbed to high places to ask why crops had failed or why a loved one had been taken. Now as I grew gradually conscious of the situation my own questions were barely different, my own answers hardly more formed: the reasons for my suffering were tied up in the struggles of angels and demons from a beyond I could not fully comprehend.

—

Just as medieval men were raising up stones of that Yorkshire village church, far away the Muslim scholar Ibn Tufail was writing his novel *The Awakening of the Soul*, a 12th century parable about the birth of human consciousness. Tufail's protagonist is a young 'everyman' marooned on an island from birth and thus forced to reason things out about his life and world for himself. When he sees fire for the first time:

> *he noticed that it always tended upwards—he felt convinced that it was one of those celestial substances which he saw shining in the firmament.*[4]

It is a beautiful insight. Sat around a fire—without doubt the most powerful and dramatic technology our earliest forebears had—early man would have watched the licks of flame always reaching and straining the same way: upwards. Raising their eyes further they would see what the flames were rising to rejoin: far, far above were tiny distant lights, and one larger light. This, they concluded, must be evidence of a 'higher' life out of clumsy human reach, a place that all lights sought to return home to.

As the fire burned low and the night took hold, we lay on the earth to sleep, watching the display of rising embers, dreaming of one day rising ourselves and making the same journey closer to the light.

Consciousness the spark within us, the Promethean fire that separated us from the other animals, vivid dreams were its most powerful and complex gift. They were perhaps the earliest form of human flight; while we struggled daily with conflict, oppression, hunger and illness, in dreaming our minds allowed what had been tied down and suppressed to lift for a while into inner skies and find release.

When reality imprisons us we need fantasies to help us taste freedom. To escape the screams of my sister and shouts of my father I would go to my room and lift away into my head. I took myself to bed one night and found myself looking down at my own body lying curled on my blankets. I was an embryo and, though I was able to see myself, I was actually inside an egg. I knew that I had to extend my legs to break the shell, but I wasn't yet able to. It was a terribly lucid dream, one that hardly needed Freud's expertise to interpret. Things were enclosing around me, a carapace that both protected and imprisoned, one that I needed to be liberated from.

Only recently have I understood why the egg was important.

What hatches from eggs are birds. And birds can fly.

—

It was a playground for me, my brother and sister, but the graveyard around the hilltop Yorkshire church was a place only visited by others in moments of vast grief. We reached it through a wrought iron gate at the back of our garden, the entrance guarded by a stone angel stood high on a plinth, a young girl with wings, writing in a book.

High places aren't just places of worship, they are also places of pain, heights we scale to ask our deepest questions about suffering. There were weatherworn graves there for babies, tombs for young men taken in their prime. Death may be medically described as 'flatlining,' but it is flat in no other way. It travels along a vector perpendicular to the Earth. It is the suicide leap, falling from a great height, the descent of the guillotine blade, the cavern below the gallows' trapdoor, the judge's final words, the slam of his gavel, a dismissive flick of the hand then, 'take him down.'

We ritualise this falling, marking the defeat by death with a rite of moving into the below, each of us ending up boxed up, lowered into the earth on ground as high up as we can afford.

For those left behind, resistance to loss begins immediately, friends and relatives gathering round the descending coffin, casting eyes to heaven and sending up prayers of resurrection—of resurgence, of 'rising again'—the human lust for altitude undiminished despite, or because of, gravity's inevitable victory in pulling each of us down into the grave.

With the mining and the smoking and drinking there were plenty of funerals in Yorkshire. Not standing on ceremony, the flies from the pig farm next door would buzz round the graveside and my brother and sister and I would watch from safe distances as the people marched up through the lychgate. 'Lych': old English for corpse, and carrying their corpses the mourners would shake their heads, confounded again as they dropped them into the hole asking: why if we were the greatest beings on this Earth should we end up buried six feet under it?

No, the sentiment seemed to be. No, we deserve more.

Down, down, down into the darkness of the grave
Gently they go, the beautiful, the tender, the kind;
Quietly they go, the intelligent, the witty, the brave.
I know. But I do not approve. And I am not resigned.

—Dirge Without Music – Edna St. Vincent Millay

What I didn't appreciate was quite how close my sister was to joining them.

The doctor at the hospital on the child ward was beginning to say he could keep me no longer because my weight was going down and down and my hands and toes were really in danger of coming off.

So Mummy, me and Daddy went up to London, Great Ormond Street. The lady we saw was the hardest and firmest lady I had met. She said they wouldn't be kind and encourage me along. They were going to be very hard and strict. She frightened me.

In the room was a mirror. It was a mirror to us, but next door there was a man looking at us through it. He could see us but we couldn't see him. I didn't like this idea one little bit and afterwards Mummy told me she didn't like it either.

She was dying. Death was creeping in, beginning to grasp at her extremities. Yet, horrified at the Dickensian regime they found, hurt by the suggestion that her condition wasn't disconnected from the emotional atmosphere within which we'd grown up, my parents refused to allow her to be admitted. She returned to Stoke Mandeville, worsened, and was finally admitted to the Middlesex in London where she remained for 3 months, a 2 hour journey by train, the nest often left empty, save me left in it with no means of flight.

—

Our disapproval at death creates a complex relationship with the above. We look there for help and become convinced that that is where the answers lie, but also shake our fists at this force that has cursed us with flightlessness, with mortality, swearing that we will one day rise to the heavens, break in and take what we are owed.

Thus, thousands of years before achieving physical flight, we performed a profound and extraordinary mental leap. Reconciled for the time being to the fact of our persisting physical grounding, we lifted off instead into religion. Our growing, sparking, conscious minds bumped against the bone lids of our skulls and, unable to rise physically to the air, created elaborate myths about the inner, spiritual world: who could reach what heights, what celestial beings existed where, and what laws needed to be followed if we were to be welcomed on high.

For Romans and Greeks this led to the development of a highly sophisticated astrology: the interpretation of the heavenly lights. Movements in the Moon and stars were both portents of the future and a book of the past. Augurs examined as oracles the entrails of captured birds, the guts of creatures gifted with flight spilled for messages taken from the sky.

In the mythology of the Abrahamic religions whole hierarchies of angels were established, instant messengers, upgraded humans who were immortal, had wings, and shone bright like fire. The link between these creatures and us mere mortals were the priests and the mystics.

My father, I see now, was a part of one of these ancient castes. Up north, all week the miners in the village toiled deep underground and on Sundays it had been his job to try to lift them. Religions have always functioned as spiritual elevators, and this is what those lamp-lit, subterranean miners surfaced for each Sunday: a vision of a higher, lighter place. In the stone church, Dad did what all his predecessors had done before him: told stories laden with vectors, a baby who'd come down, spoken of great things and had now gone back up. At his birth, Magi. Men looking up to the stars in hope of discerning great meaning, strange preparations in their stash, offerings made to strangers in low-lit backrooms, glowing ash and smoke, meandering journeys home.

The men had hacked at coughs and not said much, and in the memory of their coal-black eyes I can still see a heaviness, a stronger gravity pinning them here that had both fascinated and frightened me.

Dad had studied mathematics at Cambridge and briefly followed his father into teaching, but it was the long line of Scots Protestants from his mother's side that had won the day, him hearing the divine call and returning to Cambridge for a second time, this time to prepare for ordination.

Once the Most High has spoken, it is hard for lesser, earthly matters to carry much significance. The Shaman is rarely is a family man; his work is at the boundary between Earth and heaven, and the eternal state of countless souls depends on him.

"I tell you the truth," Jesus replied, "no one who has left home or brothers or sisters or mother or father or children or fields for me and the gospel will fail to receive a hundred times as much in this present age (homes, brothers, sisters, mothers, children and fields—and with them, persecutions) and in the age to come, eternal life."[5]

There it was in the contract: the value of your family may go up, or down. You might not get back what you invest, but if you do, you might still face terrible persecutions. Every priest is a man on commission, to be paid post-mortem, and here he was, expending vast amounts of fuel in that spire-topped tower, trying desperately to get the congregation to burn as he had, to ignite and take off.

—

A childhood can weigh a great deal. As we grow we wait for something strong enough to lift us away.

Unable to escape physically, I turned inwards to a spirituality that was something almost medieval, focused on angelic beings and the battles they waged far above us. Staying indoors and reading endlessly, to the joy of my parents I stoically worked my way through Oswald Chambers' daily devotionals, *My Utmost for His Highest*. I found there the same message holy men the world over had whispered through human history: once upon a time we *had* lived on high, had lived in the heavens, had had our own place in the pantheon. Unfortunately things had gone wrong and the gods were now unhappy with us. We had had our wings clipped, and as flightless beings our lives were a test to see if we deserved to be lifted again.

Lifted, or cast down. For if through rising lights we had conceived the heavens above, then in falling rain we had also become convinced of an abysmal below too, a place populated by the diabolical inversions of the celestial beings. It was led by Lucifer, the one-time highest angel of all who, having attempted to oust God from his throne, had been banished to the underworld. It was a hellish place of demons and torture, reserved for those who did not behave, who did not follow the revelation, who refused to obey.

This was the terrifying Christian myth that dominated the Dark Ages. Though we dreamed of flight and lived in hope of resurrection, there was also terrible anxiety about falling. The lesson of Lucifer was simple: if we were to ascend, it had to be by the right means. I was desperate to be lifted, to show myself worthy of God's blessing, of a return to heaven.

With medicine apparently failing this seemed to me the surest way that my sister would be healed and my family restored. I had it on good authority because the Bible said it would be so. A mix of Game of Thrones and Robert Crumb, the concluding book of Revelation was all whores, beasts and unfathomable architecture. Wild and fantastical, it was too weird to be preached on save for one verse just pages away from the climax. This was where I put my hope. After all the violent destruction and punishment, God arrives to live among His people, the writer setting down his transcendent vision, promising that

> *He will wipe away every tear from their eyes. There will be no more death or mourning or crying or pain.*[6]

Eden, regained. A paradise above where our struggles would finally be over. This was where I wanted to be, where I wanted my sister to be, but it seemed impossibly far away. The beautiful daughter my parents had known was falling into the darkness of the grave.

—

Somehow, they refused to let go.

In between each line in my sister's diaries is the untold trauma her illness must have caused a loving mother. She'd narrowly escaped death herself as a young girl, her own mum refusing to act on her cries of pain about an appendix that, within minutes, would have burst and killed her. Later, her own struggles with an eating disorder. Then, in September 1964, working as a nurse and her father terribly ill with cancer, her acting to 'make him comfortable.' Morphine, lots of it. Tears wiped away from eyes, no more crying or pain.

Somehow, despite the yawning darkness of the grave, my mum refused to be resigned, perhaps because this was a boundary she knew too well. She'd delivered babies into the world and ushered the dying out of it, both her and Dad employed as guardians at life's entry and exits. That they had such tenacity to hold onto their daughter's brittle, thinning, blueing, scratching fingers and stop her falling was perhaps because they were both well used to working in these shadowlands between life and death.

There were times I wanted them to let go, times when my own faith failed and I thought the only way out of all this misery would be to put her out of hers. Sometimes it felt like she was willing us to do it, and many times I had to take myself away and shut myself in my room to stop myself lashing out.

Yet somehow she clung on, and somehow we did too. A remarkable ward sister from Stoke Mandeville stepped in, tending this girl as if she were her own daughter, taking her home at weekends, working firmly and lovingly with her as perhaps only a non-doctor, non-parent then could have.

By the thinnest thread she remained connected to life, and by the thinnest thread she was slowly, slowly lifted from mortal danger.

The shadows were exorcised. Something approaching light returned. The battles were diminishing, but with their retreat came the full dawn of just how wounded we all were, how torn and bloodied the ground was, how much more than ever I wanted to fly away.

In Ibn Tufail's story, thrown about by dark forces far beyond his control or understanding, Hayy Ibn Yokdhan finally comes to rest after a storm has driven him to a far-flung island:

When the waters subsided, the ark wherein the infant peacefully slumbered was left stranded, banked up by sands, safely aground, sheltered from blustering wind.[7]

Now, only now, can *The Awakening of the Soul* begin.

Tufail's book was written during a great period of Arab culture when the Christian west was still fumbling around in the dark, the questions of life and death and suffering and meaning answered forcibly and dictatorially by the all-enfolding power of the Church. Finding its way west, it was one of the texts that lit the way for the early figures of the Renaissance. To the consternation of the religious powers, the lights of philosophy and reason were slowly turning on again, questioning the myths of the above, probing what was *really* up there.

Re-birth and Enlightenment. The dark ages were over, a new dawn rising over the hills and towns of northern Italy, clearing the runway for the invention of flight.

—

With my sister out of danger, in the summer of 1985 the family loaded into our old Peugeot estate and rumbled by road, ferry, car-train and road again to a villa in Tuscany owned by an uncle I wasn't sure I'd ever met. It was never going to be all sweetness and light with three teenagers in a car—we fought and scrapped and I kept all my shouting inside my head—but things were a far cry from the previous years. We lay in the sun and discovered a basement full of vintage red; the house was hot and dusty and crumbling and I immediately fell in love with all of it.

We were around 30 miles from the birthplace of Leonardo da Vinci and Lucca, the nearest town, had an exhibition of his designs for flying machines. Winged men, helicopters, gliders—all of this must have seemed to his contemporaries then like *Star Wars* had seemed to me. I begged Mum to buy me a book of them and spent hours marvelling over the pages of intricate drawings and fleeting sketches that all took aim at the above.

Da Vinci was born in 1452. As a baby, while lying in his cradle, a kite had flown down and hovered over him, its tail feathers actually brushing against his face. It was an event that Leonardo considered one of the most important of his life, his whole being somehow infected by this fluttering touch, his life forever directed towards the achievement of flight. He would regularly buy caged birds from the Florentine markets in order to set them free and, in 1505, published the *Codex on the Flight of Birds*—the first proper investigation into the mechanics of how birds managed to fly—which contained detailed proposals for the construction of the flying machines I saw half a millennia later.

It was a love never shared by his countrymen. Each morning we were woken at dawn by the tramping of hunters across the surrounding fields, the sounds of their shotguns so regular it seemed impossible that any birdlife remained at all. Mum railed against it all and stood aghast at the huge 'mist nets' erected in nearby lanes to trap nightingales, robins, thrushes and warblers, songbirds throttled not for augury, but to be stuffed into traditional dishes beloved since Da Vinci's day.

We might well have sampled them ourselves. On the insistence of the uncle who'd lent us the villa, one evening we had dinner with the family of the housekeeper. They spoke no word of English, we not a syllable of Italian. Communicating in hopeless gestures and smiles we were surprised to be sat at a table with only enough place settings for the five of us. As the most delicious pasta dish was served, it became clear that *we* would eat, while they would simply look on.

Nevertheless, this was a happy family table, unimaginable 18 months before. With no idea about Italian cuisine, Dad, my brother and I filled our boots with seconds and thirds of pasta, totally unaware that this was just the first of many many courses still to come. With already stuffed bellies, we were presented with cutlets of meat, vegetables and portions of delicate stews that were suspiciously avian.

To break the awkward silence the television was put on, and after some frantic pointing it became clear that a disaster was unfolding on the news. It was 22nd of August 1985. Attempting to take-off from Manchester, an engine had exploded on a British Airways plane. Fire and toxic fumes had quickly spread through the cabin and, with some of the emergency doors jammed, evacuation had been fatally slow.

Footage of this burning bird wound round and round on repeat, us transfixed, decoding what we could of the Italian commentary as the flaming wreck lay stricken back in England.

55 lives lost.

They had never made it into the air.

—

Back in 1461, when Da Vinci was still a young boy, an Italian painter called Benozzo Gozzoli was in nearby Florence finishing a painted altarpiece as shocking as the scenes we'd witnessed on TV. Cartoon-like in its story-telling, unmistakable even to the illiterate masses of this late medieval world, it made its bloody point about God's proscription of flight bluntly and violently.

The fall guy of the piece is Simon Magus, 'Simon the magician.' He appears briefly in the book of Acts, a boastful man who 'impresses all the people, both high and low.' He sees the supernatural power that Peter is wielding and approaches him, wondering what the buy-in cost would be. This is a big mistake. The Christians round on him, and from this single slip we have the root of the 'sin of simony': attempting to pay for God's blessings.

Early church writers considered Simon Magus the beginning of all heresy. One paints him as claiming to know the mind of Jesus better than Peter did, a grave accusation because it made him a Gnostic, part of an ancient heretical tradition of higher knowledge and intellectual ascent that stretches right back to Plato.

Plato's school believed that every object that we could perceive or thing that we could experience was an imperfect earthly copy of some perfect 'original' that was sited far above. The whole aim of human existence, Platonists like Magus believed, was to become reunited with what was variously called 'the Source,' the higher 'Good,' or 'the One.' Simon Magus, just like Simon Peter, wanted to reconnect with the perfect divine power above; the drama of Gozzoli's cautionary painting comes from the means of achieving this ascent.

Both men are depicted courting the favour of Emperor Nero. In an attempt to impress Nero and show that his power is superior to that of the Christian apostles, Simon Magus is shown physically taking to the air. But there is a problem, as Julian Barnes describes in his book *Levels of Life*:

> *Simon's secret rocket fuel is, however, illegitimate: he relies— physically as well as spiritually—on the support of demons. In the mid-ground, St Peter is shown praying to God, asking Him to dispossess the demons of their power. The theological and aeronautical results of this intervention are confirmed in the foreground: a dead magician, blood oozing from his mouth after an enforced crash landing. The sin of height is punished.*[8]

We wandered the Uffizi gallery that summer, the sun pounding down on the crowded Florentine streets outside, me wandering the umbral galleries within, countless walls hung with oil-dark, hanging Christs. Had it been there, I've no doubt that my 13-year-old self would have been stopped by Gozzoli's painting, subconsciously sensing so much within it from my own story. The medieval connection between physical altitude and spiritual ascension, the gasp as Simon Magus lifted away towards reunification with higher things, the shocking realisation that those weren't angels lifting him, but demons, the trembling knowledge that *only* Christ was worthy to do this work, that only he had come down from God and descended to hell and risen from the dead and carried on upwards back towards heaven, earning exclusive transportation rights along this vertical, the solemn acceptance that if I, like the Magus, accepted lift in any other form I too deserved to be punished and shot down and have my life smashed into the dirt.

Not everyone agreed. Inspired in part by Tufail's work the Neoplatonists of the Renaissance rejected divine haulage, believing instead that movement back up towards 'the One' was about the exercise of philosophy, the refining of the intellect through the art of memory. Truth didn't descend to us from God above; it was found through intellectual ascent. To philosophise was to learn how to fly. Science *was* flight.

Viewed from this perspective, Gozzoli's painting becomes something more serious than a piece of spiritual slapstick. It is anti-Plato propaganda, a warning shot fired into the theological fray: those who reject Christ and attempt spiritual elevation through philosophy and science will be identified as demonic and shot down. He was only a brush for hire, but in this commission Gozzoli found himself working to shore up the Vatican against the rising tide of Platonic ideas. This was the whole history of the city I walked through, Florence one of the prospering merchant city states, full of men prepared to challenge the long-dominant myth of medieval Christianity, but chasing away the darkness by lighting their tapers from the embers of ancient, non-Christian philosophers.

His depiction of this violent battle over the two technologies of altitude—divine resurrection or human endeavour—was a beautiful and bloody summary of the dialectic that was to power Western civilisation for the next 500 years. Yet, as the 1400s came to a close, the Neoplatonists were still weak and had to work in hidden ways, the financial, social and political power of the ruling Church and its Pope strong enough to force their ideas into the shadows. Those who practised or preached the idea of unity with the divine through higher human knowledge were branded part of the 'occult'—the occluded and hidden world of heretical ideas—and classed along with magicians and sorcerers such as Simon Magus.

I didn't know it then, but Da Vinci was one of them. In the early 1480s he received part of his training in a Neoplatonist academy sponsored by Florence's powerful Medici family and, as the Renaissance ideal strengthened, the balance of power between the Church and the Neoplatonists began to shift. The grip of 'the sin of height' was weakening.

In 1505—just as Da Vinci's 1505 *Codex on the Flight of Birds* was being published—work began on a deeply 'occult' painting on the ceiling of a new chapel right inside the Vatican itself. The immense job had been awarded to the most famous artist of the day, another alumnus of a Neoplatonist Medici academy: Michelangelo di Lodovico Buonarroti Simoni.

Working at furious pace high on a scaffold, Michelangelo completed the work within 5 years. Centuries later Goethe commented that, 'without having seen the Sistine Chapel one can form no appreciable idea of what one man is capable of achieving,' and, in his own encoded, occluded way, this is precisely what Michelangelo set out to produce—a glowing Neoplatonic testament to the brilliant heights that Renaissance man could reach.

As proof of how the world was changing, in perhaps the most famous panel of the piece, Michelangelo did what half a century ago Gozzoli would not have countenanced: in *The Creation of Adam*, man is set almost on a level with God. Adam's bare physique is not only *as* impressive, but in his greater youth he looks like a young version *of God himself*. Both are reaching out their hands, almost touching, only the smallest gap existing between their fingertips.

Such was his talent that, even in his lifetime, Michelangelo became known as *Il Divino*—the divine one. His nickname was never more true than in this painting where he dared give bold visual expression to the growing idea that, in the racing progress being made across culture, science and the arts, Renaissance man was within touching distance of becoming divine.

Sweating in the August sun, we walked miles through baking squares, Dad pointing up to the tower of the Medici's fortified *Palazzo Vecchio* soaring over the city, this only an architectural symbol of the knowledge and understanding that stretched even further, battling for dominance with the great dome of the cathedral, both buildings longing for altitude but falling out over the means. Christian or occult, dark or light, work of God, or work of man?

I was ignorant of all this as I sat with my book of Leonardo's sketches, unaware of the charged atmosphere around ideas of ascent into which his drawings of flying machines appeared in 1505. His figures were strapped with avian wings that use complex systems of pulleys and wheels to simulate the flapping and soaring the kite that had touched him so deeply.

Though he is trying to impress military commissioners, in these inked dreams of flying men Da Vinci was nailing his occult beliefs to the mast: the ascent of humankind would not be via divine means, but through mental and mechanic ingenuity. In his daring to even draw them, we see the growing confidence of Renaissance thought, so much more brash than in the cowed piety of St Peter's felling of Simon Magus.

There was defiance here that, like the first tastes of wine I took in the Tuscan heat, slowly fermented within me. If the sin of height was punishable by God, then we would now defy him as a near-equal and keep on sinning.

—

When the summer was over I found myself landed in the local grammar school, where these tensions between the 'light' world of Christian belief and the 'occult' world of my own thoughts began to pull me apart.

On the surface I was still the good Christian boy, the son of the vicar, bright and expected to 'do well.' During a Billy Graham tour — *Mission England 1984* — I'd sat in the stands of a football ground, and felt the force within me as the call was made, and lifted myself from my seat and wandered down onto the pitch to publicly give my life to Jesus. But behind the scenes, out of the spotlight, I was constantly breaking rules. I bunked lessons, drank cocktails before assembly, mixing hooch I'd stolen from a store cupboard for the teachers' Christmas party, leaving the large screw-top bottles of lager laced with soluble laxatives. I rigged a lecture hall with stink-bombs that would only go off the next morning as people filed in and folded down their seats, the

Head forced to abandon his speech to those about to do their exams, shouting above the affray that if he ever caught the boy who'd done this they'd be expelled for good.

I should have been, but I was never caught. I got away with all of it, and enjoyed nothing more than the thrill of this illicit, silent world that I kept almost entirely hidden, leaving few clues in my pious other life that it even existed.

With my sister doing better, she dropped down into my year but joined my brother away at boarding school, the hope being she'd get the attention she needed to catch up on all that she'd missed. They'd both suffered in their own ways, both been given boosts, both been launched away from the battleground.

Seemingly forgotten, I was alone in the house a lot and felt angry, and then felt guilty for still feeling angry, for still not feeling 'normal.' My sister had been very seriously ill, and now she was a lot better. Why couldn't I just get over it? There were far worse stories than mine. I'd not been raped or abused, I didn't live in poverty and wasn't inflicted with some god-awful injury. And yet, despite all this, I couldn't manage to happily get on with things, and this itself cut deep and made me furious.

Underneath, I still held on to that hope that *Star Wars* had sown: one day I would board a ship and, like my siblings, lift away from these ruins. The medieval still strong within me, I dreamed of this in physical terms: despite the horror of watching the Manchester disaster, I couldn't wait to fly. It was embarrassing. I was nearly 15 and I'd still never been on a plane.

Finally, in the summer following Italy, I got my chance. I would be going to Portugal with my best friend. Moreover, I was going on holiday with a family who didn't fight, who were relaxed and funny and didn't leave me feeling that my best game-plan was to disappear into silence.

—

In 1560, Pieter Bruegel painted Landscape with the Fall of Icarus, another myth from antiquity redeployed in support of radical new ideas. Building on Michelangelo's confidence about mankind's new elevated position, in Bruegel's painting the fall of Icarus is depicted as no more than an incidental sideshow. As the sun meekly sets in the distance, the ploughman continues to plough, the shepherd to tend his flock; the idea of punishment by God is retreating into the background. In the face of scientific and cultural progress the long medieval lists of sins punishable by eternal damnation is beginning to look rather weak.

For those leading the Renaissance, they could see the church slowly losing the battle, one of the strongest blows landed by Rene Descartes. A brilliant philosopher and keen anatomist, he had methodically sliced through the human body, searching for the soul. Unable to find it, he decided that we were little more than elaborate biological machines. That 'little more' was a problem though: his 'cogito ergo sum' held that awareness of self was the solid ground upon which all else was built—and yet consciousness itself failed to obey the laws of scientific enquiry it insisted on, refusing to be located or observed.

Descartes got round it by concluding that the *mind* must actually be the *soul*, a special part of us, implanted by God, that thus didn't need to follow the laws of the natural world. The final cut was made: because the soul was not part of the physical world, physical altitude could be divorced from spiritual consequence.

In other words, we were cleared for take-off.

—

Having never been to an airport, I had no idea about any of the convoluted business of getting on a plane: checking in, security and waiting at gates, all before actually boarding. My friend's family poked gentle fun at me, this teenager who'd still never flown. They were all experienced flyers and I was allowed to sit by the window, given the best chance to take it all in.

The 'it' had taken on some kind of mythical status. I knew that I would be thrown back into my chair, though I had no idea how strong this force be. Would I be pinned back like Han Solo going into hyperdrive?

My impatience betrayed that this was an important moment. It would be the first time I had lifted away from the ground, the furthest by a long stretch that I'd been apart from my family.

So much loomed still over me. Though my sister's eating was healthy again, the psychological toll had been immense. A bomb had exploded in our midst. Deaf, shell-shocked, hurting, confused, vengeful, we crawled around in the ruins, determined to act as if nothing had happened, refusing any assistance. Because we had God, no professional help needed to be sought. Keep Calm and Carry On.

But nothing had been dealt with, none of the fuel syphoned away. The slightest deviation risked an angry chain reaction that would quickly consume my sister, my Dad and my brother. Desperate to prevent these explosions, I kept a heavy lid on any emotional engagement. I spent my time hunkered down inside myself, protecting myself from the regular burning arguments, the searing heat of anger and the near-constant aroma of unease. I withdrew from any existence at the surface. I navigated life from just a little way beneath, millimetres only, but that toughened pane between me and the world attenuated my senses. It kept me safe but kept me down; and in the moments I had to myself I dreamed of surging up and punching a hole right through it.

Staying silent, gliding invisibly between rooms to avoid igniting the small piles of gunpowder that lay innocently under misaligned breakfast bowls or rumpled furniture, I thought I hid things well. That was the Christian thing to do. Nothing should be said or discussed, no problems admitted to or faced head on.

One concession: I had been given a dog. It was something to look after, to ease my continuing angst. In Cartesian terms, this was a soulless creature, a complex biological machine, pure stimulus-response, but day-to-day it felt more like my closest companion.

'Dogs,' Karen Armstrong notes in *A Short History of Myth*, 'do not agonise about the canine condition.'[9] So true: unlike me, my dog had no yearning for height, no desire I could detect to climb aboard a plane and understand what life looked like from above. Yet this apparent defect in its consciousness meant she was fully engaged in each moment. My black mongrel Molly lived on the surface and pursued it joyously, running and sniffing, experiencing everything, me bounding after, collar and lead dragging me for a while into visceral, sweaty happiness.

Armstrong contrasts dogs' disinterest in the question of themselves with all of humankind, and even the Neanderthals long before us. Archaeological digs of their graves from 200,000 years ago show that, unlike any of the creatures around them, they were conscious of their mortality and created some kind of myth-structure to help them cope with the mystery of this unknown beyond.

The most powerful myths are about extremity; they force us to go beyond our experience. There are moments when we all, in one way or another, have to go to a place that we have never seen, and do what we have never done before. Myth is about the unknown; it is about that for which we initially have no words.[10]

Fastening my seatbelt in that airliner for the first time, I was strapping myself to a bird that I hoped would fire me beyond my experience, offer me visions I had never before seen. This journey into the unknown, this coming surge into the above would be a means to imagine a shift in my life, to reconfigure my myth-structure, the deep story of myself.

This was the Renaissance project in a nutshell. Shedding its medieval skin, Europe wanted to get high, to look down from new altitudes and discover a new myth to live by. Through art and thought that mined the classics, Da Vinci, Michelangelo and others in the Neoplatonic tradition eased us away from spiritual angst about physical flight and our chronic fallenness. In their wake, unencumbered by the weight of religious anxiety, scientists and inventors now stepped out of the shadows that Da Vinci had had to hide in. Freed from the gravity of sin, they could engage all their faculties in the development of an actual flying machine.

—

In fire it had begun, and in fire it would be completed. For thousands of years we had marvelled at the flames rising back to their celestial home above and this became the key to our own ascension.

It is now 1782. We are in France, young Joseph Montgolfier fascinated by the way linen sheets rose as they dried over a fire in the yard. He thinks that the fire must be releasing a special gas, one that causes levity. He builds a box from the lightest, thinnest wood he can find and covers it with taffeta. Then, lighting some paper underneath it, he watches in astonishment as the box slowly lifts off the floor and hits the ceiling.

Like Da Vinci, Joseph's first thought is war: a working flying machine could surely carry bombs over fortifications and so help France achieve much-needed military supremacy.

Calling for his brother's help, the two of them vastly scale up the earlier design. (Their father is less than enthusiastic, making both promise that if their flying machine works they themselves will not go in it.) In December they light the fire under the larger box, but the uplift is so strong that they lose control of it. Laughing, shrieking nonetheless, they watch in awe as it careers off into the sky, floating a mile or so before coming to land. It is set upon by shocked peasants in the fields, and destroyed.

Undeterred, they persevere with a new spherical design, manufactured from specially cut cloth backed by paper to prevent the hot air escaping. They set about testing it, local labourers employed to hold the tether lines as the contraption heats up, the force again so great that two of the men let the rope run through their fingers while two others hold on—grasping, if only for a second or two, the chance to become the very first people to fly. To Etienne's relief they let go and drop back down to the ground, the balloon again escaping and landing on a nearby farm.

Well aware of the sensation they have on their hands, complex and secretive arrangements are made to transport the machine to Paris. Etienne will work the social scene of the French court and give the first public demonstration. The setbacks are countless—fabric ripping, the weather inclement—but finally the stage is set and the cream of French society gather.

Despite—or perhaps because of—their lack of soul, the brothers choose animals to be first passengers aboard the *Aerostat Réveillon*: a sheep Etienne called Montauciel ('climb to the sky'), a nameless duck and a cockerel. They have been scientifically selected: the sheep considered the creature most like a human in physiology, and the rooster included as a non-flying bird; as one accustomed to flight, the duck is included as the control.

On 19th September, 1783, the little menagerie of Montauciel, the duck and the cockerel are strapped into the basket of the balloon. 50 pounds of straw and 5 pounds of shredded wool are consumed in the burner. All the French royalty are here, as are the esteemed scientists of the French Royal Academy. Montgolfier is nervous but it all goes perfectly, the odd party rising up from a garden in the palace of Versailles to around 500m in a flight that lasts about 8 minutes.

Etienne has no idea what the effect will be on the creatures. No one does. Will the sheep be able to breathe? So much closer to the sun, will it burn up or its blood freeze? They make chase. The air in the balloon cools and it gradually looses altitude, landing on a lawn, partially caught in a small oak tree. The great party of trackers find it, joyfully reporting that 'the animals are in fine shape, though the sheep has pissed in its cage.'[11]

Work begins immediately on an even larger balloon. Understanding the importance of patronage and the chance this provides for social elevation, the Montgolfiers and their supporters decorate it richly with royal blues and reds, signs of the zodiac and sun-motifs that have the face of Louis XVI painted into them.

Finally, on October 15th, 1783, it is ready to be tested. They gather in the yard of Etienne's backer, the successful wallpaper manufacturer Jean-Baptiste Réveillon. They light the fire in the centre of the cradle and wait patiently until it is well established. They check the coiled tether, the lifeline back to solid ground then, shaking hands and kissing cheeks with Réveillon, Etienne takes his place in the basket.

Everyone is nervous. Etienne sweats as the ties are cut, but then relaxes as, spirit-like, the tether is paid out bit by bit and he rises up 20 or more metres into the air, the very first human to fly.

—

Was he as apprehensive as I was? Everything seemed to take an age, the long taxi out to the runway leaving me wondering acerbically as we trundled for miles around Heathrow's tarmac if we weren't going to drive the whole bloody way to Portugal.

At last, unable to see a damned thing from the tiny windows, a deep, gut-breaking roar built from below and we were suddenly accelerating down the runway, bumping and veering before imperceptibly leaning back into the air.

It was incredible. I was flying. I stared at the receding ground below, like Montgolfier able for the first time to see our world the way Jesus must have as he'd fired into the sky.

I loved it. I loved the wisps of cloud, the punching through into sunlight, the ridiculous food, the roller-coaster-like sudden drops and ascents, the drinks trolley crashing and tumbling, the sheet-white hostesses doing what they could to hold onto headrests, the white knuckle-clenching look as we careered towards the tarmac, the smack and bounce of the undercarriage, the palpable sense of relief and the way the passengers cheered and applauded as we came to a standstill. So dramatic! So polite!

It was, in fact, the worst flight anyone around me had ever been on. My ignorance had been bliss; everyone else crept down the steps from the plane, shaking and thankful to be alive, chronic turbulent storms having thrown our craft about like a rag doll.

We had just committed the sin of height, but I wanted to sin again and again.

—

In Paris, Etienne's achievement was an absolute sensation and news of it spread like fire across the West. He had an audience with the queen—Marie Antoinette—and, as hoped, his father was elevated to the aristocracy. But more than that, people jostled to ask the same questions we had once asked of seers and priests: *Tell us! What can you see from on high?*

His reports were conclusive. Not only had the sin of height gone unpunished, but—much to the delight of Enlightenment thinkers—the opposite was true. Dr Jacques Charles, who ascended in a hydrogen balloon months after Etienne, described it as 'a moral feeling.' Frederick Burnaby, who much later in 1882 flew across the English Channel in a balloon, wrote how:

> *The air was light and charming to breathe, free as it was from the impurities that burden the atmosphere near the globe. My spirits rose. It was pleasant to be for the time in a region free from letters, with no post office near, no worries, and above all no telegraphs.*[12]

Four years later, in 1868, Félix Tournachon, president of *The Society for the Encouragement of Aerial Locomotion by Means of Heavier than Air Machines,* built a huge balloon and sailed it above Paris. He wasn't the first to do so by far, but he is fascinating for being the first to return with *actual* visions of what he saw. Breaking the line of the ancient seers, his visions from transcendent journeys were not tied up in mysterious hallucinations and withheld from an unworthy public. No, when Tournachon got high, he took a camera, becoming the very first person to bring back pictures of Earth from the air; our world, from heaven.

Photography—the capturing of light, of something of the self—was an infant enough technology in itself, but here were quite remarkable images that no human had ever been able to see before. Here, finally—not through religion but an ingenious human technology—was the bird's-eye view, and with it came confirmations that the skies *were* heavenly. Tournachon wrote of:

> 'the silent immensities of welcoming and beneficent space, where man cannot be reached by any human force or by any power of evil, and where he feels himself live as if for the first time. [Altitude] reduces all things to their relative proportions, and to the Truth.'[13]

This was pure Plato, rising above the crude material earth to begin to see new perspectives on both it and ourselves, to begin to breathe hints of 'the One' as height alters our visual perception and allows us to see things in their entirety. Now the opposite of sin, *'flight'* had become just that: flight from the impure Earth, an escape from the burdens of the everyday. There were no demons to drag Montgolfier, Tournachon or Burnaby back to Earth. No, their spirits rose, lifting them further to the heavens. Ecstatic. Off the ground. Transcendent.

These first aeronauts affirmed that physical flight, just like the religious journeys into 'inner space,' was about recovering heaven. Altitude was, for these pioneering pilots, about flight to a place beyond the reach of the corrupted Earth. Height had so long been considered sacred and immortal, reserved for the holy, but now, having achieved our dream and taken to the air, things changed. It wasn't so much that altitude was prohibited because we weren't pure enough, but that we could achieve purity through flight. In the Middle Ages we had given the air to demons and witches, but now, in these enlightened times, up here we felt out of reach of the power of evil. We had risen with wings to where the heavenly host sang. In the above we could enter a place of angelic peace, a new paradise.

For all its battles with medieval Christianity, flight now emerged as a *religious* technology. At the birth of aeronautics, gravity and grave were still inextricably bound: escaping the latter was about our journey to defeat the former. Perhaps, we thought, with the invention of ever-finer flying machines we might finally escape the earth and outrun the earthen graves ordinary life dug for us.

—

That was what I had hoped for that afternoon as I'd leapt around the garden in my new trainers—not so much to be Luke Skywalker, but to get high enough to escape the aroma of decay. Around me was the slaughter of pigs, the gloaming graveyard and the stalking Ripper, family anxieties about the proximity of death.

Church had told me that our minds should be venerated for their divine spark, and I now understood that my sister had made the logical jump that her body should be denigrated for holding us down. Flesh was ballast, something to be jettisoned to speed her ascent; her soul the purer, higher part.

This was the confusing mishmash of twisted theology and warped psychopathology that fuelled our lust for lift. This was the baggage I had packed in the hold as we thundered down the runway at Heathrow. As that plane tilted its nose up and rose off the ground, I felt sure that this first ascent was somehow linked to the serious ongoing business of my quest for transcendence, for escape.

That was the ecstasy I hoped for as I took off for the first time, the long-delayed start of a journey to a place where there was *'no more death or mourning or crying or pain'* because I believed that there would be no bodies to suffer them. Weightless, finally lifting away from my family and disappearing, I could now change my story, achieving such great heights that I'd slip free from pain for good, my soul flying free.

In its pursuit of height, the Renaissance had precipitated a shift in the story of the West, countless Harvey Klings of the day no doubt writing to the authorities along the way, their quills trembling as ink spluttered onto parchment, shocked at the state of the nation's soul. There I found myself too, Leonardo's book on one side, my bible on the other, a living miniature of Gozzoli's altarpiece, determined to change the myth I lived by, sure that the high life—achieved by whatever means—would empower this transformation.

It didn't quite happen like that. The very next time I stepped onto an aeroplane it wasn't to return to Florence, to work out my struggles on the hallowed ground of the Renaissance. Another book came into my life that tore down the classical backdrop of Nero's court and replaced it with Day-Glo swirls. Like Harvey Kling, the shadow of the 60s finally crashed headlong into my life, St Peter and Simon Magus left jaw-dropped and speechless as they were wheeled off into the wings and replaced by Pentecostal preachers, astronauts and tripping hippies.

The throttle opened on a far more powerful engine, the same friend I'd be to Portugal with strapped in beside me, the two of us careering again down the same tarmac, rising, then banking west, heading to America.

We had just left school. Our parents were far behind. We were free. Kling might not like the cut of our hair or our clothes, but we were off to pay our respects to the counterculture, to the might of Apollo and the spiritual highs California had to offer.

Hell yeah, the 80s were over, and we were *flying*.

CAN
YOU
PASS THE
ACID TEST
?

My Name is _____

I live at _____

I was born _____

I am_____ tall, have _____

eyes, _____ hair, and weigh _____

I am a member of INTREPID

TRIPS, INC. and am doing nothing.

| PASTE |
| PHOTO |
| HERE |

_____
            Signature

Front / Back of Prankster ID card, December 1965

2. Getting High

The tail feathers of a kite, hovering and fluttering at young Leonardo's face, lying in his crib, something avian infecting his infancy, leaving him forever pushing for the above.

If the hawkish shadows of our sister's illness had affected me and my brother, they had sent us on radically different trajectories. To the extent that I dived down into myself, he launched upwards into life, living it to the very full.

Born in June 1968, just after his first birthday he had been lifted from his cot and put in front of the television to watch Neil Armstrong take his giant leap onto the Moon. Something ballistic must have lodged in him, his life forever under possession of a free, extroverted spirit.

He hadn't bought into religion, hadn't become the dreary dutiful son I thought I should be. I lived under heavy expectation from Mum and Dad to be the good boy who went to church and passed exams and made everyone proud but, whether I just perceived the pressure or not, as I came to the end of secondary school I knew that my life wasn't working. I wanted to change things, to be more like my brother, so when he asked me to join him at Glastonbury Festival I swallowed back my reflex and said yes.

It was 1990. I stepped out of my last A-Level exam into his waiting car, little idea what I was letting myself in for.

I remember queuing all night on jammed country roads to get in. I remember an ad hoc football game as we waited. I remember the rhythmic thud of music wafting over the hedgerows, the realisation that this wasn't even part of the festival itself, just one of the many raves that were springing up in fields around. I remember arriving, pitching our tent, then not seeing my brother again for 3 days, nor having much expectation of doing so. There were hundreds of thousands of people, countless stages and no mobiles. I remember bumping into my sister, not knowing that she'd even be there. She had forgotten to bring the poles to her tent and we laughed about this, about everything. Being here without Mum or Dad knowing what the hell we were up to felt illicit and liberating. I remember wandering the vast site in a daze, knowing among the smoke and gas and substances, the fires and dancing and the spreading smile of ecstasy, that I'd come here to shed the soft skin of childhood and attempt to fit into the baggy folds of my young manhood. Clear skies above, bright lights and stars, the feeling of being outside, with no ceiling to life.

There were riots that year on the field then given to Travellers, police weighing in, petrol bombs thrown, but with meagre means of this news spreading I knew nothing about it until later, thinking the place a kind of heaven, though a great deal muddier than I'd heard in sermons.

For my brother and I, music had always been a means of survival, a way of being airlifted out of the battle zone of the house and dropped into a different world. Since I'd been able to work a record player The Beatles had been the band I had loved most. Dad only had two albums of theirs, a rare French compilation of their early hits, and *Sergeant Pepper*. It was, and remains to this day, my favourite record. There was something endlessly fascinating, something from a world that was somehow far larger than the one I lived in. It wasn't until I got back from Glastonbury that I worked out why that was.

The festival was brilliant but, still navigating life from just below the surface, the experience exacerbated my loneliness and frustration. Why could my brother throw himself so fully at things and I could not? I'd been determined to ride it all as high as it would go, but in realising as we drove home that I'd pulled back I became more committed than ever to do something about it.

If my brother knew the secret, I figured that his bedroom must contain the answer hidden somewhere within it. While he was out one afternoon I nervously put my hand to his door and went on a raid, going in search of resources, things that he had that gave him the liberty I wanted for myself. There were records lying around that I wanted to take for a spin, magazines and clothes, cameras and other objects that seemed imbued with a better life. It was in books I put my trust though, and running my finger along his shelf a Day-Glo spine drew me, Tom Wolfe's *Electric Kool-Aid Acid Test*.

Each page went down like a tab of acid. I fell in love with every detail of the period, this decade I'd so narrowly missed, all of it brighter, bolder, better. Up until now I'd tried to take off with dust-road parables and first century fishing boats, but here was an explosion of blistering pharmacology, vibrantly coloured antics, all described in Wolfe's electrifying new journalism style set against a background of higher and higher thrusts up out of the atmosphere and on to the Moon itself.

Little did I know that this was the beginning of a long journey of exploration. The 1960s began to open itself up as a parallel world, my own struggles for flight seemingly mirrored in the major cultural movements of the time, these then resonating further the more I explored, singing something archetypal about the ancient human longing to get high.

All I knew then was that I had a year before college started and that I had to go to California. I slaved at a job, saved some money and bought a plane ticket. I was a northern lad taking off to soak up everything he could about the counterculture, stepping from a 747 out into the LA sunshine imagining I was George Harrison himself, knowing full well now why those two Beatles records of Dad's had sounded so different.

Boys from the north? A vertiginous new view of the world that left the old one looking monochrome? The comparison seemed fitting enough.

—

In 1964 'Beatlemania' was in full swing but, though the band were wildly popular, their music was pretty conventional. They turned up for work at Abbey Road studios, smashed their way through rock and roll standards and short melodic love songs grounded in everyday relationships: wanting to hold someone's hand, a gift sent 'With Love From Me to You,' and the trials of working 'A Hard Day's Night.'

Every song a story of labour or love: the extent of their revolutionary intent was to question the drudgery of the factory and the straightforward pattern of meeting, marrying and procreating. Post punk and Hip-Hop it all seems tame now, but this was heady stuff for many, and too much already for some stuff-shirts, who proclaimed this new music dangerous to society.

When myths are under reconstruction, forces of conservatism will always gather to preach grave warnings. It was the same for Rene Descartes as it was for Ringo Starr: as both drummed up energy for old ideas to crumble, others waded in with calls for their heads.

Like my parents, the band had all been born during, or just after, the trauma of the Second World War. Lennon's father was in the merchant navy and very rarely present. In 1946 he visited Lennon and took him to Blackpool, intending to steal him away to New Zealand. When an argument broke out, the five-year-old John was forced to choose between his father and mother. He chose his father, but then, as he watched his mother walking away, broke down in tears and ran after her. His father left, and John didn't see him for another 20 years.

Stories like this abounded, so no surprise then that after the ration book, after the clearance of rubble and the demolition of tenement blocks, after the grief had healed a little, after the old tales had been told and told again, this young generation wanted to rip off the torn and ragged habits that they'd had handed down to them and dance.

On a marathon session on 18th of October, 1964, The Beatles recorded no less than seven tracks: a cover of Chuck Berry's hit *Rock and Roll Music*, a Buddy Holly number *Words of Love, Everybody's Trying To Be My Baby* by the rockabilly blues artist Carl Perkins and *Kansas City/Hey, Hey, Hey, Hey* by Little Richard.

That might have been the whole extent of it—songs giving voice to a bit of hormone-drunk post-war anger against a more conservative society—but the next time the band stepped into Abbey Road in February of 1965, something had quite clearly changed. This flat music that had concerned itself with the very Earth-bound subjects of hard work and relationship troubles quite suddenly lifted off and began exploring an entirely different dimension.

At some point early in 1965, a dentist acquaintance handed after-dinner coffees spiked with LSD to George Harrison and John Lennon. Here was the kite fluttering above their cradle, the birdcage torn open. Tripping around London in a car late at night, it was as if they had stepped out of The Cavern for the first time, the low flat ceiling of the cave ripped away to reveal a vast sky above, the stale air of teenage angst, the nonsense of reluctant production-line guy meets girl exposed as entirely prosaic in the fresh, cool air of this expanded vision. Hidden for so long under their hard scarab shells, The Beatles had just found their wings.

Lennon's first creative response was *Ticket To Ride*, recorded in February 1965 and released in April, a song that, after the banality of hits about love and work, suggested the beginning of a step-change in their approach to music:

I don't know why she's riding so high
She ought to think twice, she ought to do right by me
Before she gets to saying goodbye
She ought to think twice, she ought to do right by me

She said that living with me is bringing her down, yeah
For she would never be free when I was around
Ah, she's got a ticket to ride, she's got a ticket to ride
She's got a ticket to ride, but she don't care

Here was a girl who was riding high, not wanting to be brought down, her freedom tied up with her ability to achieve altitude. Lennon wants the girl to think again, to do the right thing—but she doesn't care. He is cautious, uncertain, reflecting on those around him who had perhaps already taken off, considering—perhaps more carefully than we might give credit for—whether it would be a good thing to do, a caring thing in relation to those around him.

His decision to buy a ticket and take off after her was emphatic, and by October that same year the band were recording *Day Tripper*—a song that now had Lennon poking fun at weekend hippies, those who took acid but didn't change their lives as a result of it.

Watching the video of them play their famous Shea Stadium concert in the US in the summer of 1965—opening with *Twist and Shout* and running through their early hits—you can't help but be struck by the sense of flux. Lennon described that concert as one of the pinnacles of his career, telling the promoter that that night at Shea, 'I saw the top of the mountain.' When they play *Ticket to Ride* it sounds incongruous, introduced almost apologetically by McCartney. The hoards of girls scream nonetheless, but this is the beginning of the end. The rockabilly crooners are dying. They are playing the game still but, just a few months post-LSD now, they know a radical new direction is coming, one that cannot be played onstage, one that cannot be made visible.

Having explored working class life, labour and love, they were now flying through Inner Space, creating songs to try to communicate with those left behind. If that concert had been the top of the mountain, now they had lifted off from it and left the Earth entirely.

—

The scales fell from my eyes. It felt embarrassing in a way, finding out that the album I had blasted out around the house was a paean to LSD. It went deeper than that. We'd slung a bunch of booze into the car to go to Glastonbury—I felt this was bad enough as I was only 17— but on arrival to my complete surprise my brother became quickly involved in purchasing a whole pharmacy of items from a group of Rastafarians who'd set up a sound system in the back of a battered old Bedford van.

When I'd bumped into my sister she'd handed me a joint, and everyone around offered me everything else. This universe had surely not just been created overnight? Where had I *been* all this time, I wondered, knowing that the answer was simple: in my bedroom, reading. The shocks only continued. As I read Wolfe's book I confessed to Mum what I knew about The Beatles. She shrugged and stirred a pan of bubbling marmalade and smiled and casually mentioned how she'd and her friends had all dropped amphetamines to get them through the nursing night-shifts, the same ones Lennon and co. had used to fuel their marathon early gigs in Hamburg.

All this drug talk was eye-poppingly novel to me, but psychedelics were ancient history, inextricably intertwined with theological explorations of the above. In Greek mythology the drug of choice was ambrosia, the 'food of the gods.' It has been connected by historians to the psychedelic mushroom *Amanita Muscaria*, which could be found across Europe and Asia, and is likely also to have been the key ingredient of the mysterious 'Soma,' the ancient Hindu drink that gave rise to a whole book of hymns in the *Rigveda* dedicated to its invigorating properties:

Let Vrtra-slaying Indra drink Soma by Saryanavan's side, Storing up vigour in his heart, prepared to do heroic deeds [...] O Pavarnana, place me in that deathless, undecaying world, Wherein the light of heaven is set, and everlasting lustre shines Make me immortal in that realm where dwells the King.[1]

Then there were the native American tribes, shamans preparing peyote, ayahuasca, psilocybin mushrooms and iboga in order to get high, to break into spirit worlds, to divine the future or understand

39

what was causing illness. Because these high places were special, the drugs that offered trips there were generally proscribed, reserved as sacred initiation rites, kept apart for those in the tribe who knew how to ride them. They are now sometimes classed as entheogens—drugs that 'generate the divine'—but became more commonly termed psychedelics, a compound of two Greek words meaning a substance that 'reveals the soul.'

Across Europe, since before the time of Da Vinci, another fungus—the highly toxic ergot—had been used to help women through childbirth. It was a pure accident that this ancient psychedelic gave birth to the one of the most powerful drivers of the 60s. In 1938, its active component—lysergic acid—was isolated for the first time in a Swiss laboratory by Albert Hofmann. He'd put it to one side, and it wasn't until 5 years later that he accidentally ingested some of the drug through his fingertips, experiencing what he noted as 'an uninterrupted stream of fantastic pictures, extraordinary shapes with intense, kaleidoscopic play of colours.'

A few days later, on 19th April, 1943, Hofmann deliberately took 250mg of the drug in order to further explore its effects. He was quickly overtaken by extraordinarily powerful hallucinations and anxieties. Because of the wartime restrictions that were in place, he found himself having to cycle home, where the visions became even more monstrous:

> *Everything in the room spun around, and the familiar objects and pieces of furniture assumed grotesque, threatening forms. They were in continuous motion, animated, as if driven by an inner restlessness. Was I dying? Was this the transition? At times I believed myself to be outside my body.*[2]

He had just experienced the first ever LSD trip. Here was a white-coated Swiss scientist experiencing something of an ancient shamanic tribal ritual pushed to warp speed. The drug took him right to the extremities of experience, soaring high above his normal life, the flat world of the everyday exposed from up here as full of demons and angels, outer manifestations of a simultaneous inner depth, pressing right up against the elemental questions of his own death. He had punched a new hole in consciousness, made the transition flight to this vibrant world beyond.

Yet he wasn't dying. In fact, his doctor arrived and pronounced him perfectly well, and Hofmann then relaxed into the trip. Like the good scientist he was, he went to work the next day, wrote up his experiment and filed it with his superiors, noting that:

> *There is to my knowledge no other known substance that evokes such profound psychic effects in such extremely low doses, that causes such dramatic changes in human consciousness and our experience of the inner and outer world.*

Others had leapt and jumped, but Hofmann was the inner world's

Montgolfier: designing and testing a modern machine, he'd just flown higher than perhaps any modern man before, and returned to make a report.

Like the French brothers, Hofmann and his company now worked to leverage some economic elevation from their invention. In 1949, after the war had ended, the company introduced the drug into research institutions in the United States, convinced there might be money to be made in genuine clinical applications, especially in the understanding and treatment of mental illness.

Having come across one of these early studies, Captain Al Hubbard—a World War 2 spy who had subsequently made a fortune selling uranium—became one of its most committed proponents, taking scientists, politicians, policemen and religious leaders on trips, who, as he put it, all thought it was the most marvellous thing. Through an associate of Hubbard's, Henry Luce—the publishing magnate behind *Time Magazine*—took LSD at a dinner party at his house in 1958 and wandered into the garden where he conducted an imaginary symphony and opened a direct channel of communication with God, reporting that the two of them spoke for some minutes, God assuring Luce that things were going very well for America.[3]

Though it had arrived by accident, this was a drug long dreamed of. As early as 1920 the British writer Aldous Huxley had pondered the problem of human development, considering the question of whether there was a mental mechanism that could be tripped, a door in the mind that could be sprung, opening up a short cut route into higher states of consciousness.

> *If I were a millionaire, I should endow a band of research workers to look for the ideal intoxicant. If we could sniff or swallow something that would, for five or six hours each day, abolish our solitude as individuals, atone us with our fellows in a glowing exaltation of affection and make life in all its aspects seem not only worth living, but divinely beautiful and significant, and if this heavenly, world-transfiguring drug were of such a kind that we could wake up next morning with a clear head and an undamaged constitution— then, it seems to me, all our problems (and not merely the one small problem of discovering a novel pleasure) would be wholly solved and Earth would become paradise.[4]*

By Hubbard's time there was no doubt that this was a paradise urgently sought. The Cold War was beginning and, following Enlightenment thinking, some scientists saw the terrors of fascism and communism as the product of mass brainwashing and mental disorders.[5] Neither traditional religion nor cultural norms had been powerful enough antidotes to these evil viruses, but here came LSD as a radically new solution. Forget incense and transubstantiation and years of meditation, this was *synthetic* chemistry, clinical, clean and precise. Here, at the opening of the age of convenience—fast food, frozen vegetables and disposable razors—was a tiny, tasteless, self-administered pill that could instantly take you *right there* into life-transforming transcendence.

Hubbard—never known for his modesty—became evangelistic about the drug, talking it up with his high-level military connections and convening 'trips' all over the world, including US Senators, UN representatives, British MPs, and a prime minister.

It was, in effect, a new piece of military hardware on display. In the gardens of the palace of Versailles, Montgolfier had convinced generals not just of the tactical advantage that his machine could bring, but the total change in mindset it would precipitate too. As Hubbard stepped into the White House and the Palace of Westminster with his paper-thin vehicle to the above, this was what he was hoping to communicate. With a flying machine like this, the mysterious, problematic and poorly understood Inner Space could soon be mapped out with military precision and clarity. Taking the reins from the religious mystics, occult alchemists and delusive shamans, the so-called soul might now finally be fully revealed and understood, ending all conflicts and curing the mental problems that led to them in the first place.

—

'Earth become paradise...'

When I'd lain down the money for my flight to California, this was the ticket I'd been after, the ride I'd dearly sought. All through my sister's illness I'd tunnelled far down into myself and wanted some way of throwing light on this vast inner world I'd mined, the deep, dark seams I'd hacked at. Here, promised in ecstatic experience, was a means of flying effortlessly through it all, enlightening it, breaking its occult corridors down and bringing it to the surface where the exact problem could be diagnosed and the exact action taken to make me well.

As I touched down in LA, Wolfe's *Electric Kool-Aid Acid Test* in hand, I inhaled all of these wonderful possibilities, beckoned to me all of these means that I might become well now that I had finally fled the nest of my youth and was free to fly. I wanted the saline of the beaches and the octane of the highways, the granite faces of Yosemite and the soft dust of the Grand Canyon. But more than this, I wanted to taste the ecstasy of the 60s that were now 25 years past, to discover psychedelia for myself, to have my soul revealed. In short, I wanted what Ken Kesey had had.

The star of Wolfe's book, Kesey was born at the front of the queue for talents: charismatic, strong, athletic and academically gifted. He had excelled as a wrestler but, showing himself to be a fine writer too, he was awarded one of the highly prestigious Woodrow Wilson National Fellowships. He elected to use it to take up a place on the creative writing course in California at Stanford, near Palo Alto.

Having very little money, and being drawn to the bohemian lifestyle, he applied to take over one of a group of small weather-beaten shacks along Perry Lane, a tiny street not far from Stanford's golf course. As ever in his life, he was the one person selected from among the great many applicants.

During the writing course, Kesey initially struggled to find a subject for his novel but, working the 12-8 nightshift at a local mental hospital to earn some money, he began making notes for a story set among the patients he met. In order to boost his income a little more, a friend recommended he join a research programme they had going on there too. It was simple stuff: take a dose of whatever they were testing—LSD, mescaline and cocaine as it happened—sit through a couple of tests, take home a few dollars.

Unbeknownst to Kesey, or in fact to almost *anyone*, this was part of the top secret *MK-ULTRA* programme being run by the CIA, focusing on 'the research and development of chemical, biological, and radiological materials capable of employment in clandestine operations to control human behaviour.'[6]

The studies ranged from the plain unethical (administering drugs to patients without their full knowledge was against international codes the US had signed) to the jaw-droppingly unbelievable. In *Operation Midnight Climax*, for example, the CIA opened brothels, installed prostitutes in them, then—as late as 1965—fed unsuspecting clients LSD and observed their behaviour from behind one-way glass.

Given the high level of secrecy, security was incredibly slack. Kesey noted which chemicals were most delightful, then helped himself to the never-locked medicine cabinet once everyone had gone home. The drugs thus found their way out of the labs and wards and onto Perry Lane.

Based on his experiences, and from talking to patients judged 'insane'—many of whom he cannot then have known were being powerfully drugged without their knowledge—Kesey finished *One Flew Over the Cuckoo's Nest,* a searing indictment of the mind-closing effects of life lived under the thumb of the establishment.

No sooner had I heard about it than I tore through Kesey's book, feeling a deep affection for the American Indian narrator, Chief Bromden. Through a sedated fog, with visions of invisible wires controlling him and his fellow patients, Bromden describes a heavy, muffled world where order is kept through violent suppression. Into this claustrophobic, locked ward, comes Randle McMurphy, a bright-eyed, loud-mouthed prisoner who sees time spent in a mental institution an easier ride than labouring on a prison farm. He rips through the order and gloom of the place, introducing gambling, laughter, a fishing trip, illicit alcohol, even smuggling in a pair of prostitutes. For this he is ultimately lobotomised: the system unprepared to tolerate his acts of liberty, even while he is under their lock and key. Mute until this point, Bromden is finally raised to action. Using the immense natural strength he has for so long kept smothered, he rips out a bathroom fitting and smashes his way to freedom.

> *I put my hand on the sill and vaulted into the moonlight. I ran across the grounds in the direction I remembered seeing the dog go, towards the highway. I remember I was taking huge strides as I ran, seeming to step and float a long ways before my next foot struck the earth. I felt like I was flying.*[7]

Out from under the oppressive low ceilings of the mental hospital, a sense of the sky and the above finally breaks into the novel, just as it had for Kesey leaving his shifts on the wards at the veterans' hospital and returning to Perry Lane, his pockets stuffed full of drugs.

It was a special place during a very special time, LSD embodied in a hundred yards of broken-down real estate, and as a young man about to head to university, this long-demolished address was where I wanted to live more than anything else.

—

Like everyone on the Lane, The Beatles began to reflect more deeply on what LSD could do. Having toured the *Rubber Soul* album in late 1965 and early 1966 they had burned out and decided never to go on the road again. After around 1200 shows in just 4 years this allowed them, for the first time, space to stop and reflect. For Lennon this meant heavy experimentation, pushing acid to its furthest boundaries.

On 1ˢᵗ April, 1966, he went into Indica Books, a small underground shop and gallery that McCartney had put some money into, apparently in search of some Nietzsche to fund his thoughts. One can only wonder what would have happened to pop music as we know it if he'd stuck to his guns and bought Nietzsche's *The Gay Science*, but instead of this he came out with a copy of *The Psychedelic Experience*, written by two LSD pioneers Timothy Leary and Richard Alpert.

It was a manual for 'trippers,' a hippy smash-and-grab raid on ancient mystical writings set out in what has become known in the West as *The Tibetan Book of the Dead*. Lennon must have devoured it quickly because by 6ᵗʰ April the band were recording *Tomorrow Never Knows*, which begins with the line 'Turn off your mind, relax and float downstream,' a lyric lifted directly from the introduction to Leary's book.

The track ended up as the song that closed their *Revolver* LP released in August that year. Familiarity with it now—and the plethora of psychedelic rock music that came after—makes it almost impossible to appreciate that *nobody* had ever heard anything quite like this before. For the first time an Eastern drone sound was being meaningfully used in a mainstream Western pop song, signifying, in the words of music writer and Beatles historian Ian Macdonald,

> *A cosmic keynote resounding through space—the reverberation of the universe engendering voice of Brahma the creator, serving notice that the ensuing music will contain no tonal progress.*[8]

In Platonic currency: the sound of 'The One,' a new age dawning, a new myth beginning to be told. With the release of *Sergeant Pepper* a year later, this re-narration was complete. Dead to playing live, they were musicians transcending all other bands around them, leading Timothy Leary to declare them 'prototypes of evolutionary agents sent by God, endowed with a mysterious power to create a new human species, a young race of laughing freemen.'[9]

Leary had been a run-of-the-mill psychologist lecturing at Harvard when, in 1960, on the advice of a colleague, he took a research trip to Mexico and began experimenting with psilocybin mushrooms. Just as with Lennon, the experience radically altered Leary's approach to his work, and with Alpert he set up a programme at Harvard to explore the use of psychedelic drugs in psychological research.

Returning from his own travels to South America in search of psychedelics, the poet Allen Ginsberg persuaded Leary that the way to 'turn the world on' wasn't via Hubbard's route of working with serious-minded politicians and captains of industry. No! The place to start was with the artists!

Ginsberg had gained notoriety—and considerable wealth—from his controversial 1955 piece, *Howl*, considered the apotheosis of Beat poetry. In 1957 copies were impounded and the publisher put on trial for obscenity—a case that the state eventually lost in a landmark ruling that opened the door for the 60s to be what they were. Now a kind of travelling guru for the counterculture, Ginsberg made it his job to add to the howl wherever it was drawing breath, hence his turning up on Leary's doorstep. The poet's methods did sound like more fun, and Leary's scientific 'programme' quickly degenerated into wild parties at which Ginsberg and masses of other 'researchers' were regularly naked and highly intoxicated.

Even so, Leary got very excited about the work. 'Something big is happening to consciousness,' he wrote.

> *People are beginning to see that the Kingdom of Heaven is within them, instead of thinking it's outside, up in the sky, and that it can't be here on Earth. It's time to seize power in the universe, that's what I say - that's my political statement. Time to seize power over the entire Universe. Not merely over Russia or America - seize power over the Moon - take the sun over.*[10]

'Storming Heaven,' as one history of LSD put it, breaking into Eden via a chemical back door to bring about world peace. From the outside it looked more like raising hell though and, distinctly unimpressed with both the parties and the lack of empirical data being produced, through the fug of pipe smoke and the sound of chinking sherry glasses the authorities at Harvard decided to pull the plug. Leary and Alpert were dismissed in 1963.

Unconcerned, the two men secured a large house and carried on working and writing together out in California. Totally serious about their aims, they dressed things up in pseudo-scientific language and sent out groups of LSD-fuelled cartographers to explore and report back on the topology of the high heavens, considering themselves in the same vein as Columbus, launching ships into the wild unknown in hope of finding a new Garden of Eden, around which the whole world could unite in peace.[11]

Whoever they thought they were, the Federal Drug Administration didn't like it, and turned up to play Vatican to their Da Vinci. 'For centuries drug taking has been considered a vice,' one FDA agent said to Leary as they began a bust one summer in '64. 'Now you're not only defending it, you're suggesting it's moral, educational, even religious!' Getting high no longer sinful? It was an almost perfect echo of the early balloonists, the authorities nervous about these crazy men talking about peace and soul-revelation, moving along axes they thought they had well under control.

—

Like Harvey Kling, the FDA agent who tore into Leary could sense the world changing around him. Before these hippies had turned vices into religious rites, serious and dour 'Beat' poets and writers of the late 50s had been breaking down the edifice of straight-laced normal life, feverishly asking 'how are we to live?' LSD totally changed the conversation. With Leary and Alpert on the reading list, 'how' went out the window. The imperative was clear: ditch the tweeds, hitch your hemline as high as you dare, then an inch more, elevate yourself in some of the latest platform shoes and just... *LIVE*.

A quarter of a century later, returning from my own trip to California, off to start college, this was the single imperative I held onto. I needed to start living. I had no idea how, only that the answers I'd had before had turned out to be foolish. I didn't want to think everything through any more. I wanted to close my eyes and jump and fly, ditch the old clothes and hair and not care about the future nor worry about the past.

I watched the family car pull away from the house, Mum and Dad driving my sister off to Leicester to start her degree in English and Theatre. Hours of frenetic packing and checking and watch-tapping and shouting and hurrying fell suddenly to silence, the furniture breathing out, the tension in the wood panels relaxing.

I poured myself a drink. There was relief that this is how it had eventually happened, how she'd left. Every time I'd listened to Sergeant Pepper I'd got to *She's Leaving Home* and felt sick, taking it as some kind of prophecy, imagining coming down stairs one morning and finding Mum in tears, a note on the kitchen table, something about a man from the motor trade. No, it hadn't happened like that. She'd made it, and this deserved a large glass of Amaretto and orange, the regular tipple I'd for years sneaked out of the larder. This brambled nest was emptying. We were dispersing, departing the scene of the battle, to return only as visitors, able to control our own trajectories, pulling out if need be.

It followed me into every room, but I still couldn't talk to anyone about the hurt. Alone in the house, it now pushed through to the surface, so I lay back and put on records to fight it back down and read and brushed away what I could, telling myself that she was so much better, that it would be churlish to speak about it. Outwardly, things were generally fine, and these public impressions seemed to be what mattered.

The truth was that while the body may have healed the mind remained malignant. Though the physical symptoms were so reduced, the psychological wounds still stung like hell. I could be with her for short bursts, but any longer and I felt this magnetic repulsion, this need to push away from her in case I broke and all the septic bile spilled out. I hated myself for this, and was welcoming the prospect of university as a chance to get some space between us, hoping time would heal things.

A few days later it was my turn to leave. I was packed and ready in good time and we sped down to Bristol and before long my parents were speeding back.

Mum tried to laugh it off when I saw her that Christmas, but I could see it had hurt: her and Dad dropping me off, helping me put my stuff in my room, me clearly not wanting them to hang around, especially now that this drop-dead gorgeous girl from the year above had popped in to welcome me to my Halls. We walked back to the car, quick embraces, Dad starting the engine, me heading back down to my room, hoping that girl was still around. 'I watched you walking,' Mum said, 'wondering if you'd turn and look back and wave.' I never did.

I knew that I should have, knew that Mum would be craning her neck, hoping. It was a deliberate act of withdrawal, a statement of intent, wanting this to be mine and mine alone. I was going to live, and do so without looking back. I wish I had.

On that very first night I got talking to a guy who was doing a similar course to me. His brother lived in the city, so he knew the place a little too. We had a few drinks and he mentioned a club he'd heard was good. Again, my natural instinct was to pull back, to go to my room thankful that the opportunity had been there, but say no and slip down under the surface of things again. But, post-Wolfe, to hell with it, here was a chance to drink the Kool-Aid.

Through the rows of Clifton townhouses, down the steep hills of Bath stone and blood-bruised brick, into the concrete and tarmac speedway of Bristol city centre, older students tottering on pavements, older residents slinking in doorways, spirals of smoke from orange-bright fag-tips.

We eventually found the address, and were confronted with an empty street, a plain door with the correct number, plainly shut. We looked around and wondered what the hell to do. We'd just arrived that day and had no idea which way was up, but given that we'd come this far we thought we might as well knock. The door swung open and a huge bear of a bouncer looked us over, asking what we wanted. We could hear music in the background now and signalled that we wanted in. He took money from each of us and beckoned us on, pointing to a further door inside.

Pulling it back was as close to stepping through a wardrobe into Narnia as I'll ever get. The room was tiny—from memory holding less than 150 people—but the place was incredible. Low ceilinged, intimate, unlike anything at Glastonbury, the sound was razor-sharp and fabulously loud. In the looping lyrics the DJ promised to take us higher, in the haze of dry ice and with the impossibility of being heard, every dancer was aboard their own capsule, everyone crammed a little into themselves as they got out of their heads, the sounds and everything else ripping a smile across my face. Yes, I thought, yes; here is life and liberation and it is glorious.

—

Kesey was able to fund his own hacienda. *One Flew Over the Cuckoo's Nest* was a huge success and, free from any financial worries and with Perry Lane about to be bulldozed, in 1963 he bought a ranch and invited everyone to move out there and live the life.

With the drugs and the critical success—not to mention the message his book promoted—Kesey had a hunch that he was on a mission of sorts, a journey of psychedelic exploration that he needed some fellow travellers to help out with. He thus gathered his group of fellow 'pranksters' around him, people who had 'dropped out' and were determined to carry on the Perry Lane dream, to live out a new, unfettered life guided by free love and mind-opening substances. His ranch out in La Honda was about 20km out of Stanford, set in lush woodland within reach of the beach. With closest neighbours over a mile away it was the perfect place to throw huge parties, which Kesey set about doing with some gusto.

In 1964, when the release of his second book *Sometimes a Great Notion* meant he had to travel to New York, Kesey hit on a plan. Rather than sit around waiting for the world to change, why didn't they get out there and get some changing done? What would happen if they took their La Honda scene and transported it into small towns, outbacks, villages and stopovers far from California, turning ordinary people on as they went?

He and the Pranksters took an old school bus, painted it in psychedelic colours, rigged it with a whole host of sound equipment and took off from San Francisco for a trip across the country. Jack Kerouac's muse for *On The Road* had been Neal Cassady, so who better to have at the wheel than the angel-headed hipster himself? He'd rocked up unannounced on Perry Lane just as things were shaking down, and immediately hit it off with Kesey.

Along the way, wherever the bus stopped, they cranked up the music and held 'freak outs,' offering drugs to anyone who'd have them, hoping to open their minds to the higher place of peace, love and transcendent consciousness. This was their gospel. This was their message and ministry, the word 'drug addict' not even in the vocabulary, Kesey thinking more along the lines of the superhero comics he'd obsessed on as a child, pushing back the darkness of the cold war, challenging America to wake up and be America again.

He was a writer in good company, part of a fine tradition. In the early 1790s, just after the Montgolfier's invention of flight and amidst a similar revolutionary counter-cultural ferment, William Blake had written *The Marriage of Heaven and Hell*.

Blake was a vehement critic of the Enlightenment, hating science's obsession with the rational that made men forget that *'all deities reside in the human breast.'*[12] From his home in London he looked over to the bubbling revolution in France, to the tethers of the balloon let loose, to the rising of the people through the burning air of ideas, to the overthrowing of the clergy and aristocracy and the liberation of desire.

If the doors of perception were cleansed every thing would appear to man as it is, infinite. For man has closed himself up, till he sees all things thro' narrow chinks of his cavern.

Though he was no great fan, there are hints of Plato here, his famed story of mankind lying chained in a cave, seeing the world only through shadows cast onto a wall, philosophy not something occult but a means of breaking our chains by facing full on what had been occluded. Blake's poem is his own retelling of the tale: mankind closed up, everything seen through a narrow chink of the cavern. Only by cleaning the doors of perception would the light pour in, revealing everything in its true form: infinite. How would this cleansing happen? Blake wrote of 'printing in the infernal method,' his work a corrosive that would melt away the all that sullied the surface of things.

Taken up by successive generations of cultural revolutionaries, these lines reverberated powerfully through history and—having seen the drug he had dreamed of come into existence—it was to Blake that Aldous Huxley turned to in the 1950s, writing up his experiences with LSD and mescaline in *The Doors of Perception* and *Heaven and Hell*. This was Huxley's own printing used as corrosive, describing how this spectacular new 'acid' could melt and burn away the surfaces of conservative English life, displaying the resplendent infinity of human possibility that lay beneath.

Before Leary, before Kesey, before the counterculture had even begun, here was a major public intellectual offering his careful thoughts about the possible benefits of hallucinogens for human improvement. Describing his experiences in vivid prose, Huxley traced the history of 'vision experience' through ancient cultures and religions, common themes of herbs, gardens, intense light, controlled breathing, mantras or extended periods of songs and meditation all identified as means of gaining spiritual altitude, of spying Eden again, of breaking the chains, leaving the cave and finding the higher truth at its source. Jumping off his pages, chemicals, gem-stones and shiny materials were revealed as part of a long tradition pursued by contemplatives, occultists and ascetics trying to reconnect with the 'all deities that reside in the human chest.'

'Their faces are painted in Art Nouveau swirls,' Wolfe writes of Kesey's Pranksters, Huxley and Blake surely gathered round his desk, looking over his shoulder as he typed.

Their Napoleon hats are painted, masks painted, hair dyed weird, embroidered Chinese pyjamas, dresses made out of American flags, Flash Gordon diaphanous polyethylene, supermarket Saran Wrap, India-print coverlets shawls Cossack coats...a hell of a circus.

In short: a riot of colour, and Huxley nods sagely, recognising La Honda as in the very ancient tradition of vision induction.

Sadly, he never lived to see the flourishing of the counterculture he had done so much to create. In November of 1963, living now in Los Angeles, a serious throat condition took hold; he was in a great deal of pain and unable to speak. On the 22nd of that month, close to death, Huxley scribbled on a piece of paper 'LSD - try it. Intramuscular. 100 mg.' His wife administered the drug to him and as he fell into his last trip, she whispered quietly into his ear:

Light and free you let go, darling; forward and up. You are going forward and up; you are going toward the light [...] you are going toward the light—you are going toward a greater love.[13]

As he did so, at the very hour this man who had worked so hard to open up the doors of the mind lifted one last time towards the light, a motorcade turned into Dealey Plaza in Dallas, a chink opened in a window at the Texas Schools Book Depository, and Lee Harvey Oswald blew a hole in the back of John F Kennedy's head, his wife cradling his bloodied remains, bending over him and telling him she loved him as their car sped forward, away from the crowds.

—

A Day-Glo school bus pulling up, a band playing on top, freaky looking individuals pouring out of windows and doors, running up and offering substances... Anyone who'd encountered Kesey and the Pranksters in 1964 would have quickly understood that they were far from ordinary, but—just as in Blake's time—these days after the shooting of JFK were far from ordinary. America was, across its length and depth, an anxious place, an evangelical place, full of energy and fear and violence, simultaneously undergoing all manner of revolutions.

Following the shooting of 15-year-old African-American James Powell by police Lieutenant Thomas Gilligan, terrible riots broke out in Harlem on the east coast. Pouring money into 'Project Uplift' to employ young Harlemites, as the hastily-installed President Johnson got the east under control, in August that same summer of '64 rioting broke out on the west coast in the Watts area of Los Angeles.

Black people were on the move, demanding a narrative that treated them justly and equally. Hundreds of thousands had marched on Washington in August of 1963, but still the Civil Rights Act met with great opposition before eventually being passed in July of '64. This hardly eased national tensions. In March of 1965, protesting another death at the hands of the police, a group of 600 began a peaceful march from Selma, Alabama, to the state capital, Montgomery. They had only gone a few hundred feet when they were attacked by police and mounted state troopers, who fired tear gas at them, whipped them and beat them with clubs wrapped in barbed wire, all of this broadcast on national television.

If these pictures weren't shocking enough, from the sweating, seething jungles of Vietnam came back newsreels of flaming napalm and brutal killing. The Cuban Missile Crisis had stopped hearts dead in October 1962, and Secretary of Defence Robert McNamara had subsequently done nothing for the state of national anxiety by fully signing up to the principle of Mutually Assured Destruction: any strike on the US would mean utter annihilation for Russia too.

It was into the midst of all of this that LSD came, into the midst of this that Kesey's bus rolled, offering free trips into Other Worldly orbits, a miracle drug that promised peace for all mankind through higher consciousness. With shadowy assassinations of leading political figures, the prospect of nuclear holocaust, riots and unrest in poverty-stricken neighbourhoods on both coasts, every part of American society was being violently shaken. Who could blame people for accepting a tab and blasting off on a trip to escape awhile?

Industrialisation, consumerism, globalisation, families torn apart by war, the rising of down-trodden minorities who refused to be oppressed any more—though Harvey Kling may have been insulated from much of it, huge changes tore through the country after the Second World War. In coastal white middle class America these forces had produced the Beat poets and then the hippies, in black working class America it had generated the civil rights movement, each strata of society trying to get out from under whatever was beating them down, each trying to find their wings.

Returning from service in Vietnam, sneering, rebellious, raising a bird to the American Dream that had passed them by, these same pressures acted on young white working class men and generated a very different beast. The oldest among them had seen heavy, brutal action in the Second World War, the youngest having done things for their country that no boy should be asked to. The loud machines, the military organisational structure, the adventure, shared enterprise, comradeship and fraternity against a powerful enemy—all of these they had lost when discharged, and found again through biker gangs. Taking their name from the bomber squadrons that had razed Dresden, they were the Hells Angels, and the sight—and sound—of huge phalanxes of large and powerful men on large and powerful motorcycles further increased the moral panic in those summers of the mid 1960s.

There were sensational newspaper stories, small towns being overrun and smashed to pieces, gang rapes and bloody brawls. Their fearful name was imbued with verticals, pilot-descended steel-winged men of the above now rising up from the underworld they'd been discarded into, bringing death and destruction in their wake.

And yet, underneath the class differences, the Harley's roar was indistinguishable from Ginsberg's *Howl*. The Beat poets and Angels were compatriots in revolution and the man who perhaps came closest to being the bastard son of both was Hunter S Thompson.

Born in Louisville, Kentucky, he had grown up in poverty—his father dying when he was very young—but come to befriend some of the most wealthy and privileged boys in the state. All of them had been rebels in love with literature, but when they'd been busted and jailed for trying to buy booze underage, Thompson was shocked to see his friends all sprung by their well-connected fathers, while he, father-less, was left to rot. The judge had given him two choices: jail, or the military. Foregoing a likely glittering college career, Thompson chose to serve.

He honed his skills of irreverent description working on a forces newspaper before finally making his name as a journalist through his 1966 book on the Hells Angels, which he opened with lines from a 15th Century rebel-poet and ruffian, François Villon:

In my own country I am in a far-off land
I am strong but have no force or power
I win all yet remain a loser
At break of day I say goodnight
When I lie down I have a great fear
Of falling.

Returning from their country-crossing bus tour, seeing first-hand the different tensions and anxieties that were plaguing the nation, Kesey wanted to prove the peace-building, love-making power of LSD once and for all. Leary was continuing his 'research,' but his subjects were polite college kids. What was the point of them being turned on unless this shit worked with the really hard cases?

Who harder, Kesey thought, than the Angels? Connected through Thompson, he sat down for a beer with Sonny Barger, the Angel's much-feared leader. Kesey was awaiting trial for a charge of possessing marijuana, a little outlaw thing that gained some credit with Barger.

Kesey made his move. Hounded from towns and harassed by the police, for the first time in their history, the Hells Angels found themselves *invited* to a party.

Kesey was nothing if not bold. He was the superhero, the athlete *and* aesthete, the outdoorsman, the wrestler with a typewriter. The Angels would eat Leary up and spit his anaemic little bones out. If anyone was going to do this, to show the true power of acid, it had to be him. So, outside his ranch in La Honda, he had erected an enormous banner which read, in multicoloured, painted letters:

THE MERRY PRANKSTERS
WELCOME THE HELLS ANGELS.

The day after the Voting Rights Bill was committed to law, just as Watts was heating to boiling point, a raging squadron of Harley Davidsons roared down the winding Route 84 over to Kesey's where, for the next 3 days, they were given as much beer as they could drink and were slipped LSD for the first time, creating from two ends of the spectrum of white alienation something 'wonderful and marvellous, an unholy alliance,' Wolfe noting this all down:

The beer made the Angels very happy and the LSD made them strangely peaceful. [...] Pete, the drag racer, from the San Francisco Hell's Angels grinned and rummaged through a beer tub and said 'Man, this is nothing but a goddamn wonderful scene. We didn't know what to expect when we came, but it turned out just fine. This time it's all ha-ha, not thump-thump.[14]

—

Drugs *and* motorcycles? I laughed at the thought of my mother's two greatest fears combined in one terrifying party. These chapters in Wolfe's book read like something from the Apocrypha, a miracle worthy of a gospel, this wafer-thin sacrament casting the demons out of these herd of grunting, rutting swine, leaving them pretty much tranquillised, near as damn-it socialised.

I didn't know any Angels at university, but in the thump-thump of the club scene the Acid Jazz worked like Blake's corrosive, melting away my surfaces, opening me up to new kinds of people. Me and a couple of friends had started a band and things were going pretty well. We were played by Gilles Petersen on his radio show, and went to record in Massive Attack's studios. Next to *Sergeant Pepper,* their *Blue Lines* album was pretty much the most perfect record I had ever heard, and here we were, my friend laying down a guitar track and Daddy G nodding along approvingly in the background, me naively thinking our differences could be dissolved by music. No one in the room knew anything about me, no one was able to judge, and this experience of simply being accepted was both frightening and wonderful.

We were playing packed gigs, supporting well-known acts, and could pretty much walk into clubs for free. Another set of exams, another car stepped into, another trip to Glastonbury, the whole lot of us going in 1993, the sun shining on everything, The Orb playing and—holy shit—The Velvet Underground too, a genuine legendary act from the actual 1960s.

Music had done this. I felt that the ecstasy of it was healing me, bathing me and filling in the cavernous voids where family should have been. I was feeling it more keenly: my brother had fully launched away and gone to work in East Africa. Did I sense then that I'd hardly see him for the next 20 years? If I did, I still loved the idea of us gathering as a happy family, and, as each holiday approached, I kept convincing myself that things would be better than they had been before. They were in so many ways, but still those flash-points came around the dinner table and the old wounds split and bled.

My sister had her own scene too, and though we hardly spoke during term time I was relieved to hear news via Mum that she was building a life for herself. She had her roll-up cigarettes and backpacking tours around Europe, good friends she'd kept up with from school. We went together to help out on the same children's summer camps we'd been on ourselves, and in diluted company we got on well and would laugh and joke and drink. One August evening in a pub in north Norfolk, perched on soft cliffs, I edged back to our table with a tray of pints, and seeing her there holding court with another hilarious story my eyes began to well. The garden was dark enough and I pushed the tear back. I wanted to cry for the fact that she was well, but wanted to weep because I knew that I was not. Years of attention she'd had, and here was I, still infected, still untreated, all of this disease still crushed down somewhere inside with no way I could see of extracting it. I prescribed myself isolation. I would head back to college, to this thing I had that was away from them all, wishing that there was some way that I could make it last forever.

—

The question around La Honda was how long LSD's effects on the Angels would last. Observing the party at Kesey's, Hunter Thompson was as shocked as anyone. The biker gang genuinely scared him, and rightly so: one of them had nearly killed him when Thompson had stepped in to stop the man beating his wife and dog. But here he was, watching the acid corrode and strip away these long-conditioned reflexes of violence and suspicion. One of the Angels, Freewheeling Frank later said:

I never really became a Hells Angel until I took LSD. [It] is a medicine and not a drug. I only hope it gets in the right hands, and is used for Love rather than Fortune or Fame.[15]

It seemed to be in exactly the right hands for now. Men descended from bomber pilots were flying peacefully among their fellow human beings, these alienated rebels become peaceable mystics, sat listening to tripped-out music and tape-loops played by a bunch of Pranksters Kesey had thrown together, a band who started calling themselves The Grateful Dead.

MK-ULTRA was still top secret, but LSD had shown itself to work. It *did* bring peace. The love was spreading and the success of the party gave Kesey huge belief. What they had at La Honda was a microcosm that simply needed scaling up. Wars would stop and a transcendent global consciousness would emerge. Like Huxley said: Earth would become paradise.

Encouraged and excited, Kesey wanted the Prankster ministry widened. The Pranksters were invited later that summer to the annual Unitarian conference, to park their bus *Furthur* among the camping teenagers, some ministers freaked out by it all, but Kesey hailed by others as a true Prophet in the mould of Christ himself:

It was like the whole Prankster thing was now building up to some kind of conclusion, some ascension. A great burning column, reaching about the western horizon.[16]

Trouble was, like Jesus Christ himself, Kesey's popularity and the claims about his miracles meant the heat on him was getting turned up. LSD was still legal, but there was serious debate over whether this 'soul-revealing' drug opened up genuine religious experiences, or if it was no more than an artificial high—in other words, were these wings of angels or demons? It was St Peter and Simon Magus all over again, and plenty of people seemed to be praying for Kesey's downfall.

A year or so before, Leary himself had spoken at a conference of Lutheran psychologists, telling them that what they were seeing fitted the well-worn template of religious controversy. On the one side were new, young spiritual pioneers, confused but convinced about their ecstatic experiences, and on the other were the establishment, the priests, the Temple guards and so forth who denounced this new development as a dangerous heresy. 'The issue of chemical expansion of consciousness is upon us and you are going to be pressed for a position,' he told them. 'Internal freedom is becoming a major religious and civil rights controversy.'

Kesey, the Prankster Pope, was clear: this was so good it would be a crime to deny it to anybody.

"When you've got something like we've got, you can't just sit on it. You've got to move off it. You can't just sit on it and possess it, you've got to move off of it and give it to other people."[17]

Screw the power of the bomb to cow folks into acquiescence! Here was a far mightier mushroom cloud blowing off inside the mind that radiated nothing but pure love.

Dazzled by the miracle with the Angels, Kesey was convinced he could perform another. Going to religious camp-outs was one thing, but surely, as high priest of this emerging counter-culture, he should make divine convocation with the four biggest, most influential gods in the Universe. Surely the Pranksters should now host... The Beatles.

Having recorded and released *Day Tripper* that spring, the newly-turned on Beatles were due to finish their summer tour at the Cow Palace in San Francisco on 2nd September, 1965. It was just 3 weeks after the Hell's Angels had come to La Honda, and, having had it work so well last time, the Pranksters created another huge banner, this time announcing:

THE MERRY PRANKSTERS
WELCOME THE BEATLES.

Kesey could read between the lines of their new song. He knew they were turned on, and he had it all mapped out: The Beatles would play the gig and then come out to La Honda for a decent freaking party with the Pranksters. They were Prankster people. No matter that Kesey had actually *met* the Hell's Angels; he had no personal connection with The Beatles at all, but he now felt in total control: everyone could, at will, be brought into their thing. The sign would make them come, and the gods would meet, and a new era would be upon the Earth...

Except the gig was monstrous. As every Beatles gig now was—hence their giving up touring immediately after. Tens of thousands of teenage girls screamed incessantly, even during the support acts. During songs, between songs, it made no difference, and nobody, especially not the Pranksters in their seats high up in the gods of the venue, could hear a single note.

Even more smashed on acid than ever, thousands of flashbulbs popping each second, the trip turns bad, the sound of screaming unbearable but then doubling again. Wolfe describes the girls waving their arms around, 'a writhing, seething mass... like a single colonial animal with a thousand waving pink tentacles.' Kesey becomes convinced that the whole thing is going to implode. All he can see is cancer, poison, madness, a creature out of control, about to snap and devour them all. He orders the Pranksters to leave, his young girlfriend moaning that she'd 'come here with a bunch of old men who never saw a rock 'n' roll show before,' all of them on a downer, but trying to pull up again, heading back to Kesey's ranch because the sign had said WELCOME THE BEATLES and they would *surely* come.

They didn't. When they reached the ranch hundreds of people were flocked on Kesey's land, swarming around in expectation of the miracle, but as the night drew on and the band didn't arrive it became clear that this was one that even Kesey and his Pranksters could not deliver. They were utterly downcast.

The Beatles didn't go out to Kesey's ranch, but instead went home and recorded *Tomorrow Never Knows*, its extraordinary, ground-

56

breaking drone and Eastern guitar sounds somehow a more perfect, heady distillation of everything that Kesey and The Grateful Dead had been aiming at.

The Beatles didn't follow the Prankster's bus out to Kesey's ranch, but somehow, from somewhere, had their own bright idea to get an old bus, paint it up and travel the country doing acid and making a movie, a *Magical Mystery Tour...*

The Beatles didn't take up Kesey's invitation, but someone else's instead, driving from their gig at the Cow Palace in an armoured car to spend the evening with... Elvis Presley.

Elvis? That washed-up melamine *square.* That *un-turned-on throwback?* What the *fuck?*

—

Inexorably, the months and years were turning. I entered my final year of university and too soon Christmas had come and gone, finals now looming, that summer an event I simply could not see beyond.

At break of day I say goodnight. When I lie down I have a great fear of falling.

The days of walking home from clubs, the dawn just beginning to rise, buying bottles of milk from the milkman rattling on his early rounds, the blissful silence and the cool air after the hours of heat and noise, saying goodnight as day broke... all of it was ending.

In old language I'd 'gone up' for my degree, and now, inescapable as gravity, I had to come down. The band was falling apart as people decided they needed to study, to equip themselves for what was next. Except I had no idea what was coming next. When I lay down, all I knew was this great fear of falling, of the unknown period beyond this place where I'd have to actually begin living for real.

One cold spring evening the phone went in the house and someone shouted upstairs for me. It was Mum. She sounded upset. The dog I'd been given for my birthday all those years ago had died. They'd buried her under the bird table. I couldn't speak. I held on while she said what words of comfort she could, and hung up and went upstairs to my room and wept.

She'd seen me through, her black coat and wet nose, her thumping tail and playful bark leading me onwards, not letting me sit or mope, always onwards in excitement, ever hopeful. She'd seen me through to this point, and now she'd lain down, unable to do any more.

Mum and Dad had moved the year before, out to a village in the next county, a new house where my brother and sister and I no longer had a room to call our own. All of this I cried for, adrift and homeless. Having turned my back, determined to be free, to make my own way, I now found family giving me what I'd wanted, not pushing for information or pressing me about what I was going to do. Everyone else seemed to have something sorted out—a job, an in, an opportunity or idea. Wasn't someone meant to have helped me with this? While I was blagging pints at 5am, shouldn't someone have been pushing me into milk-round interviews with banks or engineering firms?

For near-on three years I'd strived to stay aloft, convincing myself that in those high places I'd become whole. Now, to my horror, I found that I hadn't. I'd blown it. These high times hadn't healed me at all. They had helped me escape for a while but now, like a horizon I couldn't glide over, graduation was hurtling towards me, a dark night falling, with me alone and chartless, rolling into the unknown, with no direction home.

—

Tired and dispirited at The Beatles' no show, their powers for the first time shown to be limited, the Pranksters hit the first waves of turbulence that would only later bring down the whole counterculture.

A few short weeks later, the very same Hell's Angels that Kesey had turned on to peace and love now turned up at an anti-war march in Oakland. Chanting 'Hare Krishna,' Ginsberg was there at the front of the crowd of students, Pranksters and hippies, when Sonny Barger and his gang appeared and began ripping down banners and attacking the protesters, yelling, 'go back to Russia you fucking communists!'

Pre-warned that things might get nasty, Ginsberg had already made a contingency plan: if there was any trouble someone should put The Beatles' hit *I Wanna Hold Your Hand* on to get everyone dancing together. Trouble was, The Beatles were like salt in the wound for the Pranksters right now, so Kesey talked to Barger in person and the Angels pulled back a little, though they continued to sling abuse at the marchers and tried to pick fights.

Having been heroes of the bohemian left just weeks before, now they were being hailed by the political right, and they loved it. Barger, something of a notorious celebrity himself, sent a telegram to President Johnson with a message that read like a pitch for *Apocalypse Now*:

> *On behalf of myself and my associates I volunteer a group of loyal Americans for behind-the-lines duty in Vietnam. We feel that a crack group of trained gorillas [sic] would demoralize the Viet Cong and advance the cause for freedom. We are available for training and duty immediately.*[18]

After the heady success of the La Honda party, this clash with the Angels was a sobering moment for the Pranksters, and everyone in the scene who had put their faith in the power of LSD. Hunter Thompson was there documenting it all, later calling the confrontation 'an historic schism in the then Rising Tide of the Youth Movement of the Sixties.' For a few blissful weeks, Kesey and the others had believed in the miraculous power of acid to bring peace, but now, with violence breaking out at a goddamn *peace march*, that dream was over, this attempt to reconcile working class biker-dropouts with upper middle class students trashed by Thompson as a 'doomed effort.'

Soundtracked by *Sergeant Pepper*, the 'summer of love'—regarded as the apex of the counterculture movement—was still to come in 1967. Yet to those on the inside of things, as '65 turned to '66 the writing was already on the wall. The Beatles hadn't come, the Angels hadn't been pacified, the war in Vietnam was intensifying and the civil rights movement was still brutal. Earth would not be made paradise, not this way.

Kesey, not willing to go down without a fight, tried to crank things up nonetheless, and changed tack. Rather than expect people to just turn up at his place, he decided that they needed to get out again and start proselytising. The Grateful Dead were up and running properly now and gathering a following. They became the house band for a series of 'Acid Tests,' large scale events in concert halls with roaring guitars and tape and film loops all mixed in as Neal Cassady rapped away on a mike, others chanting, lights flashing, the Pranksters synthesising as best they could the experience of a trip, no drugs actually being given out officer, no sir, but—as the saying went—'never trust a Prankster,' and if anyone helped themselves to the free Kool-Aid, well they might just find that it had been electrified.

Under the hood though, the mission had changed too. The bus trip had aimed at switching on the masses, the Pranksters believing they could usher in a new era of psychedelic consciousness, making war and division a thing of the past. That had failed, so now the aim was 'to get hundreds, maybe even thousands, synched up ... to leave the planet!'[19] Escape was the driver now: if they couldn't stop wars and help people live in harmony, they might as well take off for a different world and leave the rest to it.

Thousands did come, all of them stoned, all of them looking to become part of this emerging scene. After the first few Tests things began to get more serious, and Kesey was approached by event producers who saw a chance to take the format and polish it until it was like, as one put it, one of Billy Graham's crusades. In other words: mass market.

Kesey was torn. On the one hand he still hankered after this vision of LSD precipitating a new world order, but on the other—post Angels—that was looking like a more difficult proposition. With all the recent trouble there were those who wanted to keep the drug within the bohemian intellectual scene, preserve its use for those who knew how to get high properly, not as an inebriant for shit-faced undergraduates or violent gang members... but Kesey had said it himself: when you've got something like we've got, you can't just sit on it. Even under pressure, a messiah has a duty to share.

One of the apostle-Pranksters was a well-organised young hippie idealist called Stewart Brand, and he and Kesey decided to go all out, headlining Brand's three day 'Trips Festival' with an Acid Test on the Saturday night. Jesus, things were getting complex though, and the authorities were looking for a way to get him. Like McMurphy—his protagonist in *One Flew Over the Cuckoo's Nest*—Kesey's rebellious, fun-loving antics had been tolerated to an extent, but were now beginning to land him in pretty serious trouble. In April of '65 the La Honda ranch had been busted by the police. His lawyers had managed to keep stringing things out with various legal arguments, but the whole Hells Angels thing that summer had ramped up the heat and late in '65 he had to take a charge of dealing drugs to minors, agreeing to three years probation and six months on a work team.

January 1966, final plans for the Trips Festival being made, Kesey was sat out on the roof of Stewart Brand's apartment, smoking a joint, looking forward to the biggest, grandest Acid Test ever, relaxed, flicking pebbles into the neighbours' yard, watching them rise and arc and fall. Suddenly the police are there, investigating complaints of stones being thrown, so Kesey slings his bag of marijuana onto the pavement below. The cops find it. This is it. This is serious. He's contravened the terms of his probation. No way out of it, he's going to face definite time inside.

While the lawyers tried to sort it, the Pranksters did the Trips Festival, but police were crawling all over. It felt as if the system was closing in. Determined to avoid jail, Kesey made a bold plan. Claiming that he intended to jump off a cliff to kill himself, he left a suicide note in a truck, slammed it into a tree, and stole away to Mexico. The religious overtones were too obvious to miss: the messiah was dead, impaled on wood.

Some of the Pranksters began to join Kesey down in Manzanillo, but the scene was not good. The prophet of the high life didn't like living underground, and he began to plot a way back into the US. He'd started reflecting on the whole thing, on the Angels on the Acid Tests and the counterculture, and began talking about a radical new direction: going beyond acid.

Owsley, the great acid chemist who is supplying most of the scene, comes down to Mexico for a sit-down with Kesey, who says he's tired of 'opening the door and going through it and then always going back out again.' Unsurprisingly, Owsley sees this as bad for business, and freaks out:

'Bullshit Kesey! It's the drugs that do it. It's all the drugs, man. None of it would have happened without the drugs'—and so forth.

Kesey keeps cocking his head to one side and giggling in the upcountry manner and saying: 'No, it's not the drugs. In fact'—chuckle, giggle—'I'm going to tell everyone to start doing it without the drugs.'[20]

Not just opening the doors of perception, but putting chocks under them. 'Storming heaven,' was how Leary had put the exact same idea to Owsley, and now Kesey was saying it too, talking about life as shadows on the cave wall, murky representations of the higher True Forms, the chemicals unchaining them for a few hours, but them needing to go further, an elite band of students taking off the hinges, opening a free path to the transcendent. Blake's vision would become a daily-lived reality, Huxley's dream would be fulfilled, man returning to The Source 'in his primal state of innocence.'[21]

There must be something in the air, because right then in August of '66 a new band break onto the scene. They call themselves The Doors and have clearly done their background literary work too.

The gate is straight, deep and wide,
Break on through to the other side
Everybody loves my baby, everybody loves my baby,
She gets high, she gets high
Tried to run, tried to hide,
Break on through to the other side.

It wasn't much of a hit, but the mood of breakage, energy, and escape resonated with Kesey's idea of a final assault. Yes-sir, Kesey says to Owsley. What with Vietnam and mutually assured destruction...with Earth becoming hellish it was time to stop making return trips, to get out of here for good.

At least, that was one side of it. Kesey then sneaked back from Mexico and gave a clandestine interview with the Village Voice, just as 'Break on Through' was released, railing about the state of the counterculture:

LSD has reached the stature where Babbitt begins to take it. It used to be Hells Angels and Bohemians, but now the son of the hardware store owner in Des Moines is taking it.[22]

He might as well have accused Harvey Kling. George Babbitt was the protagonist of Sinclair Lewis' 1922 satirical novel about middle-class American conformity, Des Moines the capital of Iowa, about as far from the countercultural coast as it was possible to get. Only a year before Kesey had been the one out on those roads trying to get Babbitt to take it, but here was Kesey the elitist, Kesey the winning athlete, Kesey the one who had, against all the competition, got onto the Stanford writing programme, and then, with crowds of others trying, been the one selected to join Perry Lane. The extraordinary had become ordinary, and Kesey wanted to push on higher.

If anyone was going to storm heaven, to make it to the mountaintop, it would have to be someone special. After the Angels, after The Beatles, Kesey no longer believed in taking the masses along with him. Not only did LSD not work as they'd hoped and bring about mass peace and love, it had also just been made illegal—something that many heads now began blaming Kesey for. The net was tightening. He was chased down by police in October of '66 and jailed, awaiting trial.

It was time to eject, to lift off and escape for good. His lawyers made a plea to the judge. He was an important man, someone young people looked up to. He'd been a student of LSD for a long time and learned many things. Down in Mexico he'd had a revelation, a vision of 'going beyond.' The judge pushed his glasses up the bridge of his nose, wondering what kind of BS this drop-out author was going to try now, hearing something about pulling kids away from LSD, reluctantly thinking it had to be worth a shot, looking Kesey sternly in the eye as he read out the conditions, bailing him to pull this stunt, this drugs education event, after which he'd see out his sentence.

Kesey walks, stands on the steps of the courthouse, the usual gaggle of journalists and heads gathering round with wire-bound notebooks and microphones as he announces the last great act of the Prankster ministry. Halloween night, 1966, he tells them. The Acid Graduation.

—

'...in this warehouse, and this is where we're going to do it. We're going to have the Graduation here and it's going to be our scene.'[23]

My own life at college hurtling blind towards a precipice, I knew that this was what Wolfe's book built up to, this final act, this last supper of the Pranksters.

Though desperate to project otherwise, the resurrected Kesey was exhausted and full of doubts as he pulled back on his buckskin shirt and gathered everyone around him again to explain what they were going to do.

Kesey's voice picks up and he starts assigning tasks: Page in charge of setting up a stage and chairs. Roy Seburn to decorate the place with a lot of cloth hangings. Faye and Gretch to get food and drink.

He had secured Winterland—with 5,000 seats one of San Francisco's best venues—but at the last minute the owner had pulled out. A major political rally was booked in for a few days after, and rumours were flying that the Pranksters would spray an invisible coating of LSD on door handles and into the ventilation, sending unsuspecting Senators tripping. All Kesey had now was a broken down old warehouse.

The Pranksters gathered in the dust that Halloween night in '66 knowing that the next morning their leader would be returning to jail. They gathered knowing that the Hells Angels hadn't been miraculously pacified and that The Beatles—a band now unwelcome in many parts of the US for claiming to be bigger than Jesus—were not within their powers of attraction.

They gathered knowing that LSD hadn't lived up to the enormous hopes they had had for it, that as of 3 weeks back it was now illegal, that Kesey, playing fast and loose with the drug, was partly to blame. Richard Alpert—who had, along with Leary, sacrificed his academic career over his hopes for the drug's spiritual potential—was most vocal, decrying its use in 'manic screaming orgies in public places.'

They gathered knowing that a lot of people in the scene were pissed at them... pissed, but still fascinated. Kesey is interviewed as a guest on local TV, people holding up cards reminding him to say the promised words that LSD is dangerous, but he's refusing to take the prompts.

'Ken, can you tell us something about the message you're going to have for the kids at this Acid Test Graduation?' the TV guy says, and Kesey smiles his big Oregon smile and winks and says, 'I'm going to tell them, "Never trust a Prankster."'

Never trust a Prankster! Maybe this Graduation thing was all a ruse. The whispers went round the hip joints of San Francisco. Maybe it was going to be the biggest, baddest Acid Test of all.

Knowing all this, Kesey, the one-time messiah, pressures building on every side, desperately tries to lift his followers one last time, preparing them for the final push, up and through the veil:

> *These costumes are not for a Halloween party but for the liberation of dead souls...churchly vestiture, in truth... They're like freaking faëries out of A Midsummer Night's Dream, duelling shirts and long gowns of phosphorescent pastels like the world never saw before, Day-Glo death masks beaming out in front of the instruments.*

On the most occult night of the year the Pranksters kit out the San Francisco warehouse with every piece of electrical equipment they can lay their hands on. Audio, lighting, staging, decoration, the whole place rigged for the ceremony, the night arriving and hundreds and hundreds of heads turning up, most of them dumb to the reality, still in mythic awe of the miracle Kesey had pulled with the Angels—some of whom have roared up in their leathers demanding to be let in— everyone intrigued to see what the returning, back-from-the-dead trickster has planned. Could he do it again? What with his temporary reprieve from jail and talk of 'going beyond' the place is also crawling with reporters and TV crews, trying to get the scoop on this coming ascension.

Finally, with the Day-Glo colours set against the vast backdrop of the civil rights movement, assassinated presidents, ongoing war, the threat of nuclear annihilation... with the fights with the Angels, the disappointment of The Beatles, the drugs charges, the outlawing of LSD... with ancient shamans, priests, Blake, Huxley, Hofmann, Leary and Ginsberg ringing in their ears—with *all* of this the music begins to play and loop, people dancing and smoking, Neal Cassady standing bare-chested like a circus master, speaking to the crowd, drawing them towards the doors, readying them for the breakthrough...

Hiding all these conflicting thoughts, Kesey takes the stage, a single spotlight beaming on him as his commencement speech begins, preparing his disciples for flight with very deep messianic talk about the journey of humankind, onwards into a brilliant new post-Enlightenment myth:

> *'I believe that man is changing...in a radical basic way...The waves are building, and every time they build they're stronger. Our concept of reality is changing. It's been happening here in San Francisco...I believe there's a whole new generation of kids. They walk different...I can hear it in the music...It used to go life - death, life - death... but now it's death - life... death - life.'*

That ancient, primordial theme of death again, and the desire to escape it. *O Pavarnana*—the hymn to the mystic drink in the Rigveda—*place me in that deathless, undecaying world, wherein the light of heaven is set, and everlasting lustre shines...* All have slugged the Kool-Aid, imbibed the holy soma, beckoning in the Brave New World, whatever form it will take.

The wildly pioneering *Tomorrow Never Knows* had only a month or so before hit the airwaves as the parting track on The Beatles' new *Revolver* LP. *Turn off your mind, relax and float down stream*, Lennon sang. *It is not dying, it is not dying. Lay down all thoughts, surrender to the void, it is shining, it is shining.* Music like nobody had ever heard, sounds and words that needle Kesey as he looks around at the crowd, imagining them choosing Elvis over... over *this*.

He pushes the thought away, and with the smoke billowing and the vibrant colours and with the anticipation of the cream of high society before him he's like Étienne Montgolfier, the balloon readied, the tethers there to be cut, this journey about to begin that no human has ever achieved before...

'There are moments,' Karen Armstrong writes, 'when we all, in one way or another, have to go to a place that we have never seen, and do what we have never done before...' If new myths are going to be born, these trailblazing flights must be undertaken...

But every time Kesey gets the atmosphere right and the thing begins to rise the TV crews keep puncturing, extending microphones, giving orders in stage whispers. Frustrated, he nonetheless pushes on.

> *'For a year we've been in the Garden of Eden. Acid opened the door to it. It was the Garden of Eden and Innocence and a ball. Acid opens the door and you enter and stay a while...'*

All of this is pure Blake and Huxley, and Kesey, a learned man of letters, plays them beautifully, standing on their shoulders, reaching for the above they had longed for. But just then a quartet of cops come in, poke around, break the atmosphere again. Word begins spreading that it's really not a Prank and *there's no goddamn drugs being served*. It's all feeling like hot air or—more worryingly—like there's some rip in the fabric, in-rushing cold drafts sending the balloon descending.

Kesey desperately tries to explain, how they need to lift off and step through the door for good, but it's complex and subtle and there are too many punctures and the vibe is leaking fast. It's like the Palace of Versailles, the rain pouring, Etienne riled, the Lords and Ladies impatient, ignorant of just how bloody difficult this is. People begin to look around at each other, a little embarrassed, like this thing isn't going to fly. The true believers in the core join hands in a circle and close their eyes tight, waiting for the moment of energy... *Turn off your mind, relax and float down stream.*

Kesey is still working hard to create lift-off, a corporate transfiguration, chanting and chanting *Hare Krishna Hare Krishna* and for a moment, Wolfe tells us, *'he pops out of the time warp into the silver haze of...The Universal Mind...'*

This is it! He has returned to the Source! At such a great high that he can perceive the unity of all things! This is the psychedelic experience! His soul fully revealed!

But then there's more noise and he's back on the ground. It won't work. It can't work. The doors won't budge. The nuclear reaction won't start, these mere sparks too weak to light this new sun.

'We almost had it,' says Kesey, opening his eyes for the first time. 'We would have had it. There's too much noise...'

People start to mill around. There's embarrassment and confusion and they drift away, go to other parties, places where there's less bullshit, more drink, more drugs. Then one of Kesey's children begins to cry, to scream in fact, and Wolfe describes this piercing, singular noise reverberating through the warehouse, one lone voice imploring someone to tend to the kid.

'The - child - is - crying - Do - something - for - the - child - first'

Kesey says nothing. His eyes are shut tight. The high keening sound rises from the circle with the kid's scream weaving through it. Fantastic mind power crackle - Goldhill registers the energy

THEY'RE ALMOST

But the girl on the other side doesn't let up: 'See - about - the - child - A - Child - is - crying - and - no - one - is doing - anything - about - it'

ALMOST HAVE IT - PRESQUE VU

' - Why - is - the - child - crying - Doesn't - an-y-bo-dy - care?'

Too tied up in trying to birth a new consciousness, nobody cares for the newborn. Perhaps Lennon had been right all along. Perhaps those with a ticket to ride *didn't* really care, those who flew high didn't do right by the rest they were leaving behind.

Tragically, wrenchingly, it comes to an end. Cassady draws the Graduation to a close, the hundreds now down to just 50 or so as dawn comes, the wan rising sun shedding grey light on their dashed hopes, the bright new star they had set their hopes on cold in the morning, extinguished.

WE BLEW IT! they chant, a mantra the Merry Pranksters now repeat over and over as they lament the coming death of the counterculture, their failure to storm heaven, to bring peace to Earth or even eject away from it for good.

The Summer of Love hasn't even happened yet, but they already see it. So much shit and hurt and aggression and oppression, and this thing they had discovered had promised to lift them away from it all, up and away from the violence and war and division, returning them to Eden. But it hadn't. It couldn't.

Their eyes open and they are still on the ground, this revelation still smarting but the bloody wars still going on, the racial tensions still smouldering, the fear of nuclear apocalypse still palpable, the doors of perception still shut, the new world of peace and love not born, the book ended, our Graduations over and me literally reeling in shock with them as the curtain falls on this time of ecstasy, the blackness of the unknown days ahead gaping as the chant rises, me mouthing silently along with them,

WE BLEW IT!

WE BLEW IT!

WE BLEW IT!

Me, at corner of Haight and Ashbury, 1990

3. Altitude Sickness

In 1971, following his success documenting the Hells Angels, Hunter S Thompson was hired by Sports Illustrated to cover the Mint 400, an off-road motorcycle race out in the desert near Las Vegas. He felt it an opportunity worth taking, not so much for the story as a chance to get away from California and spend time with the prominent Mexican lawyer and activist Oscar Zeta Acosta. They wanted to get out of town to discuss the killing of the TV journalist Rubén Salazar by the Los Angeles police during an anti-Vietnam war march.

Their trip—and a second that followed shortly after—he wrote up in a complex amalgam of fact and fiction as *Fear and Loathing in Las Vegas—A Savage Journey to the Heart of the American Dream*. If Wolfe's book had been what had launched me into university, Thompson was what so many students were reading when I'd got there, passing it round as a triumphant victory roll of soaring hedonism.

I remember skimming it then, late at night, a friend's copy. Only later did I give Thompson more sober time to explain, and there I found a very different book, a lament on the failures of the decade just past, the heart of the American Dream damaged and hurting.

Thompson had been there for the whole thing. He'd been there for Kesey's party with the Angels, there when things had turned violent at the Vietnam march, there when the Beatles hadn't shown, there for the failed Graduation.

He'd also been there in 1969 when The Grateful Dead put on a chaotic free concert in Altamont. The Angels—still the toughest men the band knew—had been asked to provide security around the woefully inadequate stage at the bottom of a long hill. Thompson had watched as the crowds had surged and the Angels thrown themselves happily to their task, meting out beatings as The Rolling Stones played, Jagger's calls for 'these cats to cool it,' falling on deaf ears. When Meredith Hunter—a tripping 18 year old African American—attempted to climb onto the stage, one the Angels attacked him with a knife and killed him.

If the violence at the anti-war march in '65 had been the first symptoms, here at Altamont at the end of the decade were the death throes of the counterculture, the final nail in the coffin of the hopes of acid to bind people together in peace.

It was a death that was simultaneously played out on-screen in December that same year with the release of *Easy Rider*. Starring Peter Fonda as the Kesey-esque hippy-cum-Captain-America and Dennis Hopper as the longhaired, leather-clad Angel Billy, they are joined on their rambling journey of liberation by George, played by Jack Nicholson. At one stop they make in a diner the three face a torrent of abuse and have to flee, and as they camp out under the stars that night George bemoans the demise of America:

> *It's real hard to be free when you're bought and sold in the marketplace. But don't tell anyone that they're not free, or they'll get real busy killing and maiming to prove that they are.*

That's precisely what happens that night: George is bludgeoned to death, leaving Wyatt and Billy fleeing their assailants, their trip descending into darker and darker places, ending up in a New Orleans graveyard during Mardi Gras, tripping on acid with two prostitutes.

Despite making lots of money selling a consignment of cocaine at the opening of the film, despite the amazing motorcycles they'd then bought, despite all the high times, Wyatt knows they've failed.

'We blew it!' he laments, precisely echoing the Pranksters' chorus at the end of the Graduation. Despite drugs and free love—in essence everything that the counterculture had to offer—it had all left him feeling empty, down, chronically low.

'Why don't you get a haircut?' a trucker shouts as he overtakes the two riders leaving New Orleans. When Billy gives him the finger he draws a rifle from his cab and kills him, before opening fire on Wyatt too, the film closing as the camera lifts away from the road, Wyatt's bike exploding in flames.

The trucker, that all-American man of labour, his wheels fixed to the road and his eyes only for the horizontal ahead, guns down both the Angel and the hippie for daring to lift off, daring to flip the bird at the life of conventional graft, sending them crashing to the tarmac in flames, a new Simon Magus felled by the new dominant power, blood oozing onto the ground.

Riding east from the west coast in search of high times, *Easy Rider* was a violent update of the story of Kesey's journey with his Pranksters in '63, who had also headed east with a trunk full of drugs. Where Kesey's road-trip to turn America on had led to hopes of peace and love, *Easy Rider* tore all this bullshit down, adding a tragic and bloody ending.

With *Fear and Loathing,* Thompson now took the baton from Wyatt and Billy and handed it to his own semi-fictional protagonists Raoul Duke and Dr Gonzo, who also screeched away heading east from LA in a souped-up drug-fuelled Chevy convertible.

In '66 Kesey and co. had blown it.

In '69 Billy and Wyatt had blown it.

This was '71, and Duke and Gonzo roared away with an attitude of... *fuck it.*

They had no mission to expand the minds of others, nor to turn the country on to peace and love. They weren't even seeking transcendent experiences or a way of making fast money. Theirs was utterly, darkly, stinkingly, nihilistically a narcissistic trip into heat and sweat and monstrous behaviour. Fuck the money, fuck mind-expanding human progress, fuck psychedelic journeys for the improvement of society, fuck global consciousness and the birthing of a new post-Enlightenment myth, and fuck trying to end wars.

All of that had been tried, and all of it had failed.

Unlike Blake or Huxley, Thompson didn't see acid as something to corrode away the pretensions of society, something to reveal the true divine nature of humanity beneath. 'I've had friends who used LSD to really explore things spiritually,' his first wife said, 'but for Hunter, it was really more of an escape.'[1] Drugs were not about opening up the mind but destroying it, burning through it with pharmacological napalm, a scorched-earth strategy applied to the cortex, memory reduced to ash. LSD wasn't so much psyche*delic* as psyche*cidal*, there to dissolve any pretension that *anything* lay beneath.

> What sells, today, is whatever Fucks You Up—whatever short-circuits your brain and grounds it out for the longest possible time.[2]

In one particularly desolate scene in *Fear and Loathing*, Thompson's alter-ego Duke returns to their hotel to find Gonzo in the bath aiming at exactly this: getting *very* fucked up, smashed on every chemical they have, screaming along to a tune that he is playing over and over. Duke threatens to kill him for making so much noise, and Gonzo wills him to go ahead, thinking there'd be no better way to go than just as a particular bar of the song soars.

> "Let it roll!" [Gonzo] screamed. "Just as high as the fucker can go! And when it comes to that fantastic note where the rabbit bites its own head off, I want you to throw that fuckin radio into the tub with me."

> I stared at him, keeping a firm grip on the radio. "Not me," I said finally. "I'd be happy to ram a goddamn 440-volt cattle prod into that tub with you right now, but not this radio. It would blast you right through the wall-stone – dead in ten seconds." I laughed. "Shit, they'd make me explain it—drag me down to some rotten coroner's inquest and grill me about... yes... the exact details. I don't need that."

> "Bullshit!" he screamed. "Just tell them I wanted to get Higher!"[3]

The mantra of the committed hedonist: higher and always higher, right unto the brain-exploding point of death itself.

—

My Higher Education was ending and there was nothing I could do about it. I pumped my brain as full as I could and did my finals and tried to forget about the future, obscuring and hazing it in the time-honoured fashion of students finished with exams. Glastonbury that year was to be the last hurrah for us all before vacating our house and going our separate ways. We arrived and sneaked under the fence as usual, gear thrown over the top, tramping across to find the spots we'd camped in before. The weather wasn't great and perhaps the threatening clouds bore down on everyone, the atmosphere immediately different. Where I'd once laughed at the catatonic crowds milling, the groups of people drinking and drinking and falling and vomiting and leaving the fallen to lie in muddied patches of grass, now I felt uneasy and sad, a depression rolling through.

On the Saturday night a bunch of people pulled guns on each other. No one was hurt, but word of it spread and tensions rose, a fractious stench infecting the whole place. The next morning we heard that someone had been found dead, sprawled out from an overdose. Some laughed, most shrugged it off, all carried on intoxicating, me wanting to be somewhere less toxic, the silence of that one stilled pulse haunting my final night.

Ignorant of the riots that had torn through the Travellers field and blissfully unaware of the Molotov Cocktails arcing through the sky into lines of police, my first Glastonbury had been full of hope. I'd seen technologies of flight on offer and believed whole-heartedly that they would heal me. Now the opposite was true, the people not getting high out of hope, but because of the lack of it. 'Depressive hedonia,' the lecturer and writer Mark Fisher called it later in his book *Capitalist Realism*, his own students knowing that things are bad, but knowing too that they can't do anything about it, theirs a depression caused *'not by an inability to get pleasure so much as by an inability to do anything else except pursue pleasure.'*[4]

Leary, Huxley and Kesey—I'd once seen all this as a festival of their ideals, a celebration of better living through chemistry. Now all I could see were hardcore Thompsonites, today's bestsellers being whatever Fucked You Up, whatever short-circuited the brain and ground it into the softening Somerset mud for the longest time possible.

—

When Kesey went to jail his followers scattered. Neal Cassady ended up back down in Mexico where, with fellow-Prankster George Walker, he became something of a show himself, getting high, rapping his stories and racing cars. Yet the man of speed was beginning to flag too. He took aside one young follower and gave them some advice:

'Twenty years of fast living – there's just not much left. Don't do what I have done.'

As a young writer, Thompson had worshipped Cassady, partly because he was another man who had lived life 'looking for the lost dad he never had,' someone else who, fatherless like John Lennon, had had to 'figure it all out on his own.'[5] On February 3rd, 1968, barely 15 months after the Acid Graduation, Cassady was walking along some railroad tracks, trying to make it to the next town one night after a wedding, when he was caught in a storm. Wearing only a t-shirt and jeans, he caught a chill and went into a coma. He was found the next day and carried to hospital, but died within hours.

The death of this fellow seeker, this man whom Thompson considered 'flat-out amazing,' hit hard, no doubt contributing to his bitterness as, at the end of *Fear and Loathing*, he became more reflective, more scathing about the harm the great false hopes for LSD had caused.

All those pathetically eager acid freaks who thought they could buy Peace and Understanding for three bucks a hit. This was the fatal flaw in Tim Leary's trip. He crashed around America selling "consciousness expansion" without ever giving a thought to the grim meat-hook realities that were lying in wait for all the people who took him too seriously.[6]

His hedonistic bender to the heart of the American Dream boiled down to this sour residue: the failure of acid to change anyone's material reality. Kesey and Huxley—both men of privilege—started out wanting people to take drugs as an act of expanding their consciousness. According to Thompson—ever the scarred underdog, the poor fatherless boy left to rot in jail—for most people the reverse was true: they didn't get high to find heaven, they got high to escape hell.

The fulcrum of *Fear and Loathing*, when Duke does eventually divine the location of the heart of the American Dream, it's 'main nerve' is in the bar of one of Vegas' largest casinos, Circus-Circus. For Thompson, the whole 60s trip turned out to be just that, a circus, a freak show.

'You can wander [in] any time of the day or night and witness the crucifixion of a gorilla—on a flaming neon cross that suddenly turns into a pinwheel, spinning the beast around in wild circles above the crowded gambling action.'[7]

It is here—among the rolling of dice and cutting of cards, where nature is crucified and then kitch-ified, and crowds gather in the round to step away from meat-hook realities—it is here that the dream is focused, not on world peace, but on escape.

Having invented the drug and become convinced of its powers to change human consciousness, Albert Hofmann ended up agreeing with Thompson. An excellent chemist, in his 1980 book *LSD - My Problem Child* he also showed himself to be an astute social scientist, expressing powerful opinions on why the drug had enjoyed such a rapid uptake in the 1960s:

[It] had deep-seated sociological causes: materialism, alienation from nature through industrialisation and increasing urbanisation, lack of satisfaction in professional employment in a mechanised, lifeless working world, ennui and purposelessness in a wealthy, saturated society, and lack of a religious, nurturing, and meaningful philosophical foundation of life.[8]

This wasn't a drug that emerged to bring about a new consciousness, but to enable flight from the struggles of modern life. Despite his reservations, Hofmann remained convinced that, carefully controlled, LSD could have been an effective remedy, a powerful part of a doctor's repertoire to help with the treatment of alcoholism and mental illness. Its descent all the way from transcendent entheogen right down to recreational trip was a tragedy for him partly because it prevented further research with the drug, but more widely because it exposed just how desperate people were to escape the grim narrative of their daily-lived reality.

This is precisely what Aldous Huxley had predicted 50 years before. It's a weird discovery, finding that he had briefly taught George Orwell French at Eton College, but here it is, Huxley writing to his former pupil to congratulate him on the publication of *1984*. Now literary equals, he also took the chance to contrast the different dystopian visions that he and Orwell had imagined.

Huxley's fantasy about the 'ideal intoxicant' had formed part of *Moksha*, published in the 1920s. By 1932, *Brave New World* showed him as being more cautious. Contrary to the heavy-handed state oppression of *1984*, in Huxley's world the masses are conditioned into supine obedience via the facile meeting of their desires. As he explained in his letter to Orwell:

> *Within the next generation I believe that the world's rulers will discover that infant conditioning and narco-hypnosis are more efficient, as instruments of government, than clubs and prisons... The lust for power can be just as completely satisfied by suggesting people into loving their servitude as by flogging and kicking them into obedience.*

In this brave new world sex is open and frequent. Material needs are all met, and, because everything is simply thrown away, there is full employment as more and more always has to be manufactured. However, realising that the masses will still hanker after something deeper and more meaningful in their lives, the state gives them a regular ration of a hallucinogen, a chemical ecstasy that gets rid of the need for religions or social gatherings, and is even wonderfully hangover-free.[9]

Kesey, Leary, Cassady, Lennon and Thompson, were that 'next generation' that Huxley referred to, one that, as Hofmann described, 'discovered [LSD] precisely at this time in order to bring help to people suffering under the modern conditions.' It was also the generation that initiated the *MK-ULTRA* programme of narco-hypnosis, the one that wooed the masses into loving their servitude to consumer culture, that began the hypnotic drip-feed of advertisements and the heavy projection of the terrible spectre of communism.

Altamont and the Acid Graduation served as a wake-up call for many, slapping them out of their hypnosis, their brave countercultural world revealed as no more than a fantasy that had helped them cope with the fear and horror of real life.

—

As I left Glastonbury, these fields that had book-ended my college days, the grim meat-hook reality of my own plight began to catch up with me. With no job to go to, no idea what I wanted to do with my life, and in no healthier mental state than I was before, I panicked, pushing back against the hedonistic escapism, returning to what I felt I knew best. As one fantasy crumbled, I jumped into another. If the Electric Kool-Aid hadn't healed me, perhaps a dose of spiritual psychedelia would.

My guilty secret: as other band members had slept off late nights I'd taken myself up to the highest point of Bristol, in under the towering spire of a church in Clifton. One connection made on my first night in the bar had taken me to the ecstasy of clubs and music; another made on my first Sunday—a girl casually saying she was heading to church and did I fancy joining her—kept me in regular contact with the Most High. Strange currents of guilt and nostalgia mixed to draw me there through all of those hedonistic years in college, and now that these were over I re-immersed myself fully in them.

Though I couldn't square these two circles of my life, I was unaware that others had done right through the 60s. As the summer of '67 came around, with Kesey locked up and the Pranksters dispersed, Leary attempted to take things back in a more serious direction with his 'League for Spiritual Discovery,' venerating the drug as its sacrament and couching its formation in explicitly religious terms:

Like every great religion of the past we seek to find the divinity within and to express this revelation in a life of glorification and the worship of God. These ancient goals we define in the metaphor of the present—turn on, tune in, drop out.

Huge speculation for sure, but perhaps the highly literate Thompson noted one possible Latin translation of 'turn on, tune in' as *circumroto, circumspice*: Circus-Circus indeed. Either way, by the time he'd passed through Leary's scene of spiritual discovery Thompson was disillusioned and pissed off, and *Fear and Loathing* is his testament—not to the power of drugs to bring to birth a new world, but to their impotence.

By the time Thompson had written and released his book, Leary had also been arrested for possession of marijuana, comparing his arrest and treatment to that of Christ as the hands of Pilate and Herod. Carefully formulating answers to a test to assess his mental state—a test *he himself* had written while still employed by Harvard—Leary wangled his way into an open prison, from which he escaped and absconded to Algeria in September of 1970.

From there he eventually sought refuge with a high-powered arms dealer in Switzerland called Michael Hauchard, who effectively imprisoned him while he tried to conjure a lucrative film deal about Leary's life. Managing to extricate himself again he went to Vienna, then Beirut and Kabul, hoping to settle in Afghanistan as it didn't have an extradition deal with the US. Yet before he could physically attach himself to Afghan soil he was arrested by US agents on the plane as it opened its doors at Kabul airport.

Leary was really in deep trouble now, facing 25 years or more behind bars. Coming face to face with this meat-hook reality of his own he turned snitch in 1973, giving evidence for the State in exchange for his freedom as old associates and friends were prosecuted. Largely ostracised for his betrayal, he saw out the remainder of his years as a cardboard cut-out celebrity, living off his drop-out soundbite, vending memories of the Summer of Love, latterly taken to parties and clubs in a wheelchair where, like a circus sideshow, he was fed cocktails of illicit drugs by still-eager acid freaks until he died.

—

Steeped in the Christian story, I could see that both Leary and Kesey considered themselves in the mould of Jesus Christ. Both had had disciples around them, both their mysterious parables, both set upon by the authorities because of their discovery of a dangerous, subversive liberating new myth to live by. Both became leaders of communities formed around these beliefs that had levels of inclusion and exclusion. Whole chapters of *The Electric Kool-Aid Acid Test* were given over to who was in or out of the Prankster inner circle, and Leary capped the number of people who could join his League For Spiritual Discovery at 360.

I pictured Thompson sitting at his typewriter writing *Fear and Loathing*, thinking about Leary's imprisonment, fuming, grieving, struggling to make sense of it all, this exclusivity smacking of every other religion that had come along before, every paternalistic, privileged and powerful elite.

> *What Leary took down with him was the central illusion of a whole life-style that he helped to create... a generation of permanent cripples, failed seekers, who never understood the essential old-mystic fallacy of the Acid Culture: the desperate assumption that somebody—or at least some force—is tending that Light at the end of the tunnel.*

> *This is the same cruel and paradoxically benevolent bullshit has kept the Catholic Church going for so many centuries. It is also the military ethic... a blind faith in some higher and wiser "authority." The Pope, The General, The Prime Minister... all the way up to "God." One of the crucial moments of the Sixties came on that day when the Beatles cast their lot with the Maharishi.*[10]

The Beatles? Again? The band kept turning up in my life. Soundtracking my childhood, and central to Kesey's downfall they now reappeared as a focus of Thompson's loathing for shacking up with a guru in August of 1967. Having released *Sergeant Pepper* in June they were struggling to deal with the incessant and unquenchable furore that engulfed them. Beatlemania was more rampant than ever, but same old crush of teenage girls was now joined by serious critics like Kenneth Tynan, who declared their new album 'a decisive moment in the history of Western civilisation.'

76

They needed to escape, and that August they booked a retreat in Wales with Maharishi Mahesh Yogi, pioneer of the practice of Transcendental Meditation. Just two days in came the tragic news that manager Brian Epstein—their mentor up to that point—had committed suicide with an overdose of barbiturates. The band were distraught. Still grieving, still reeling from the currents of public opinion, they took off *en masse* in February of 1968 to India, to the Maharishi's ashram.

Just 10 months after Kesey's own effort The Beatles were about to try the same thing, heading off to an intense finishing school to undertake an attempt at graduation. Harrison made pretty much the same little speech that Kesey had:

> *LSD isn't a real answer. [...] To get really high, you have to do it straight. I want to get high, and you can't get high on LSD. You can take it and take it as many times as you like, but you get to a point that you can't get any further unless you stop taking it.*[11]

What with Cliff Richard going all Billy Graham, the media were ready to pounce and mock more pop faux-spiritual weirdness. Sensitive to this, Harrison tried to justify all this mystical Eastern stuff. 'It helps you live life to the full,' he added. 'Young people are searching for a bit of peace inside themselves.'

Except the truth of it was, many under the Maharishi were making far bigger claims than that. There was the Natural Law Party, who claimed that by following his regime of compulsory meditation all wars would cease. Then there were those who believed that the transcendental element wasn't just spiritual: if you practised hard enough you could achieve yogic flying, your body 'spontaneously lifting up,' giving 'great clarity of consciousness, energy, exhilaration, and unboundedness.'[12]

Unfortunately, LSD-free and struggling to get the same highs without it, disappointment and frustration quickly set in among The Beatles. Mia Farrow had travelled with them, and the band accused the Maharishi of sexual harassment of her. Pissed off, thinking they'd been had, one by one they left.

Hunter Thompson, writing after all of this, was wanting people to see that the gurus and Popes and military leaders and acid trips were all part of the *same* bullshit: ecstatic, soul-revealing experiences that promised connection to a lost father-figure and salvation from the mundane grimness of real life, all peddled by corrupt elites who cared nothing for what happened when the comedown inevitably came.

Father-less, he was perhaps more desperate for these promises to be delivered and more hurt when they weren't, the brutal iconoclasm of *Fear and Loathing* more courageous than that managed by the more privileged and comfortable Huxley in *Brave New World*. Angry and bruised, each page lashes out, severing with a blunt and bloodied knife any link between drug use and spiritual quest, exposing all of it—all attempts at transcendence—as no more than a flight from the painful reality of violence and alienation, exacerbated by the mechanising and industrialising West.

I can't help see something of Thompson in Gozzoli's altarpiece, his writing, like Peter's prayer, an exposé, a puncturing of a magician's power, proclaiming the secret rocket fuel illegitimate, sending Magus, Leary, Kesey, the Maharishi and the Pope crashing to the ground. Peter was 'the rock,' the best parts of him focused on the Earth. He was the outspoken ruffian, a working hunter, a man who knew the boat—his vehicle—inside out, a little of the Hells Angel lodged in his heart, shooting a man down for talking bullshit about the above, leaving blood and broken teeth.

—

Leaping in my garden as a child, leafing through my bible as a teenager, leading the way to the dance-floor as a student, there was an ache in all these things for true psychedelic experience. I wanted my soul to be opened up and shown to be loved, to feel a Force acting on me, a light tending me. I threw myself up, grasping for an above in hope that each attempt at ecstasy might heal my hurts, unable to see that each was another mechanism for escaping them.

Deaf to Thompson's insights I came down from university and, like Kesey and Harrison and everyone else, decided that I needed to make my own attempt to 'go beyond.' I'd been doing things all wrong. The True Form of things was not in the thumping chemical beats and flashing lights of ecstasy. I needed to graduate, to move up to a purer, higher spiritual version of them.

I moved to London and took a job in a church. I'd been away from home for three years. I'd grown up. Time had passed. Surely it would be fine to move into a flat with my sister? We took an ex-Council place not far from Parson's Green. Neither of us earned much, but neither of us had to. The capital hadn't quite yet gone mad.

Old patterns quickly re-emerged. Weakened by distance, the magnetic forces that distorted every interaction with her I found untouched by time. But I thought I could beat it. Pushing the music and clubs into the background, the religious part came back to the fore, shape-shifting smoothly into a new version of myself, one I prayed and prayed would rise above history and be healed. If these different sides seemed incongruous to others, to me they were two engines pushing for the same above, ones that I'd coupled as far back as that first trip to California. What I hadn't figured then was just how closely they had been bound together by events in the 60s.

There's a photo of me at the corner of Haight and Ashbury in San Francisco, the Vatican City of the counterculture, smiling into the camera, a happy pilgrim in my year out before college. The next day my friend and I had taken the train back down to LA then gone on to Anaheim, to a church that was a kind of Mecca for Christians at the time, both of us excited at what we might experience. The place was enormous, the size of a shopping mall, and we went in and sang for hours and threw our hands in the air and fell to the floor, the divine surging through us.

I knew better than to tell the people that our previous stop had been the centre of the LSD counterculture, having no idea that the country-rock choruses we were singing had grown out of the psychedelic movement, nor that the church's emphasis on 'signs and wonders' had come straight from a hippie who had met Jesus while smashed off his gourd.

—

Lonnie Frisbee had been right there in '67 at the Summer of Love and had taken to reading the Bible while high. During one trip he had a powerful spiritual encounter and joined the 'Jesus Freaks,' walking the beaches of southern California and converting the young people he met there. 'No more LSD for me,' the Larry Norman song went, 'I've met the man from Galilee.'

With his first class Haight-Ashbury credentials Frisbee become something of a guru to the flocks of disillusioned hippies stuck in California, lost and disorientated after Kesey's graduation had flopped and the great hopes of the LSD counterculture had been dashed. He would tell them his story—another charismatic leader going 'beyond acid'—and then take them all off to church in their 100s and 1,000s.

Frisbee threw out the organs and hymns and replaced them with the acoustic guitars and long, rambling songs familiar to anyone who'd taken acid and hung out on the beach. With the dreary hymnals went the conservative, straight-laced ideas about God and, drawing directly from his experiences on acid, in came his teaching that ordinary people could encounter the bedazzling power of the Most High.

Yes Lord! This was super-hero theology, and those who were turned on were given divine visions, supernatural power to perform miracles, heal people, raise the dead, cure blindness and see the future. He called it 'power evangelism' and, seeing what was going on, John Wimber—a musician connected to The Righteous Brothers and pastor in the Calvary Chapel churches that Frisbee was now helping to lead—invited him to speak at his branch over in Orange County, about 40 miles from LA. With his focus on the miraculous, Frisbee's visit kick-started huge growth in Wimber's church, spawning a new sect that Wimber and Frisbee led together: the Association of Vineyard Churches.

Fresh of the train from Haight Ashbury, this was the church I found myself in, careful not to let on I'd just come from a hot-bed of liberal sexuality and drug-fuelled ecstasy, clueless that the very foundations of the Vineyard had been laid in that culture.

My ignorance was perhaps excusable: Lonnie Frisbee was written out of the history of the church for revealing to Wimber that he was gay. Shunned and exiled by the very ministry he had founded, his name had been completely erased. Moving to San Francisco—he'd actually been there when I was passing through—he'd contracted AIDS and died a few years later in 1993.

Hofmann was convinced that the drug that he had invented had become so popular among highly literate young people because it offered a way of dealing with the intense anxiety they felt over industrialisation, civil unrest and the prospect of nuclear holocaust. LSD was going to bring an end to all wars. LSD was going to bring in an age of peace and love. When it failed to bring paradise to a broken world people became lost and disillusioned and Frisbee's 'power Christianity' was the most obvious thing to jump to. Promising the same ecstatic highs and the same utopian future, it benefited from being a legal, 'clean' technology of flight. With it, Middle Class Christian America had just found a way to enjoy their own trippy counterculture.

This is my father's own story. Anxious, exhausted, worn down by his labours and unsure about the future, just after the 60s had closed he had gone on a trip from our home in Sheffield with his church youth group. There, as they had prayed for him, he had had his Lonnie Frisbee moment, an overwhelming spiritual experience, something psychedelic, his soul laid bare, a great revelation that there was a loving force tending the light.

20 years later, I found myself in the same situation: working for a church, proud to be doing God's work but feeling desperately insecure about my life. Though omnipresent, for some reason God had moved on from Orange County and Sheffield, and the best trips were now to be found in a church in Canada. They called it 'The Toronto Blessing,' and one of the pastors of my church went over and tried it and brought some back to share. Its supernatural highs included hysterical laughter, falling over, roaring like animals, running and dancing and shaking and convulsing. Apart from the fact that we kept our clothes on, Ginsberg and Leary would have been right at home.

It was, so the preaching went, Pentecost all over again, a reference to the church's 'Bicycle Day,' to the innocent psychedelic experience Jesus' followers had had soon after he had been crucified. Unsurprisingly, this had been a terribly traumatic and anxious moment in their lives. Their leader had been executed, there was a big rumpus over where his body had gone and they had been forced into hiding, both Romans and Jews out to violently stamp down their heresy. We see them frightened, alienated from their communities and families, disenfranchised and impotent, their future uncertain. As the story in the book of Acts opens, they are meeting in secret.

When the day of Pentecost came, they were all together in one place. Suddenly a sound like the blowing of a violent wind came from heaven and filled the whole house where they were sitting. They saw what appeared to be tongues of fire that separated and came to rest on each of them. All of them were filled with the Holy Spirit and began to speak in other tongues, as the Spirit enabled them.[13]

Separating out the stuff, one for each person, to be placed on the tongue. And so the trip begins. Extraordinary power! Language like you never heard before! Flames were meant to rise *up* to rejoin the heavenly light, but here was that light descending in flame, in person, to them, to be swallowed down in one. Jesus had once proclaimed 'I and the Father are one,'[14] and here was the adoption rite of his followers into that perfect paternity, these men and women who had shunned their families, given up everything, pouring out onto the street, unchained, released from the cavern, empowered by The Source.

'Something big is happening to consciousness!' Leary had proclaimed, and years later, as we revelled in this Toronto phenomenon, after long periods of chanting we rose in chorus to announce that 'God is powerfully at work here!' 'Jesus has conquered the grave,' we sang over and over, the excitement of ecstasy bringing a belief that transcendent peace would soon break out in the midst of our anguish and stress and there would be no more death or crying or pain...

And then, in all of this, in floods of tears and crushing pain, I lost my grandmother.

'Keep on with the music,' she'd whispered, labouring for each breath at the end, me moistening her lips with a sponge on a stick, her squeezing my hand as I'd cried by her hospital bed, ashamed that I had no career or prospects to leave her with a sense of pride in me.

Gathering round her coffin didn't feel much like victory to me, but which way could I go? All I knew was to push harder, to leave her funeral and pray more, sing more, raise my hands further and trip higher and ever higher into the religious ecstatic.

—

The background to Frisbee's own experience had been in the Los Angeles church of St Mark where, in Easter of 1960, Pastor Dennis Bennett had explained to his middle class, white congregation that he had just had a Pentecostal encounter with the Holy Spirit. They were shocked and horrified. This was a country struggling with civil rights and racial segregation, and Pentecostalism was black religion, black and poor.

It had begun in the 1920s, around the impoverished area of Azusa Street, a group of fasting believers feeling the power of God come among them. They'd shaken and jumped and rolled on the floor and the LA Times had reported 'wild scenes,' including 'the gurgle of wordless talk by a sister.'

Just as with the traumatised and anxious early church in Acts, this outbreak of ecstasy had come to a disenfranchised and violently suppressed community. It was Hofmann's thesis all over again: tripping as means of coping with oppression; not so much about *revival* as *survival*. Nothing in the holy rolling or jumping or roaring changed the brutal fact that their black bodies were powerless in the face of white supremacy, but this ecstasy offered a means to lift away

81

from it and, wrapped in a myth of transcendent, divine power, survive it too—survival itself being a radical political act at a time when those who stepped out of line were hung from trees.

As the 50s had rolled around, the blues, the music of hope in slavery, had jumped from poor black communities and been taken up by white middle class musicians needing a way to deal with their poor, broken, jilted hearts. It never quite sounded the same.

When Pentecostalism made the same jump a decade later, similar losses were made in translation: well-off, middle class Christians conducting spiritual power from above was very different to poor black and Hispanic Christians doing so. Yet, in those post-war years leading up the 60s alienation, dislocation, anxiety and the trauma of impending annihilation were being felt right the way across the social spectrum, from sensitive poets to working class men returning from bomber command to students and religious communities.

For the Middle Classes who couldn't countenance the escapism of drugs or the thrill of roaring motorcycles, ecstatic religion *was* their counterculture, *was* their acid trip, *was* their snarling Harley Davidson. It *was* their psychedelia: their way of affirming in a faceless world that they had soul.

Thompson had seen Leary and Kesey and The Beatles all flip from acid to something beyond, all of them lifting their vision and talking of a great force tending the light. But if the LSD version of the counterculture had failed to change anything, if all it had been was a desperate circus of fear and loathing, the question urgently needed posing: could a spiritual ecstasy hope to fare any better?

—

'Isn't this sublime?' a friend comments, looking out over the mass of slain bodies on the carpeted expanse of the nave, a guitarist picking out the bones of a song that had long-since breathed its last, the keyboard player frowning, wondering if this was a progression he could follow. It's right in the middle of the craziness flown over from Toronto, after the death of my grandma. A half-fried neurone with a weak spark attempts to ignite a memory I had from a college lecture on thermodynamics. *Sublimation*. A body changing from solid to gas, without passing through the intermediate liquid state.

The civil rights struggle still years from maturity, Pentecostals of the 1920s move directly from the solid fist of brutal oppression to the gaseous ecstasy of spiritual liberation. Under intense heat and pressure they ascend into the sublime, the talk of heaven and healing and divine provision an *out of body* experience, souls soaring while physical bodies lack liberty.

40 years later, hippies, biker gangs and disillusioned heads make identical moves, hailing the sublime highs they have found as places of great freedom, even as the ground remains unchanged. Here is George Harrison, crying out that 'young people are searching for a bit

of peace inside themselves,' the solution to the lack of peace around them not political activism, but drugs and meditation to achieve a little tranquillity within themselves alone.

Here is Timothy Leary, speaking to the group of Lutheran psychologists, demanding that internal freedom is becoming a civil rights issue. His equating of the struggle to see LSD accepted with that of the struggle to have minorities seen as equals is an act of purest sublimation, allowing him to pretend to be part of the fight while others marched, others were beaten and others gunned down.

Here too is Bob Dylan, stepping onto the stage the night after Kennedy was shot, opening with the song he'd written in more hopeful times just weeks before, convinced that 'the times, they are a-changing.' The crowd just don't get the irony that *nothing* had bloody well changed, and scream and burst out into great applause when the song finishes, leaving Dylan in state of shock, wondering whether this whole 'protest song' movement was in fact a way of avoiding the issues.

I couldn't understand why they were clapping, or why I wrote the song. I couldn't understand anything. It was just insane.[15]

This was the insanity: all the activist songs he'd written and toured through endless Beat coffee shops—taking aim at real targets, at real politics, at real problems of injustice—all of it had ended up with him heralded as the Great Force tending the light, the saviour of protest music, the man whose sublime music meant that further material action was somehow unnecessary. Forget marching or standing up to the police; put on a Dylan record and find a little peace inside yourself.

Well screw that, he says, and turns away, refusing to be that person, meeting up with Ginsberg and becoming profoundly affected by *Howl*, taking his own trips with LSD soon after and realising that it was he who was a-changin'. He turns lyrically inwards, cranks up the sound with electric guitars, drowns out the calls for him to be the prophet and no longer asks what we actions we might *do* but 'how does it *feel*.'

There in turn was my Dad, and here I am too: stressed, unsure, grieving, seeing no way out, making the same move and lumping for the ecstatic even as, deep down, I know that this act of sublimation will do nothing to change the things that dragged me down in the first place. I am praying for a miracle, something to rid me of these fetid innards without ever having to open them up to anyone. There in the congregation are my father and sister, these relationships way more broken than I can admit. She is working in a shop until something better turns up. We're both stressed. My anxiety at church and at home is constant, not to mention the guilt at my anger towards her and my inability to engage emotionally with her, so in the face of all of this I shut my eyes and raise my hands and tilt my head to heaven, pretending that a great power is at work in me, not bringing about anything as practical as a proper job or career, not empowering me to walk me over to meet my family's eyes and say the unsayable, but performing galactic level transformations in the Other World, a place where I am, for a precious moment, a son in whom the Father is well pleased.

Aldous Huxley, tripping on mescaline, was asked by those observing how he felt about other people.

> 'One ought to be able,' I said, 'to see these trousers as infinitely important and human beings as still more infinitely important.' One ought—but in practice it seemed impossible. This participation in the manifest glory of things left no room [...] for concerns involving persons.'[16]

He had wanted the psychedelic experience to be transcendent vision that radically improved empathy for others, one that,

> in [Meister] Eckhart's phrase, is ready to come down from the seventh heaven in order to bring a cup of water to his sick brother.[17]

It wasn't. The drugs took him to a place of great contemplation, but it was 'a contemplation incompatible with action, even the very thought of action.' It was a contemplation that found trousers fascinating, but left no room for people.

Kesey's baby is crying, one sole person willing someone to come down from their trip and tend the child, but no one does.

Next to me in the pew my girlfriend is crying. She has sat down. She has had enough. She has sang as much as the rest of us, prayed as hard, lifted her hands just as high... but nothing. No shaking, no divine laughter, no speaking in tongues, no roaring like a lion, no bedazzling vision of God's glory. Nothing.

For weeks it has been like this: me and my friends tripping off into the divine ecstatic, and her left alone, seemingly unable to fly. I am torn. Isn't God infinitely more important than people? Doubts keep nagging, moments where I see things that seem forced, people falling to the ground just to be done with it. It takes such a lot of time, hours and hours in services, and our relationship is suffering. I want more than anything for her to share this ecstasy, but it never happens for her. We are good Christians, and don't allow ourselves more earthy pleasures, but the temptation and guilt around this, coupled with the illusive *petit mort* she can't reach in our prayer meetings, builds to a head so I do the only thing I can think of and withdraw.

I break it off. So much crumbles with this separation, and only after we have split do I understand that it was our increasing closeness that had driven me further into heavenly flight. This woman I loved had wanted me to open up; she also knew my sister well, and had wanted to go with me back to that place of pain and begin to deal with it. I couldn't. As she'd drawn closer and tried to help me, I'd pushed higher, taken off out of her reach, up into a sublime paradise beyond criticism, because what could be more vital than spending time with God?

The relationship over, all the laughing and roaring subsided. I stopped shaking, but the whole experience had left me shaken. For the first time I felt unwell in my mind, admitted to myself that this was a problem, accepted that there were things within me that were causing people pain, things that weren't going to be prayed away. The physical shift was unmissable: having been the enthusiastic guy on the front row of church, I became the skulking presence in the last pew, moving closer each week towards the back door. Yet from this new vantage point I could, for the first time in my life, watch what was going on, see the sublime move taking place, see the great focus on trousers, the desperate projection of great transformation in the heavens precisely because there were material issues that were simply too difficult for people in the congregation to face. The music starts, eyes are shut, hands are raised to Pan and everyone lifts away. The hangover-free high. Brave New World.

Saturday nights and Sunday mornings: via one means, and then another, over those years from college and beyond I'd pushed for dazzling highs, feeling in clubs and churches that I was about to be raptured. 'Smoke the Jehovah-juana! Get smashed on god-ka!' I've heard one American pastor teaching recently, his ministry all about encouraging addicts to switch from one ecstasy to another, not for a moment questioning what is driving their need for altitude.

Forced to look into the soul that these psychedelic experiences had revealed, I found that I had re-enacted my sister's condition more than I'd dared accept. Under great tension I too had wanted to be rid of my body, to become *ex stasis*, to abdicate responsibility for my shitty situation to great highs and then the Most High, to lift off from Earth and land up in Eden.

Félix Tournachon had described his pioneering balloon flights as taking him to 'where man cannot be reached by any power of evil.' This wasn't true. Even up in the highest places of ecstasy, darkness had always followed me. Despite the extraordinary new thrusters the 60s afforded them, as Kesey saw, as Ginsberg found out, as Huxley and Leary died knowing, as Thompson knew all along, as I eventually understood: the veil is not pierced, paradise is not gained and unity with the Father is not achieved. The doors of perception resist our attempts to break them and, despite our very best efforts at height, we always fall, always come back down.

After years of pursuing enlightenment, the light, I had to conclude, was untended. Could anyone doubt my sincerity, anyone question my fervour? I'd applied myself to daily Bible study and prayer, attended church after church, sung my heart out, fasted, waited on God, sought the Holy Spirit, going as high as any fucker could possibly go, and yet this ecstatic path had proven fruitless.

Transcendent experiences hadn't healed the pains I had buried. In promising to do so, they had elevated me away from them, only to fall back down into greater depression when these wings inevitably failed.

Left untreated they darkened, the sublime crashing into a psychotic hell, shorting mental circuits and fucking me up. Wildly oscillating between sanctifying my wounds as Christ-like and tearing away from them in various ecstasies, I'd hurt myself and others, the light of all my relationships warped and bent by this black hole within me. I had to step away, abandon all these ecstasies, be content with a different chemistry, a new level of equilibrium. I had to walk out of the church and pull the heavy door behind me.

—

Human beings are extraordinary complex systems, kept in a state of 'normality' across fluctuations in temperature, pressure, energy and sensation. What drugs and other ecstatic interventions do is disturb these equilibria by radically changing inputs beyond the limits of our body's ability to normalise them.

Huxley knew this, understanding the link between mental equilibrium and chemical stimulation, appreciating that many suffered conditions that meant they had no choice over their trips to 'Other Worlds,' no control over the messages whispered in their heads, no ability to discern if they were angels or demons.

> Many schizophrenics have their times of heavenly happiness; but the fact that (unlike the mescaline taker) they do not know when, if ever, they will be permitted to return to the reassuring banality of everyday experience causes even heaven to seem appalling. But for those who, for whatever reason, are appalled, heaven turns into hell, bliss into horror.[18]

One of the darkest horrors that this produced in the 60s was in the crimes of Charles Manson.

Having been in prison a number of times, Manson had settled into the heart of the happenings around Haight Ashbury in the summer of '67. He'd looked like the archetypal head: hooking a lot of acid, being a bit of a freak-out, even going as far as mimicking Kesey and The Beatles by gathering his band of (mostly female) followers in an old bus, decking it out with pillows and throws.

Just like Frisbee, he witnessed firsthand the disillusionment of large numbers of vulnerable young hippies after the failures of the Summer of Love. Where Frisbee gathered them into the family of the church, Manson exploited these vulnerabilities to a dark and chronically abusive level, and by 1968 he had welded his own 'family' together under his powerful, charismatic leadership, become father to another small rump of the fatherless.

Incited by the assassination of Martin Luther King, he became convinced that The Beatles' tune *Helter Skelter* was a divine proclamation of the beginning of a bloody racial war against black people. Between May and October of 1969 he led the family in a truly horrific series of murders and mutilations, one of the darkest moments of the fucked-up underbelly of LSD and the corrupting power of 'vision experience.' Only much later was Manson diagnosed as a paranoid and delusional schizophrenic, no one able to know just how severely his psychedelic drug use had triggered his descent into such grave evil.

The murder at Altamont, and now this. In many ways, Thompson's entire road trip in *Fear and Loathing* was an attempt to outrun the horror of the collapsing, blissful naiveté of the previous few years as these shocking events of 1969 sent the whole previous decade's highs crashing down behind him.

As I closed the door on one period of my life it was as if to hide from view my own razed wasteland that lay behind me. I felt bitter about these wasted years. Anger grew and multiplied in me, furious that, looking always upwards, I'd squandered so many opportunities to push my life in a different direction. I had a degree, but no work skills to speak of, my head so long in the clouds I had no idea which direction to walk in once I found myself back on the ground. What the hell was I going to do with my life on Earth now that I wasn't shooting straight to heaven?

A number of very dark months passed in genuine fear and self-loathing, my dreams savage, my reality distended. Only now do I see that, in some ways, I got away lightly.

In 1990, Timothy Leary's daughter Susan, her childhood so chaotic and unstable in the shifting shadows of her father's life, walked up to her sleeping boyfriend and fired a bullet into his head. Ruled unfit to stand trial, while held in jail her own fragile equilibrium finally gave way. She tied a shoelace around her neck, stood on a chair and rocked it over. She was 42.

Thompson had to run for the rest of his life, the massive success of *Fear and Loathing* becoming a monkey on his back. Having created the Duke character as a way of saying the things that couldn't be said, he found the blurring distinctions between ego and alter-ego increasingly hard to cope with.

When invited to speak he wasn't ever sure they were inviting Duke or Thompson. 'I'm not sure who to be,' he says in a 1978 documentary on him for BBC's *Omnibus*.

> *I'm filling with hate and rage even thinking about it. [...] I'm really in the way as person, the myth has taken over, I find myself an appendage, I'm not only no longer necessary, I'm in the way, it would be much better if I died...then people could take the myth... But that's my problem. I'm going to have to kill off one life, and start another one.*[19]

We had handed his book around and laughed at his exploits and binged as we did so, unaware that this High Priest of student bacchanals had become more withdrawn and chronically depressed as his body had become gradually more decrepit. Underneath the

Duke character was a chronic life of alcohol and drug addiction that demanded the very best of his energies. Having taken so many uppers and downers and experienced such powerful hallucinogens, what he struggled to find afterwards was level ground, any state of personal balance.

'Someone who suffers truly unimaginable energies and such dark mood swings,' his first wife Sandy noted, 'will inevitably attack his external world in a desperate attempt to relieve his inner world.'[20] Raging, angry, violent to people around him, The American Dream, he'd concluded, was to 'remain dreaming constantly; never wake up.' His fear, his loathing, was having to face up to the fact that he himself was now awake and, despite all the drugs in the world, he couldn't get back to dreaming.

In 2005, aged 67, wheel-chair bound and no longer able to care for himself, he sat in his writing room, in the aftermath of a storming row with his carer, suffering a particularly bad low. The football season was over. He could no longer swim or walk. 'Act your (old) age,' he wrote, perhaps finally understanding that, having so long confounded the rivers of time with so many substances, its tides were rushing in on him. 'I'm always bitchy. Relax—this won't hurt,' he assured himself, the page always having been the place where he'd negotiated with his demons.

The clattering of his typewriter had been almost as constant as the ammunition rounds he'd fired off at his Aspen ranch. Now the house had finally fallen to silence. In all his writing—whether on Nixon, Vegas or the Kentucky Derby—he had taken aim at this great fantasy of American greatness, to lampoon it and haunt it through the grand figure of Gonzo. He had said all he could, but it had never been enough. Gonzo had demanded everything of him, this Faustian pact with an untiring, never-slowing, always funny, always up, always boundary-pushing maniac finally driving him to do what he'd known he would have to, neither able to live while the other survived.

One last lever to pull, one final period to fire into the vellum.

Pulling open the drawer of his desk, he picked up his gun and shot himself in the head.

—

No one in the house ran to him, everyone thinking that the crack of the bullet was simply the sound of a book dropping to the floor.

They were right, in a way. Finally the work that had defined Hunter could slip away to the ground. The drug-fuelled Vegas trip that had haunted him was finally exorcised. In a flash of brilliant light his life-long torment of having to keep Duke high was gone. His savage journey was over; he would never wake up.

He'd railed against Leary and his constant drive to find meaning in height, but these two prophets of the psychedelic world both yearned for altitude even after death: Thompson had his ashes fired out of a cannon, Leary had his attached to a rocket and blasted up into space, both still falling slowly out of the sky in invisible particulates, dissolved in raindrops, tiny fractions of these two remarkable men now in everyone.

'Something big is happening to consciousness,' Leary had said at the beginning of the 60s. 'People are beginning to see that the Kingdom of Heaven is within them, instead of thinking it's outside, up in the sky and that it can't be here on Earth.' *Forward and up; you are going toward the light,* Huxley's wife had told him as she'd given him a last dose of LSD before he slipped into death.

They'd both been wrong, and Thompson knew that we had blown it. The psychedelic experience hadn't worked. The most comprehensive mapping of consciousness had not located paradise, not offered a way to return to Eden, not broken our chains, not led us from the cave and lifted us up to the Universal Mind.

Through a sober reading of his work I understood this from Hunter. But I also knew from my own savage journey to the heart of the Christian dream that ecstatic religion hadn't delivered on its promises either. I had poured my very soul into fabulously convoluted doctrines and outlandish trips into the Inner World, desperate for an experience of the light, longing to be united with a Father in Heaven.

Now that the maps had been shown to lead nowhere, where could I turn? Anger hissed and smoked in me, pressure building to thrust me off in a new direction. The flat my sister and I shared was finished. She moved to north London while I headed south; a river snaked between us.

'It's time to seize power over the entire Universe,' Leary had pronounced as the 60s had waned, 'seize power over the Moon— take the sun over.' Like me, Thompson had been left fuming and fulminating, so many people from churches to acid tests hurt in the fallout of this failed ecstatic revolution. Ecstatic religion was done, yet my lust for flight was undimmed. I wanted new vehicles to help me scale different heights, still believing I could rise above my hurts.

He'd been wrong about so much, yet maybe Leary was onto something: with rockets and lunar modules, power *was* about to be seized over the Moon. Perhaps there was hope yet. Perhaps the answers lay in an entirely different realm, not far out in the inner world, but high up in outer space, out towards the fast-combusting sun.

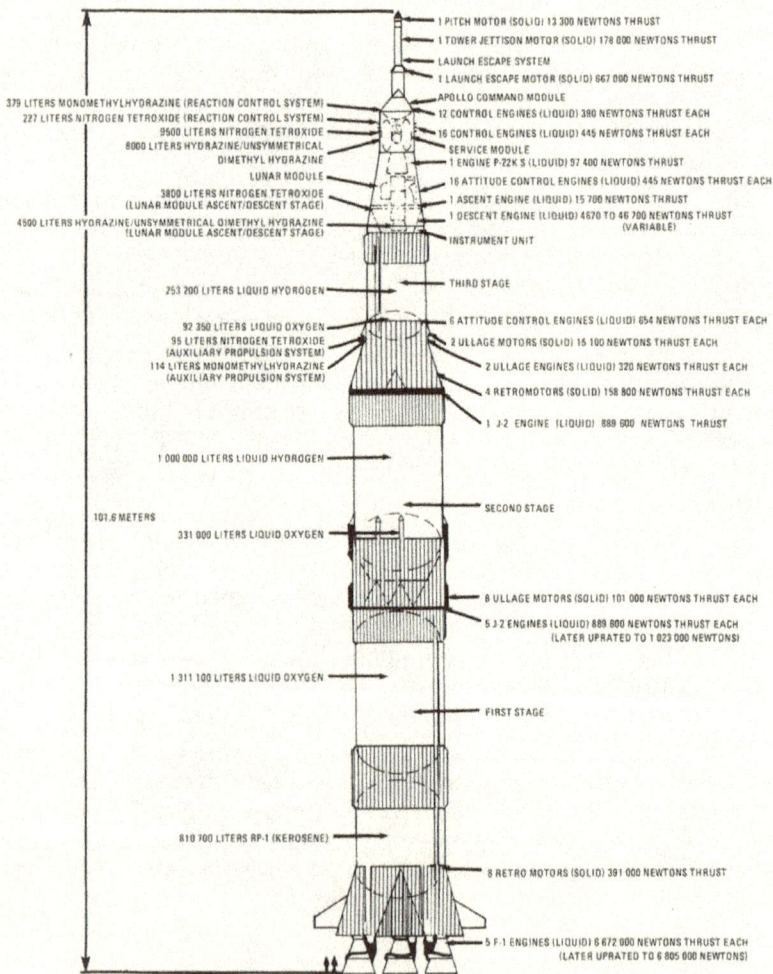

1 PITCH MOTOR (SOLID) 13 300 NEWTONS THRUST
1 TOWER JETTISON MOTOR (SOLID) 178 000 NEWTONS THRUST
LAUNCH ESCAPE SYSTEM
1 LAUNCH ESCAPE MOTOR (SOLID) 667 000 NEWTONS THRUST

379 LITERS MONOMETHYLHYDRAZINE (REACTION CONTROL SYSTEM)
227 LITERS NITROGEN TETROXIDE (REACTION CONTROL SYSTEM)
9500 LITERS NITROGEN TETROXIDE
8000 LITERS HYDRAZINE/UNSYMMETRICAL
DIMETHYL HYDRAZINE
LUNAR MODULE
3800 LITERS NITROGEN TETROXIDE
(LUNAR MODULE ASCENT/DESCENT STAGE)
4500 LITERS HYDRAZINE/UNSYMMETRICAL DIMETHYL HYDRAZINE
(LUNAR MODULE ASCENT/DESCENT STAGE)

APOLLO COMMAND MODULE
12 CONTROL ENGINES (LIQUID) 380 NEWTONS THRUST EACH
16 CONTROL ENGINES (LIQUID) 445 NEWTONS THRUST EACH
SERVICE MODULE
1 ENGINE P-22K S (LIQUID) 97 400 NEWTONS THRUST
16 ATTITUDE CONTROL ENGINES (LIQUID) 445 NEWTONS THRUST EACH
1 ASCENT ENGINE (LIQUID) 15 700 NEWTONS THRUST
1 DESCENT ENGINE (LIQUID) 4670 TO 46 700 NEWTONS THRUST
(VARIABLE)
INSTRUMENT UNIT

253 200 LITERS LIQUID HYDROGEN

THIRD STAGE

92 350 LITERS LIQUID OXYGEN
95 LITERS NITROGEN TETROXIDE
(AUXILIARY PROPULSION SYSTEM)
114 LITERS MONOMETHYLHYDRAZINE
(AUXILIARY PROPULSION SYSTEM)

6 ATTITUDE CONTROL ENGINES (LIQUID) 654 NEWTONS THRUST EACH
2 ULLAGE MOTORS (SOLID) 15 100 NEWTONS THRUST EACH
2 ULLAGE ENGINES (LIQUID) 320 NEWTONS THRUST EACH
4 RETROMOTORS (SOLID) 158 800 NEWTONS THRUST EACH
1 J-2 ENGINE (LIQUID) 888 600 NEWTONS THRUST

1 000 000 LITERS LIQUID HYDROGEN

SECOND STAGE

101,6 METERS

331 000 LITERS LIQUID OXYGEN

8 ULLAGE MOTORS (SOLID) 101 000 NEWTONS THRUST EACH
5 J-2 ENGINES (LIQUID) 889 800 NEWTONS THRUST EACH
(LATER UPRATED TO 1 023 000 NEWTONS)

1 311 100 LITERS LIQUID OXYGEN

FIRST STAGE

810 700 LITERS RP-1 (KEROSENE)

8 RETRO MOTORS (SOLID) 391 000 NEWTONS THRUST

5 F-1 ENGINES (LIQUID) 6 672 000 NEWTONS THRUST EACH
(LATER UPRATED TO 6 805 000 NEWTONS)

Schematic of Saturn V Missile,
two human figures included for scale.

4. Into Orbit

Hunter's gunfire. The smack of type into paper. The anguish of fathers and children, pressing so hard into things that the skin is pierced.

Kesey's sky-high world had begun crashing back to Earth late on in 1965 as he'd watched the tiny stone satellites he and Stewart Brand were throwing arcing down from their rooftop and smashing onto the pavements below. The neighbours got pissy. The cops were called. Kesey and Brand were smoking weed, finalising the details of the Trips Festival, Brand's big idea that would take off in January of '66. Kesey slung his stash. It got found and he got busted. Just weeks after the disappointment of The Beatles, here began the horrible series of months that would see him dragged into the legal mire, faking his own death, disappearing to Mexico and returning for the fated Graduation, the bright hopes of acid extinguished before the sun had even risen on the Summer of Love.

Wolfe would eventually write the defining document of this journey, and later still Thompson would later rake over its bones. *Hells Angels* came out in '66, a solid enough, pre-Gonzo piece of work, but the year before a young Italian journalist called Oriana Fallaci published a book-long letter to her father, pioneering the highly subjective, impressionistic, fully immersed style that Thompson and Wolfe would later rise so high on.

It started in 1957 with the launch of Sputnik 1.

'Do you remember, Father? The spark of light ran across the TV screen, so small and weightless that I could have picked it up on the tip of my little finger and put it in the palm of my hand. Father! Isn't it extraordinary, Father?'[1]

He had been reading his newspaper and lowered it reluctantly, grumpily saying no, he did not find it so. But his daughter persisted: that spark of light was the beginning of a journey. 'We'll go to the Moon!' she gushed at him. 'To the other planets!' This only roused him to great anger.

'What's the use of going to the Moon? Men will always have the same problems, on the Moon or on the Earth; they will always be sick and wicked, on the Moon or on the Earth. They tell me that on the Moon there are no seas, no rivers, no fish, no woods, no fields, no birds. I couldn't even go shooting or fishing.'[2]

The hunter. The crack of gunfire in the Tuscan dawn, their country house just outside Florence. A mist of young thrushes rising from the cherry tree, their number reduced each time he shoots, his daughter approaching with the bag, scooping up the clusters of felled birds.

Fallaci disagrees with her father. While she walks with him she aches for the Moon; he strides and shoots, and riles at speed and flight, just as his own father had, a man who had thought planes were evil birds, putting on his hat and going out into the street, brandishing his stick at the sky and shouting: 'Bastards! Bastards!'

Though he kills them, her father claims to love the birds and fish and animals; he does not want to risk losing them because of rockets trying to reach the Moon. But his daughter is headstrong and determined and argues with him and tells him that it is mankind's destiny, that yes, we hunted and gathered, but we grew able to do this because of our ache for invention. And it is this same ache that made us envious of the birds, so we stole their wings and flew higher, always higher and shot away on them to see beyond the closed door of the sky.

'For the love of God, Father, if a door is closed don't you have the urge to open it and see what's behind it? Isn't the story of man a story of closed and open doors?'[3]

They return home as a storm rides through. The Doors. Break on through to the other side: this is what the young Fallaci wants to do. But her father shakes his head, standing and pointing and saying, 'you can open it. But if that door is the last door, where will it take you? I'll tell you where: headlong into the void.'

Long before Leary has caught up and pointed onwards to the Moon, with some trepidation, Fallaci decides to grasp the handle and push at the questions this poses. She flies to America in '63 and spends months interviewing everyone involved in the space programme, all the time thinking of her father and 'the abyss that divides two generations,' unsure which side she wants to be on, nor what she will find on the other side of the door, questioning what the space race will bring and where humanity is running to, finding her world permanently altered as her mission unfolds.

If Sputnik 1 had been the beginning for Fallaci, that small spark of light floating across the sky had ignited an explosion of panic in Washington. Crippled by the Second World War, suffering more casualties than the Nazis, USA and European Allies combined, the USSR was thought to have been a spent and broken force, yet by 1949 they had developed their own atomic weapon, and just 8 years later had won the race to put the first man-made object into orbit.

The potential fusion of these two technologies into a nuclear bomb delivered from space had created hysteria in the White House. As the satellite circled above people gazed up from American streets, wondering at the power these bastards now had, silently colonising the sky above them. Lyndon Johnson, Senate Majority Leader at the time, was quite clear:

'The Roman Empire controlled the world because it could build roads. Later—when it moved to sea—the British Empire was dominant because it had ships. In the air age we were dominant because we had airplanes. Now the Communists have established a foothold in outer space!'[4]

Whosoever is the Most High has the most power and American politicians and generals knew that, left unchallenged, the Soviets would soon have dominion over the whole world. Unfortunately, their first attempts to match Russian achievements had been farcical. Hurrying to catch up with *Sputnik 1*, in December 1957 NASA had broadcast live the countdown and launch of what was to be their first satellite. As the now-familiar digits descended—FIVE, FOUR, THREE—the Vanguard rocket fired into life, raised itself a mere mouse-leap off the ground and promptly exploded in flames, much to the enjoyment of Khrushchev and the dark humour of the American media, who dubbed the whole thing 'KAPUTNIK.'[5]

The first satellite, the first man in space: the Soviets beat America to everything. As the 1960s opened, along with all the other pressures of civil strife and disaffected youth, the US faced this colossal pressure to regain the upper hand. People were frightened, and NASA's very public early failures had brought shame on the nation.

To add to national woes, in 1961 a CIA-backed counter-revolutionary force had landed in Cuba on the Bay of Pigs, aiming to overthrow the communist government of Fidel Castro. To America's shock, Cuban forces destroyed them within three days, and Castro began turning to the USSR for support.

The whole operation had blown up in JFK's face and so when, in September 1962, it was announced that he would make a speech declaring that the United States would put a man on the Moon by the end of the decade it seemed laughable. If we couldn't even land a team of soldiers on a beach, how were we going to put a crew down onto the lunar surface? Americans were depressed, losing faith, anxious that their national myth was being shown weaker and less dominant, Russia like a wild beast, huge, powerful and seemingly unstoppable.

The Cuban Missile Crisis just weeks away, clear evidence already existing of huge military build-up on the island, when Kennedy got up make his speech at Rice Stadium the stakes had become astronomically high. The USA was running a distant second in the space race, had been shamed militarily and technologically and now had nuclear missiles aimed in its face just 90 miles off the Florida coast.

As he rose to speak, the President had to become the all-American seer, the high priest of the American Dream who would spur the nation to transcend itself, to believe again that its myth could still win-out. But Kennedy had a problem. He knew that he couldn't defeat Russia in a war, not without destroying most of the Western world in the process. He needed to rise above all of this, to find a new way to prove their status as the leading super-power. To gain the upper hand he needed to go even higher than they had. *This* was what a successful voyage to the Moon could do.

> *Only if the United States occupies a position of pre-eminence can we help decide whether this new ocean [of outer space] will be a sea of peace or a new terrifying theatre of war.*

He couldn't march into Russia, but he could colonise the Moon, and in a sublime piece of oratory Kennedy inspired the faithful to gather their gifts and make the appropriate sacrifices and perform this miracle. It was this speech that finally proved irresistible to Fallaci. She had to go to leave her fields and follow the stars and see this thing that was happening.

—

'One wish, one thing you could do in your life,' a friend asked as a bunch of us sat out in a field camping one summer, tins of lager foaming at our mouths, a collection of empties crushed and fallen in the grass. The fire smouldered, throwing up gentle flows of curling smoke, grey waterfalls running backwards.

As much as LSD, the space-race was an entheogen, a technological enterprise that generated divine feelings within people. It had done for Fallaci, and did so for me: rockets with awe-inspiring power taking brave pioneers on trips to previously uncharted planes, punching open the thin membrane of the sky, tearing the amniotic sac of our protective atmosphere and shooting out into a vast and cold and frightening-but-wonderful universe.

Post-church, post-club, I needed a new world. The inner one of the ecstatic, the music and the power-religion, had failed to deliver. I wandered for months in London, wondering what I could do, angry at life, depressed, wishing I knew how to make all this work in a way that others around me seemed to find so easy.

It was a clear night for camping, but there were few clear answers. People groaned and vacillated about adventures they'd like to have, or lovers. Hung full above me, sparks from the fire spluttering up across its round face, my answer was immediate and definitive: to hell with the odds of coming back, I'd go to the Moon. I was drunk but unshakeable. We laughed and argued and someone called me a lunatic.

—

In his speech, Kennedy sketched out what would be needed: $5.4 billion for one thing, as well as new alloys and materials not yet invented. All of this would go towards building a rocket that could carry a lunar module and lander unit into orbit, yet the most important part of this payload would not be spacecraft or high-tech machinery, it would be the American values of hard work and old time religion. This was what drove the quest to get high: to plant the flag, to colonise the land, to have Earth looked over by the God who blessed America and hated communism.

Trouble was, as the 60s got going there were two very different Americas getting high in two very different ways. Thomas Paine, the head of NASA, gave an angry speech at Worcester Polytechnic Institute about this struggle between what he called 'Potland' and 'Squareland.' Potland was Kesey and Thompson and the Hells Angels; as he put it, 'ranks of bright young adults goofing off,' wasting away with riots and social unrest and protest marches and getting high on drugs.

Squareland, by comparison, was where things Paine proudly saw things getting done. Things like missions to the Moon and good, honest hard work. As an article in *The Evening Dispatch* put it:

> [NASA scientists] are men and the sons of men and women who still believe that Boy Scouts are good, that divorce is bad, who teach Bible classes on Sunday, enjoy church suppers and Parent-Teacher meetings, who wash their kids' mouth with soap, who regard sexual license as wicked, who respect the American flag and observe the Fourth of July.[6]

Yuri Gagarin had returned from the first ever human orbit in 1961 and been quoted as saying that he'd 'flown into space, but didn't see any god there.' This was exactly the kind of godless communism that couldn't be allowed to propagate any further, and the Squareland folk of NASA were determined to transport their own narrative into space, unload it and stabilise it in orbit.

Thus, as Kesey and his *Merry Pranksters* were crashing rudely back to Earth in an abandoned warehouse at the end of 1966, far over on the East Coast a rocket was burning with far greater thrust, firing astronauts James Lovell and Edwin 'Buzz' Aldrin out of Earth's atmosphere and 120 miles up in the heavens. This was the last of the *Gemini* missions, and on them Aldrin completed three ground-breaking spacewalks, proving for the first time that astronauts could undertake complex work outside of a space vehicle.

Paine must have glowed. Here was a Squareland man in space doing what regular Square guys did down below: putting on a suit and going to work. Officially, the cosmonaut Alexei Leonov had performed the first spacewalk in 1965, but the air pressure in his suit had made it so stiff he'd not even been able to reach round to press the shutter on his camera. In fact, he'd been paralysed so quickly that he'd almost died, unable to work the airlock to get back inside his ship. Aldrin, in contrast, had worked on his for over 2 hours.

It was in this almost mundane picture of domestic activity—a man tinkering with a machine—that NASA began, finally, to crawl past Russia into a space-race lead. If they had to concede that Gagarin was the first *human-in-space*, for Squares, hard-working American Aldrin was the first true *space-man*, getting up and putting a shift in.

That was Monday to Friday sorted, but if space was going to be all-American it couldn't just be a place of hard labour. Sundays meant Christian worship too. John Glenn—the first American to orbit the Earth—had been quick to appreciate this devotional, religious dimension to his work, and at the press conference when the inaugural *Mercury* group of astronauts were introduced to the media, he started off on a sermon:

> *"I am a Presbyterian... I take my religion very seriously... We are placed here with certain talents and capabilities... there is a power greater than any of us..."*

High on acid, in *Heaven and Hell* Huxley had waxed lyrically about gem stones and shiny materials being venerated for their resemblance to the glowing marvels seen with the inner eye of the visionary. And here now, parading in their stunning silver space-suits and sparkling glass helmets, the Mercury 7 looked like living deities, like angels walking among us, about to ascend into the sky above. These weren't even flights now, they were *missions*. The astronauts were American *missionaries* sent up to the heavens, and when asked for a show of hands of those confident they'd return safely, Glenn had gone the whole religious hog, raising *both* hands high in the air, the very call-sign of the middle class Pentecostal.

Probing how they'd selected these men, one of the doctors confided in Fallaci:

> *I can tell you this: when NASA began looking for astronauts, we spent a long time discussing the psychological requisites necessary for an astronaut, and the result of our discussion was that we ought to look for them among the priests. Young, healthy priests qualified in engineering, in chemistry, in medicine, in geology.*[7]

Sexually controlled, apparently. Emotionally stable. Men under authority, able to face death.

NASA rejected this idea and went not for priests but test pilots, men who already thought themselves gods. Having written *The Electric Kool-Aid Acid Test*, Wolfe had gone on to document these Pranksteresque navy fliers who happily strapped themselves into experimental machines, hardly having a clue what kind of trip they were about to take. As they soared far above, this was their 'acid test': how far could they push the envelope? Wolfe was satisfyingly frank about those who didn't quite make it, those left behind in the wake of the true heroes, choking on their dust, nursing fat lips, left spluttering for sobriety or simply rejected by the top brass:

> *A career in flying was like climbing one of those ancient Babylonian pyramids made up of a dizzy progression of steps and ledges, a ziggurat, a pyramid extraordinarily high and steep; and the idea was to prove at every foot of the way up that pyramid that you were one of the elected and anointed ones who had *the right stuff* and could move higher and higher and even—ultimately,*

God-willing, one day—that you might be able to join that special
few at the very top, that elite who had the capacity to bring tears
to men's eyes, the very Brotherhood of the Right Stuff.[8]

For Wolfe, Chuck Yeager was all of this personified. An instinctive flyer, a dazzling World War 2 hit count, totally calm under pressure, he was a 'good ol' boy' who necked a skinful of drink, fell off a jumping horse and broke two ribs just two days before he became the first person to break the sound barrier in the experimental Bell X-1 jet, doing so with only one good arm, the other one still so damned painful he could hardly move the sonofabitch. Squareland resident? Never.

Yet Yeager was a dying breed, part of the line of gung-ho aviation pioneers that stretched right back through Howard Hughes, Antoine de Saint-Exupéry, Charles Lindbergh and Amelia Earhart to the Wright Brothers. Progress had been so fast since their first cloth-covered plane that Orville Wright had been alive to witness Yeager's going through the sound barrier less than 45 years later.

Brave and brilliant they might be, but Yeager's sort weren't the kind that Paine wanted tainting the newly formed NASA, and one undercurrent of Wolfe's book is something of a lament at the gradual reining in of these half-crazed stick and rudder men, the slow toning down of the colour as the political stakes got higher. Anyone who knew Yeager would have had him top of their list to be selected to move up from supersonic jet planes to become one of the first American astronauts, but he wasn't eligible: he didn't have the prerequisite college education. You can feel the sneer in Wolfe's writing, the blinkered hierarchies not recognising lowborn Jesus Christ himself in a flight suit, rejecting his miracle talent because of some pieces of goddamned *paper.*

Asked if he regretted not being selected, Yeager himself was blunt: not one bit. He'd seen the early experiments, the fruit flies sent up, the rabbits and monkeys that followed, most of which did not survive. In November 1957 Laika—a stray from the streets of Moscow—had become the first mammal to orbit the Earth. Despite Russian propaganda to the contrary, Yeager knew she'd likely over-heated and died within the hour. That was not the kind of crap you pulled with elite members of the Brotherhood.

No, according to him, the guys who were chosen for the *Mercury* missions—America's first attempt to put a man into space—were no more than 'spam in a can,' no more than the sheep, duck and cockerel who'd been strapped into Montgolfier's balloon basket. They were to have no controls, nor any window from which to see to use them. Everything would be done remotely. In fact, so little was there going to be to do that the proto-NASA's initial call for graduate volunteers mentioned circus daredevils, parachutists, submariners, divers and arctic explorers.

—

In another life, Kesey's co-pilot, Stewart Brand, might himself have signed up. Though he is a kind of countercultural Forrest Gump, turning up in the background of some of the major events of the period, Brand was far from the typical hippie, one that probably would have fooled Kling's radar if the two had ever met. He'd corresponded with Huxley in the 50s about *Heaven and Hell*, but had also taken officer training in the military—becoming a qualified parachutist—and had a degree in biology. Never sporting a beard, never growing out his hair, he was always the man who'd make sure that things actually got done. If Kesey's trip was all about 'who's on the bus?' then Brand was his sidekick, making sure that said bus left punctually, with some gas in the tank and a set of tyres that would get them there. He'd been the one who'd seen potential in scaling up the Acid Tests, and begun organising the Trips Festival.

In January of '66, as the weekend of it had approached, he'd begun a publicity drive, attaching a large banner with the word WOW hanging below three weather balloons and sailing them up above San Francisco's convention centre.

'Look at it go right into the sun!' he yelled into the PA he'd hired, to the bemusement of the tourists and business-folk milling around. 'It's trying to get a little closer to the sun before it burns its wings off.' A little nod to Icarus, just to see who got it.

Like Fallaci, the vertical remained a fascination for Brand and the summer after the Trips Festival had gone off he'd been lying on his back on North Beach, a dose of acid to the good, staring at the tall buildings in downtown San Francisco, noticing that, as they rose to the sky, they weren't quite parallel.

It dawned on him that, at a certain huge distance, the curved horizon of the Earth would close and the whole planet could thus be framed in a single photograph. Such a viewpoint was impossible for a human being... *but wait*, he thought, *hadn't NASA sent up satellites to do exactly that?*

Well, yes they had, and back in '63 Fallaci had been interviewing astronaut boss Deke Slayton, asking him what sort of landscape they might expect when they finally landed on the lunar surface. With the Moon being so much smaller, Slayton had explained, it would look like you were always standing on the brink of a nearby precipice, the Earth looming huge just beyond. 'Think of sitting on the Moon and looking at the Earth,' he'd mused, predicting that it would make a very fine photograph.

Brand knew none of this, but as the Lunar Orbiter 1 unmanned spacecraft had launched that August in '66, just weeks before Kesey's Acid Graduation, he figured that if they had rigged some kind of on-board camera to snap shots of the Moon's surface, surely someone would have also thought to mount one pointing back at Earth?

Brand being Brand, within a week he had had thousands of button badges made up with simple text, demanding in bold type:

WHY HAVEN'T WE SEEN A PHOTOGRAPH
OF THE WHOLE EARTH YET?

He spent the next months hiking around the country, selling badges at 25c a pop, seeding this question to anyone who would listen. Sure enough, in 1967 NASA bowed to pressure and did release a 'Whole Earth' picture taken from a weather satellite. Smudged, grainy and only in black and white, it wasn't the mind-blowing shot that Brand had envisaged. For that he would have to wait another year, but when it was released its effect was just as powerful as he had hoped.

'Earthrise' was shot in December 1968 aboard Apollo 8, the very first mission to rocket away from Earth and put a manned spaceship into the orbit of another celestial body. As they circled the Moon the crew witnessed Earth 'rise' above the lunar horizon—something no human had ever seen before.

On board was William Anders, operating the shutter of a specially modified 70mm Hasselblad 500EL camera. The first Whole Earth picture had been shot remotely but the Earthrise photograph that he took was something else. It drew the viewer in, inviting them to place themselves with the crew, this tender human experience of seeing our planet emerge from the night, edging its way above the pocked lunar surface, a fragile, green ball upon which all of history has been played.

Squarelanders may have taken the shot, but, encouraged by Brand, Potland jumped on it. Whole Earth ideas were suddenly everywhere. Hippies began talking about Gaia and 'Mother Earth,' the Apollo photographs the go-to images to illustrate ideas about the vast and deep interconnected coherence of life. Unwittingly, astro-engineering had unleashed a new wave of ecstatic, esoteric religious fervour.

—

Fallaci had divined this already, years before any Apollo craft had lifted away and made the transit to lunar orbit. From her strong Catholic upbringing she could see that astronauts were a religious sect. 'Unwittingly, childlike,' she noted, 'these men were looking for God.'

For America, desperate to defeat the godless communists, the space race became an overtly spiritual quest. Even before Glenn had preached at the Mercury press conference and lifted his hands to heaven, God had been called upon to side with them.

May, 1961. Al Shepard is ready to be thrust briefly into the above and become the first American in space. He is due to splash down in the Pacific ocean and aboard the *Lake Champlain*, the naval chaplain has assembled the whole crew, eyes raised to heaven, scanning the sky for their angel, prayers sent up for his safe return:

Dear Lord who hears us, now that a precious life is about to be flung into the heavens, we are filled with fear... Dear Lord who hears us, we thank Thee for giving us men ready to sacrifice their existence to open up for us the doors of space.[9]

Fallaci reports it like an ancient, primal ritual, the priests congregating in hope that their endeavours will be favoured, offering lives up as tithe. Shephard had been woken at 1 that morning, immediately alert, getting up and asking for breakfast: rare steak, eggs and ham and orange juice. 'He seemed,' she reports the doctor who attended him saying, 'like a man getting up to go hunting.' Not for birds, but for gods: sat atop the smoking gun, firing him bullet-fast to puncture the soft, dark underbelly of heaven.

As the missions became more courageous, so the Christian fervour escalated. As Earthrise was witnessed for the first time in 1968, the Apollo 8 crew soundtracked their taking of photographs by broadcasting the opening words of the book of Genesis to Mission Control.

A year later, as Aldrin and Armstrong waited on the Sea of Tranquility, readying themselves to exit the lunar module, Aldrin asked for radio silence, took the communion elements that he'd secreted aboard and performed a short Eucharist, reading from Psalm 8:

O Lord, our Lord,
how majestic is your name in all the Earth!
You have set your glory
above the heavens.

No less than a chorus of conquest, the celebration of an enemy vanquished.

Sneaking the elements aboard such a complex and sensitive flight was a serious breach of mission guidelines, but Aldrin escaped sanction purely because NASA saw the fervoured cheers from Squares that followed, and feared the backlash it would cause if they punished him.

Others followed suit. Apollo 12 took a crusader's cross and a Christian flag on their mission. Those on the fated Apollo 13 were carrying hundreds of Bibles on microfilm, provided by the Apollo Prayer League of Houston who wanted to use them in evangelistic missions when they returned to Earth. The Apollo 15 crew recited Psalm 121, and declared to all that they 'explored the surface of the Moon with the power of God and Jesus Christ.'

Observing all of this was Norman Mailer, researching for his own book on Apollo, *A Fire on The Moon.* He went to the launch of Apollo 11 and was almost physically blown away, the television pictures simply unable to communicate the almighty power and gut-thumping force of the Saturn V rocket taking off.

'Finally,' he screamed above the roar, 'man has something with which to speak to God.'[10]

Not priests as astronauts, but astronauts as priests: the finest specimens of our race sent to intercede for us.

Sitting with the writer Raymond Bradbury in preparation for all her meetings with the people on the space programme, Fallaci had put to him the connection between breaking the force of gravity and breaking the hierarchy of heavenly beings. He'd vigorously agreed, considering all attempts at altitude to be super-human, all these miracles of flight a form of blasphemy. Now with the Saturn V Mailer saw the unforgivable sin of height, committing wonderful heresy, pulling God by the coat-tails, this hissing, shaking, steaming mass of pressurised energy, shouting to the heavens above and the communists below that Eden had better watch out because we were on our way.

'The Earth has become too small for us,' Fallaci had said to her father as the book opened. 'We must look for other myths and other dreams.' Break through our atmosphere and change the heavenly order. She belonged to a generation that was dizzy about these vast horizons opening, unsure even which way to explore. 'Where are we running, and why?' she'd asked.

Here in Mailer and Bradbury was part of her answer. We went to the Moon in search of Eden. We went to the Moon to storm heaven, fleeing the fallen Earth that had so long held us captive. In the grip of the Cold War, in the midst of our bloody battles with a powerful enemy, we reached to the above in hope of a more pure, unblemished place.

I picture my sister in her hospital bed and think yes, to achieve this we made men weightless.

—

Was this why I looked longingly up at it? From the chaos of my life did I see a vision of perfect place?

Fallaci knew: the search for Eden had a long history among explorers tired of the fight. Centuries before she had walked these shores, her fellow Italian Cristoforo Colombo had been the first European to set out and find the Americas.

Columbus' *Book of Prophesies*—released in 1505, the same year Leonardo had published his codex on bird flight—explained how his missions had been part of the fulfilment of predictions found in the Bible. Even on a horizontal axis, early Renaissance Earth had still presented great mysteries, the unknown worlds across the seas clouded in as much mystery as those above in the sky.

Columbus not only wanted to find new lands of unbelievers in order to see them converted, but was convinced that paradise would be found beyond the ocean's horizon. High up on a rocky crag in Venezuela, untouched by floodwaters that he believed had swamped the Earth in Noah's day, he was briefly convinced that he had rediscovered the Garden of Eden.

This quest to locate heaven had been vital to the expansion and strengthening of his own tribe's myth. During Columbus' lifetime, Spanish Catholicism faced its own 'Cold Wars' with rival tribes and nations, the years leading up to his first voyage seeing a gruelling 10 year conflict with the Islamic Emirate of Granada, as well as constant battles with other European states for dominance of the New World of the Americas. Locating the primal utopia of Eden would be the Holy Grail, their control of this powerful territory a means by which their narrative could be shown to be righteous, their enemies crushed under their feet.

Yet, despite having sailed to the farthest stretches of the planet, Columbus still couldn't find it. A pilot-priest, the explorer died a broken man in a monk's habit, no closer to understanding where heaven was hiding.

All horizontals exhausted, within 10 years of his death a Renaissance poet called Ludovico Ariosto had moved the search to an entirely different axis. Amidst more brutal conflict between Islam and Christianity, in 1532 he published *Orlando Furiouso*, within which the protagonist, Astolfo, meets St John at the top of a mountain. Astolfo is searching for a cure for his master's ills, but the saint points him on further, saying,

Wholly must you leave this nether sphere;
To the Moon's circle you I have to lead,
Of all the planets to our world most near,
Because the medicine, that is fit to speed
Insane Orlando's cure, is treasured here.[11]

In other words: there would be no cure on Earth for the war between religions or nations. Peace would only be found far *far* higher, onward right up to the lunar surface.

I could see it in myself and my sister: in times of great upheaval the search for Eden always intensifies, always projects itself to the highest place in the imagination. For those in the 1600s that focus became the Moon.

It is 1609, and Johannes Kepler has just discovered the very laws explaining the movements of the planets that would allow Armstrong and Aldrin take aim at the lunar surface. He writes to Galileo, full of familiar frustration and fear at the continuing wars and tribulations throughout Europe, explaining his desire to escape:

'I want to leave the Earth and go to the Moon. [...] Let us create vessels and sails adapted to the heavenly ether.'

A few years later, in 1611, the Italian monk and Platonist heretic Tommaso Campanella also writes to Galileo setting out his similar belief that paradise would be found there. Like Columbus, his 'scientific' justification points back to the flood. If a Venezuelan cliff-top wasn't high enough, then surely the Moon was the only place distant enough to have escaped the rising waters and remain uninfected by Adam's sin?

Drawing extensively on Campanella and Kepler, in 1638 John Wilkins publishes his *Discourse Concerning the Discovery of a New World in the Moon*. He has recently founded the Royal Society, and in this scholarly work affirms that 'Paradise is in a high and elevated place, which some have conceived could be nowhere but the Moon.' Explaining his 'contempt for these Earthly things,' he predicts that, 'so soon as the art of flying is found out, some of their Nation will make one of their first colonies on the Moon,' going on to muse that those who do so will be so happy as the warring Earth will be so far away.

300 years before Apollo, in a similar time of great wars and apocalyptic anxiety, humanity was looking up from the bloodstained Earth and pinning its hopes of peace on the pure white Moon above.

Unfortunately for Wilkins, in 1642, just after he'd published his discourse, a child was born in the English countryside who would dash his hopes. The infant was so small at birth he could fit into a quart pot. He grew up poor, weak and badly bullied at school and, seething at the cruelty of his classmates, he determined to outstrip them intellectually. By his wits he worked his way up from nothing and on to a scholarship at Cambridge University.

Having reached these dazzling academic heights, in 1665 an outbreak of the plague forced the college to shut down. Most students would have been delighted with this unexpected holiday, but with little interests other than his work, he returned home and continued to study under his own steam. Thus, by the time Cambridge re-opened in 1667, he—Isaac Newton of course—had developed the theory of differential calculus, written a groundbreaking paper on optics and devised the laws of gravitation.

Attempting to explain why the Moon didn't simply crash down into the Earth, Kepler and Wilkins had concluded that the sun, Moon, stars and planets must be made of a pure, 'higher' stuff that, unlike everything on the depraved Earth, did not 'fall.' With his new theory of gravity, Newton tore down these pseudo-theological interpretations, replacing them with scientific ones: it wasn't that the Moon didn't fall, it was that *everything* in the universe was falling.

This was shocking enough yet, perhaps even more disturbing to Kepler's view of the heavens, was Newton's 1668 invention of the reflecting telescope. When the first astronomers used it they were shocked to discover that the Moon was far from Edenic.

This couldn't be paradise. It was no more than a pocked wasteland of dust and rock.

—

Right at the end of the decade, on 21st July 1969, it was into that dust that mankind finally took one giant leap. As Neil Armstrong stepped off that ladder and his feet pushed down a fraction of an inch into the lunar surface, it was as if an enormous door had just been kicked in. Never before had any human being, in all our hundreds of thousands of years, stood on ground that wasn't Earth.

If it felt dramatically alien—millions upon millions far below watching on their TV sets, stunned and speechless as this spaceman bounced across the Moon—the hours building up to this event had been jaw-droppingly ordinary. True to the values of Squareland, the two astronauts had been instructed to get some sleep and eat some dinner. Sleep hadn't come to either, but they'd eaten a square meal, then done what good squares did: 'washed up.' After all of the rocket-fuelled heroics—Armstrong *only just* finding an appropriate landing site before their fuel ran out—it was this beautifully domestic task that precipitated hours upon hours of monotone, paint-dry TV coverage, the whole world waiting and waiting because putting away the dishes had taken far longer than planned for in the mission schedule. Potland critics fumed. 'Only America,' journalist Michael Hoffmann complained, could 'take a miracle and turn it into a bummer!'[12]

There were huge celebrations of course. But no sooner had the astronauts returned safely than Fallaci's questions resurfaced in earnest. What had it all been for? LSD had faced criticism for sending people on pointless trips to sky-high places; now Apollo came under fire for doing the exact same thing. Newton had already shown that there was no Eden to be found there, and it hadn't taken Armstrong and Aldrin to work out that this was no New World of great material resources.

Why then had we gone? That it had been an extraordinary feat was never in doubt, but what had been its purpose? Down below, people were dying in their droves, many at the hands of American soldiers wielding napalm, firing indiscriminately into Vietnamese villages from helicopter gunships, others beaten by police at civil rights marches, millions more still anxious about the ever-present spectre of nuclear annihilation.

'Why do men climb the tallest mountains and voyage to the Moon?' Raymond Bradbury had been asked, hunting for answers to Apollo. 'We go because we are nearer the stars, and if we reach the stars one day we will be immortal.'[13]

For thousands of years this song had essentially remained the same: we got high to escape death, offering our tithes to priests and shamans who gathered them to make costly trips to the heavens, interceding on our behalf, asking for absolution for sin, reopening the way back to paradise, a new Eden, a new Earth out there somewhere.

Finishing and publishing her book in 1965, all of Fallaci's interviews had taken place in an atmosphere of great optimism and excitement, one where the stars—and immortality—really did begin to feel nearer. 'The Moon is only a staging post!' NASA administrators and engineers had gushed. The real goal was Mars, and then on out into the galaxy!

Amidst all the violence and Cold War nuclear anxiety, more than ever America needed this hope. At the beginning of the decade JFK had pledged to land a man on the Moon and now, as Mailer put it,

Four assassinations later; a war in Vietnam later; a burning of Black ghettos later; one New York school strike later; one sexual revolution later; yes, eight years of a dramatic, near-catastrophic, outright spooky decade later, we were ready to make the Moon.[14]

Kennedy had announced that the mission would be done 'for all mankind,' but after 10 years of national lunacy, when it came to it there was only one desperate reason why the deed was done. As Armstrong and Aldrin hammered a pole into a useless lump of rock and dust hundreds of thousands of miles away, as they hung from it a limp and windless Stars and Stripes and prepared to leave again, they did so in the face of huge divisions, trying to prove to the world that America was still strong, that somewhere out in the infinite universe there was a United States that was still in a state of unity.

But, more than that, in the face of possible annihilation at the hands of their enemies, they did it as a kind of prophetic religious act. These flights into space were performances of a mystery play that assured the faithful that, if the unthinkable happened and the beloved country of the Pilgrim Fathers faced a fresh apocalypse, there would a new, virgin land to flee to.

This was the true meaning of the Moon, right in the title of Fallaci's book. We went there to begin the process of flight to another world, in case our own was snuffed out.

We went to begin preparations for this terrifying eventuality: *If The Sun Dies.*

—

What happens if the energy that has sustained life burns out? What happens if Helios turns out to be a mere finite source of heat? What happens when the Light of the World dims and weakens and loses the battle against the shadows?

'For a year we've been in the Garden of Eden,' Kesey said at the Graduation. Acid had opened the door to it and they had stepped through, and he had tried to gather them close and thrown in intense music and lights, hoping to build the energy to create some kind of fusion, a new star born in a warehouse in San Francisco.

For a moment he had popped out of the time warp into the silver haze of the Universal Mind... They'd almost had it, but this tiny sun that had glowed for a moment had died. They had blown it.

The door that Blake had promised would lead to Eden had been the last door; they had stepped only into a void, one full of fear, and loathing, one into which all manner of violence would soon rush.

We have been here once before, and so has Blake. In the gardens of the Palace of Versailles, Etienne Montgolfier struggles with poor weather, cloth and thread. It is 1783, and he is sweating, worried that the lords and ladies of French society will not care for his invention. He could not be more wrong.

Outside the gates of the palace, crowds regularly gather. They are hungry. While the King continues to borrow and spend extravagantly—showering his wife Marie Antoinette with diamonds—the poor die of starvation. When the grain crop fails, which it regularly does, the price of bread rockets and the people of Paris come to protest the King, to demand that he acts. But the feasting in Versailles never stops and the King does not act, other than to throw those who agitate and organise and demand a more just ordering of society into the terrifying basements of the Bastille.

Because of this there is revolution afoot, one that Blake reads greedily of back in London. The known world could face slaughter; the shining monarch may have to be extinguished. Etienne's own father is not immune to these troubles, nor immune from the anger and emotion that crackles through France. He wants to be ennobled, to be lifted above all this into the protective orbit he assumes aristocratic society will provide, and now his remarkable sons might just afford that opportunity.

Etienne is finally ready. The King has suggested that two criminals be put into the basket—they are subhuman animals after all—but Montgolfier resists, and the sheep, duck and rooster are installed. The straw is lit and the heat rises. The balloon, painted in rich ensigns to impress and pay tribute to the royal party, lifts into the air; the court gasps with joy.

The King's generals leap on Montgolfier, desperate to have his invention. France is dividing against itself and perhaps the best way to prevent the growing shadow of civil war will be to direct anger upwards, to crane the people's necks away from their abject poverty to look in awe at the above. Rather than destroy the Earth below, why not discover a new one above?

But it is too late. The sun is already dimming into dark night. The *Ancien Régime* is out of fuel. It is consuming itself, is no longer trusted to sustain the people. The gardens at Versailles had been Edenic, but now the heavy doors protecting the elite have been breached. Whatever chances they had to keep their elevated position have gone. They have blown it.

Montgolfier's principle backer, Jean-Baptiste Réveillon, had made his fortune selling flocked wallpaper to the rich. He suggests in a newspaper that free market economics would lower both the price of bread and wages, words that the hungry Parisian mob take unkindly to. The same garden from which Etienne first rose is later overrun with angry rioters.

The cracks in French society cannot be papered over, even with the spectacle of a flying machine. For men who cannot afford bread, flight is like cake: it is unattainable, part of the above which they rise up to rupture, to pull down, the very necks that strained upwards in marvel at the balloon, now set on the block, Monsieur Guillotin's heavy blade descending.

And yet the principle is established, and others take note. It came too late to save Louis XVI, but perhaps flight *can* divert the anger of the people away from unjust governance, away from the vitriol the masses feel about the way the powerful arrange the world to suit themselves? Thus, when Tournachon sails with his camera over post-revolutionary Paris, he notes the way the streets fall into perfect cartographic order, how the movements of the people can be traced and observed, how, up here, man cannot be reached by any human force or by any power of evil.

—

The powerful know that control of the sky is vital to their continued domination. This is what the French learned too late: if the people will rise up, the state must use miracles of technology and rise above them further still. So, when the sun is at risk of dying, when a United States is threatening to fall apart, light blinding fires under powerful rockets and send them up to puncture the sky.

Give the poor pictures from such high vantage points that they understand that, though the whole Earth can be seen to be turning, there will be no revolution. There cannot be, because when a Squareland white Christian nation has reached the pure white pseudo-Eden of the Moon, the people of Potland, the hippies, the blacks, the disenfranchised Vietnam veterans, the bikers and beatniks will conclude that there is no means of rising above the God they call the Bright Morning Star. They buried him in a tomb, but three days later he rose up, this son who will not die, this omnipotent, ascended being who is now the Most High, who has conquered death itself, who is eternally victorious and has ordained this state of things with Nixon in the White House and communism nearly vanquished.

Alongside the Stars and Stripes, the Apollo 11 astronauts left a plaque, which read:

> HERE MEN FROM THE PLANET EARTH
> FIRST SET FOOT UPON THE MOON
> JULY 1969, A.D.
> WE CAME IN PEACE FOR ALL MANKIND

The signatures of Aldrin, Armstrong and command module pilot Michael Collins seemed appropriate enough below this text, but what rankled for many, muttering in the background as the world went wild was Nixon's name inscribed beneath them all.

Quiet voices asked from the sidelines: after all of the violent struggles of the preceding years, how could three white men and a white President be said to represent all mankind? With all the slaughter continuing in South East Asia, how could three Americans pretend to come in peace? One journalist suggested that the plaque should have read, 'Here men first set foot outside the Earth on their way to the far stars. They speak of peace but wherever they go they bring war.'[15]

Back in Italy, Fallaci's father nods in agreement. He has been right all along, and underneath her love of space, his daughter knows it too because the family had lived through the German occupation of Italy and its subsequent liberation by the Allies.

Interviewing Deke Slayton, she is hit by this thunderbolt: he revealed that he had been a bomber pilot flying missions over German-held Florence. He had bombed the beautiful bridge right by her house. Working for her freedom, he was a hellish angel, terrifying this young girl as he circled and dived.

Had anything changed? Were the missiles any different now that they aimed at the Moon? Released in 1969, Kurt Vonnegut's *Slaughterhouse-Five* thought not. 'Dresden was like the Moon now,' he wrote, drawing a startling parallel between the bombed out ruins of the city and the barren wasteland of the lunar landscape. The desolated, lifeless rock was a message to all of America's communist enemies, a symbol of what she would do to all who dared oppose her.

For the Vietnamese, for the Palestinians, for the impoverished African Americans, the extraordinary display of power that delivered victory over the Moon was a chilling warning about white, western Christian might, one that seemed to carry totalitarian overtones from another recent regime similarly intolerant of tainted elements within its population.

Interviewed about the Saturn V rocket that had finally allowed man to speak with God, the man who had built it had warned that countercultural and racial divisions in American society were worrying signs of national rebellion.

He felt that the only way to restore order—both inside America, and internationally—was a great display of state power. Space could do this. It was a moral substitute for international violence, the huge power of missiles turned not against other people, but upwards to the Moon.

He pointed at his Saturn rocket. 'At last man has an outlet for his aggressive nature,' he said, going on to emphasise—as Ariosto and Kepler and so many balloonists and star-gazing scientists and early aeronauts had done before him—the moral importance of flight in the quest for a new, peaceful utopia on this divided Earth:

Here then is space travel's most meaningful mission: on that future day when our satellite vessels are circling Earth, when

men manning an orbital station can view our planet against the
star-studded blackness of infinity as but a planet among planets,
on that day, I say, fratricidal war will be banished from the star
[sic] on which we live.[16]

The most important rocket scientist in history was placing his own work at the centre of the drive to end war on Earth. The man whose technical brilliance would power the awesome Saturn V missiles was convinced that these earth-shattering, thundering machines were what was needed to press a broken American society back into shape.

Using dramatic, almost divine displays of force, American military officers like William Anders now had the entire world in their viewfinders. Now that this had happened, he believed, any attempt at war would be fruitless. It was America, *über alles*.

Who was this man, this great redeemer of America and herald of global paradise? None other than Wernher von Braun, one of Hitler's most important captains.

—

What happens when the sun dies?

Fallaci interviewed von Braun and found herself horribly captivated by him, unable to understand why until she realised that he smelt faintly of lemon... Yes, that was it, that same lemon soap that the German soldiers had used, the ones who had come that beautiful sunny day during the war, looking for two Yugoslavians hiding out with her family in an abandoned convent.

They had found them in the well, laughed and taken them away and shot them.

'These men who will go to the Moon or to Mars,' she wrote, 'and they don't even know what happened in Poland in Yugoslavia, in France, in Italy, in places called Dachau.'

Born into a wealthy, powerful aristocratic family, von Braun was given a telescope by his mother when he was 8 years old. He became obsessed with space, and set about learning all he could to become a rocket scientist. Fallaci notes with horror that, in his apartment at university, he and his friend Constantine Generales set a bicycle wheel on a powerful electric motor, in order to test the effect of high g-forces on living things. They would tie a live mouse to the rim and increase the speed until the rodent burst like a grenade. Generales would go on to become NASA's lead in space medicine.

Later, needing a place to test out his inventions, von Braun's mother suggested Peenemünde, a desolate place on the Baltic coast where his grandfather had gone to hunt ducks for sport.

In 1939 von Braun met Hitler. Nazi Germany wanted to overcome and destroy its enemies and von Braun gladly lent his shoulder to the wheel, convincing Hitler that terrifying rocket-powered ballistic missiles would do the job best. He returned to Peenemünde to refocus his work. The pinnacle of his achievements, his pride and joy, was the *Vergeltungswaffe Zwei*—'Revenge Weapon 2'—that became known simply as the V2. Brilliantly exploiting Newtonian mechanics and perfected in 1944, thousands of them rained terror down on London.

They were the first manmade objects to reach sub-orbital space, flying to a height of around 130km before turning and beginning their descent. Bearing down at more than the speed of sound, they carried no audible warning before them, whole tenements suddenly obliterated, families swatted like fruit flies and burned like dogs.

The casualties in London were horrendous, but more chilling is the fact that the V2 is perhaps the only weapon to have caused more deaths in its construction than its deployment. Von Braun experienced first-hand the terrible treatment and brutal suffering of the slave workers from the Mittelbau-Dora concentration camp that manned the V2 production line. He knew what was going on, but ignored it, working tirelessly to get Hitler his 'wonder weapon,' promising that once London fell, he would aim 30,000 more V2s at New York and Washington, and another 30,000 at Moscow.

But it was not to be. If they had perfected it 6 months earlier, Germany would probably have won. Now, as 1945 opened, Peenemünde was being obliterated itself. Russian forces were approaching from one direction, Americans from the other. The dream of a pure Nazi state was dying. On 29th April Hitler knew that the game was up. He hastily married Eva Braun and consulted a doctor on the best way to commit suicide. Drugs and bullets, came the answer, so deep in his underground bunker, he bit on a cyanide pill and fired a bullet into his head.

What happens when the sun dies?

His Führer dead, his rocket facility blown to smithereens, his enemies closing on every side, von Braun has to decide what to do. Gathering his key scientists and engineers he stands and makes a speech.

> 'Germany has lost the war, but our dream of going to the Moon and to other planets isn't dead. The V2's aren't only war weapon, they can be used for space travel. To one end or another, the Russians and the Americans will want to know what we know.'[17]

Staying and fighting is out of the question, and escape is impossible. They have to surrender, but to the Americans or the Russians? Russia has suffered von Braun's work directly, and America has not. They vote unanimously to hand themselves over to American forces, hoping that their expertise would be a bargaining chip that will save their lives.

It worked. To prevent a brain-drain into the USSR, President Truman had ordered the round-up and wholesale transport to the US of all leading German scientists. He had expressly told his agents not to include anyone who had been anything more than a nominal Nazi party member, but his order was ignored, secret military agencies deciding that certain talents couldn't be allowed to go to the enemy.

Along with 120 of his key men, von Braun was taken to America under 'Operation Paperclip,' his Nazi record expunged and fake political notes and employment records 'clipped' to his file. An adept shape-shifter, he played his new role beautifully, becoming an evangelical Christian and lead scientist in the development of Redstone, the first medium-range nuclear missile, little more than an updated version of his beloved V2.

When NASA was formed in 1958, von Braun's rocket group was brought under its wing, his propulsion expertise conscripted to help get Armstrong to the Moon. Full of god and spaceships, the man who had created the revenge weapon had morphed into the all-American superman, making grand speeches about the ability of his missiles to bring world peace.

This troubled Norman Mailer greatly, and in his pieces on Apollo for *Life* magazine, he identified a heavy piece of Nazi shrapnel still lodged in von Braun's ideology. Who was this man who, since a young boy, had yearned desperately to leave Earth and reach other planets? Who would do that, other than a god or a devil? In all of his work he had sought peace through terror, bidding to end war by convincing his enemies that resistance was futile.

All the glories of space, the dazzling human achievement of Apollo, the carefully selected, prime-specimen white men in pure white suits standing up to the overbearing black sky, this all-American trip to the Moon—all of it had been fuelled by a man who had worked tirelessly to lift the Aryan race to assured immortality.

The triumphant footage, the ecstatic crowds rejoicing at the totem in their hands... there is a chill to it now, a cold shadow of the man who is never seen, the scent of lemon soap, the one who demanded an all-powerful response to opposition, gases mixing, injecting, igniting, men crammed into air-locked capsules, pumped full of gas.

—

At last man has an outlet for his aggressive nature.
Now man has something with which to speak to God.

In the confluence of Mailer and von Braun's words there's a primordial current of ancient religious yearning and brutal tribal warfare. Our shouts to God are so often tied up with violence towards those branded heretics, those who are communists, those who are Jews or hippies or disabled or migrant or homosexual or black or dirty or impure.

The sun god Apollo speaks in such thunderous tones that all enemies of his power are shaken into obedient conformity. When Harvey Kling wrote to the President, he described in delighted tones the wonderful welcome he'd had from the Japanese people, apparently blind to the brutal omnipotence his presence represented. Thinking that they had clapped and shaken his hand for no other reason than he was an American, he'd perhaps not realised that he was only half a day's train ride from Hiroshima, a city that his country had annihilated just 25 years before, one suitcase-sized package delivering burning, atomising hell, a tiny sun falling to Earth, ushering in a breathless, choking night.

The Land of the Rising Sun had been extinguished and the pure Aryan dream overcome. Von Braun had signed up with the Führer because he had wanted society to be purified, and was prepared to use great force to achieve this. Tempted by their already-advanced weaponry, his response to the countercultural divisions he'd witnessed in America was the same one Hitler had demanded to deal with the sullying of Aryan society: a ferocious display of state power, one that would leave no one in any doubt of the risks of dissension, even as it was couched in the language of delivering a utopian final solution.

And yet, to von Braun's horror, the sun was dying again.

When Fallaci had sat down with him in 1963, the room 'suddenly as full as an eggshell is full of egg,' he'd been supremely confident: they would reach the Moon by the end of the decade, and Mars by about 1985 or 1990. Then Venus. Then Alpha Centauri. Apollo 11 had succeeded, and there had been worldwide fanfare and a genuine sense of joint human achievement. During Aldrin and Armstrong's 45-day celebratory tour to 25 foreign countries, the world *did* seem a more peaceful place. We had done this together! We could all get along!

But the bullshit couldn't last. Paine had berated Potlanders for burning time and money on getting high, but now the accusations came firing back: unreal amounts of money and resources to put straight white guys on the Moon? And what had it achieved?

Quiet before, dissident voices now strengthened and interest sapped quickly from subsequent missions. The Moon hadn't turned out to be made of cheese, but lunar landings were fast becoming cheesy. Apollo 13 was in danger of boring the public until the famous pronouncement that 'Houston, we have a problem.' The potential for disaster saw a surge in media attention, but by the time Apollo 17 had lifted off from the Moon late in 1972, my parents too bored of it all to lift me from my cot and show me, everyone in the program knew that missions 18 to 20 had been shelved.

That was it. 6 trips to the Moon. NASA's funding was slashed, the apparently limitless resources suddenly exhausted by the whim of Congress. Space was done. Dusted. It was over. Apollo was dead, the sun god extinguished. They had had plans to establish a permanent lunar base, to push deeper into the solar system, but Nixon, his own star collapsing in the face of the Watergate scandal, said no.

Paine was vocal and furious at the President's lack of vision, not realising that, for the White House, it was mission accomplished. As the 60s had opened they had been underdogs, but now, as the 70s began, the American myth had emerged victorious. Soviet strength had been vanquished; explain again, what do we need a base on the Moon for?

Von Braun seethed at the budget cuts, at the last three flights grounded. He fought with the White House, but what could he do? He might be the greatest rocket scientist in history, but he'd also been a member of SS. The ice was always thin. He quietly retired in 1972, and died of cancer a few short years later, his gravestone reading:

The heavens declare the glory of God
the skies proclaim the work of his hands.

There was no mention of the Earth.

—

I was by now living in the bombed out remnants of von Braun's conceit, South London pockmarked with post-war constructions thrown up over the crater sites of V2 hits and other ordnance.

Understand the visual symptoms and you see the disorder everywhere: neat rows of Victorian houses suddenly, rudely interrupted by low cost, high-density dwellings erected in great haste, brutalist estates raised on razed ground, housing some of London's poorest ecstatics, who gathered in throngs at Pentecostal meetings or sucked on pipes in broken corners. No Sea of Tranquility here, the long reverberations of the V2's terror was still keenly felt in their desperation for sublime flight.

Drawing inspiration from von Braun's achievements, Hal Lindsey funded the bleak theologies of escape that these poor urban communities clung to. In 1969 he published *The Late, Great Planet Earth*, announcing that,

Astounding as man's trip to the Moon is, without benefit of science, space suits, or interplanetary rockets, there will be those who will be transported into a glorious place more beautiful, more awesome, than we can possibly comprehend.

An apocalyptic, divisive diatribe of 'prophesies,' Lindsey's book went on to be the best-selling non-fiction title of the following decade. In his interpretation of Revelation 21, Christians would be lifted to a city that needed neither sun nor Moon, for the glory of the Lord would give it light. It was a doctrine of flight back to Eden, a divinely elected elite lifting away from the sin-filled poverty and darkness of Earth.

Not to be outdone, now that the bright sun of LSD had been extinguished, in his post-jail years Leary began hailing space exploration as the means by which a new utopia would be created. He summarised his ideas with the acronym SMI²LE: Space Migration, coupled with Increased Intelligence and Life Extension. Presumably considering himself worthy of a place on the list, 5000 of the human race's finest specimens would be sent away from Earth to begin a new Edenic civilisation on luxurious HOMEs—High Orbiting Mini Earths.

Where was Thompson to call this bullshit out? I scoured his work for any mention of Leary's plans for space, or even of Apollo or von Braun. A totalitarian system casting the spell of liberty? A lifeless wasteland masquerading as Eden, his nemesis Nixon right at the centre of it all—surely this would have been fertile ground for his writing?

Just as with the drugs, just as with religion, here was a technology of power that promised to deliver peace, that held out the hope of Eden but was no more than a means for a tiny elite to pedal a myth that helped them lift away.

'You're really writing one lifelong book called *The Death of the American Dream*' a friend had told him. An autopsy of the collapsing black hole of the Stars and Stripes. Biographies were clear that Thompson had taken these words to heart, making the absence of any comment on the stinking necrotic fantasy of Apollo even harder to take.

—

If the sun dies we have to find a new world. It took me a while to work out what I could do once the ecstatic, dazzling orb of church had faded and exhausted. Abandoning the prayer room for the clean logic of the classroom I finally began training to be a teacher. Mathematics. *Scientia est potentia.*

The first school I was sent to felt like being thrown into an inferno. My training had been done in quiet lecture rooms, vast rolling lawns stretching out beyond the windows as we wrote notes and made polite talk of classroom management. The vision we had been given was of ascent through the power of the intellect, children from difficult backgrounds lifting themselves up from their poverty through careful study.

We might as well have been training for the long-jump on the Moon. The brutal gravity of 30 teenagers who did not give a damn about pedagogical theory was a bruising landing. I was punched and kicked, had cigarette lighters held against my clothing, shouted and sworn at daily and regularly threatened with violence.

'I know where you live!' one boy screamed as he burst into the office I shared with some colleagues. Earlier that week I'd caught him throwing a can of Coke down the stairs and he'd bluntly refused to pick it up, telling me to fuck off in the process. After a meeting with his parents, during which he'd kicked off with the head teacher, he'd run up the stairs to find me. 'I'll track you down and I'll kill you!'

I had no choice but to pick myself up and learn how to survive. It was both exhausting and exhilarating. The kids poured in from the surrounding council estates, and drained out at the end of the day taking the best parts of me with them, leaving me empty, tired, frustrated at my inability to make learning stick, but also genuinely inspired, working with extraordinary colleagues and wonderful children for whom life had served up plate after plate of shit.

It was such an imperfect art: logical and rational mathematics explained quite clearly, these pure pearls soon thrown down and trodden into the ground, some students laughing and some throwing rubbers and some working diligently, and some happily forgetting everything by the next day. Other days were less happy, dragging in tensions from home, squeezing the pressures of teenage life through my classroom door, me the safest outlet for their aggression, the one authority figure who wouldn't smite them.

With no God to direct all this collected anger onto, lacking any model of how I might begin speaking up about my own still-raw, untreated wounds, I swallowed it all down and, trying to protect those around me, turned it on myself. Anger turned inwards, or, as it is better known: depression.

For the first time I owned up to this as part of my inheritance: an ancient seam of blackness running through my father's side. It expressed itself most obviously in a fierce inner drive to succeed and lift myself above my pain, a Newtonian rage that sought to out-perform others.

Von Braun had his V2, and I my own Revenge Weapon, a terrible internal anger falling silently from the edge of space each time my own astronomic expectations of myself and others failed to be met, me desperately and expertly guiding it inwards, blowing huge holes in myself, ones I quickly built over, throwing up flimsy refuges, places no one could expect to live.

Sandy Thompson—Hunter's wife of 17 years—said of him that 'he shot out of the womb angry.'[18] That felt too close for comfort. I'd always painted my sister as the angry one in the family, but I saw it now: she was no more so than the rest of us, opting to let it vent and burn off, rather than syphoning it down into underground tanks as I did, compressing and cooling it until it detonated somewhere deep within the mine, another part of me crumbling, suffocating, trapped.

The 60s were meant to be all flower-power and the Summer of Love, but the wide array of means by which people took off for the skies was perhaps testament to the vast sumps of bitter fuel that needed expending. The pent up anger of the Second World War shot angrily out of the wombs of those who had lived through it, giving birth to those who would grow up in the 60s amidst Vietnam, the toxic poison of racism, the regular assassinations of public figures and the constant spectre of nuclear war.

In 1956, full of serious Beatnik angst, the first production of John Osborne's play *Look Back in Anger* had taken London by storm. Now, 40 years later, the mood of hippie escapism that had come immediately after returned for my own E generation, the upstart band Oasis releasing *Don't Look Back in Anger,* a perfect, blinkered reaction to the dismantled Britain that Margaret Thatcher had left behind.

Firing away from things rather than dealing with them, that was me. Cloaking my inner storms with extraordinary care, done with God and the ecstatic but now fighting them with sharp edges of books, I pushed always ahead, convinced that I could out-think this thing.

The DNA of depression was coiled in a double helix with the curse of perfection. I became the angry ideologue, wanting the world to line up straight, reaching for such intellectual heights that everything would fall into perfect order under my feet below.

Was this why von Braun had lusted after space? At certain altitudes you can no longer hear the screams or bullets of the concentration camps. From the divine perspective, Earth always looks heavenly. You can't see the gang rape and mutilation, the murder of unarmed civilians, the seething unrest in the Middle East or the widespread torture of academics by Maoists in China. The seas are tranquil, the land gentle hues of greens and browns, spacemen none the wiser about children screaming in hunger, loggers ravaging a forest or militants beheading school-girls.

Had he worked to climb away to a place where his own wounds and sins would disappear into tranquillity? If he had, I found myself following the same trajectory, desperate to find a way to still the waters raging in me.

—

'Fly me to the Moon,' Sinatra sang in 1964 as American began to go crazy for space. 'You are all I long for, all I worship and adore.' He was perhaps unaware of how ancient this line was connecting conquest of the Moon to romance and love and the ache for human fulfilment.

In Plato's *Symposium*, Aristophanes gives a long speech about the nature of love. He explains how there were once not two but three sexes: man, woman and man-woman, and Plato details their astrological origins:

> *The man was originally the child of the sun, the woman of the Earth, and the man-woman of the Moon, which is made up of sun and Earth...*[19]

In this state we troubled the gods because of our might and strength. So Zeus hewed us in half, split us down the middle, dividing us into man and woman in the process, and threatened to split us further if we didn't behave.

Love, for Plato, was no more than the pursuit of the whole, the recapturing of this long-lost perfect state of union, making one out of two.

It's here that the Summer of Love and the conquest of the Moon are bound together in a writhing, grasping Platonic embrace. As we penetrated the lunar surface we saw the erotic rejoining of heavenly bodies meant for one another since the dawn of time. Reaching the Moon was a symbol of human wholeness. It was the climax, akin to the orgasmic moment of finding oneself utterly complete in love for another. As Lennon had put it, channelling Plato perfectly, *all* you need is love.

Believing him, I married on US Independence Day in 1997, my many flaws coming together in desperate hope that may be *this* would make me whole, this other person would fly me to the Moon and fill-in all that I lacked. Because of the deep Christian seed within both of us, we'd contrived never to have been to the Moon before. This was it, our Apollo 11, lifting from Earth, jettisoning material at each stage, falling, falling, searching for a place to land, Tranquility Base, this one small step for me a giant leap in so many other ways...

That we slowly crashed and burned wasn't her fault. I shouldn't have staked so much, walked into things out of such a place of need. It gradually dawned on me that marriage hadn't meant peace had broken out within me, that in this long-awaited union I had not found a wormhole through to a brighter sun.

—

In my hope that it would is the erotic re-framing of the *Earthrise* photo. From the 1968 perspective of this soon-to-be-conquered Moon, Earth was perfect: round, plump and gorgeously calm and serene. Before Altamont, before *Easy Rider*, before Charles Manson, from this rose-tinted altitude, imperfection, death and pain and suffering could not be observed, nor the cries of needy children be heard.

Fallaci, Deke Slayton and Stewart Brand had all foreseen the psychedelic, Platonic power of this far-out shot, but the false sense of order and wholeness it offered was blown away by another photograph, one taken from a height that took not days, but decades to reach.

In 1977, 9 years after Anders took his groundbreaking picture, NASA launched the unmanned *Voyager 1*, primarily to probe other bodies, but also carrying a 'Golden Record' of pictures, telemetric data and recordings of music and human voices curated by the astronomer and author Carl Sagan.

This initial mission took until 1980, from where the probe began moving towards the outer reaches of our solar system. That took another 10 years. In 1990, after a long campaign, Sagan successfully persuaded NASA to turn Voyager's cameras on one more time, roll around and point them back towards Earth.

Earthrise is astonishing, but the photograph taken from a distance of 6 billion kilometres on Valentine's Day that year is something else entirely. Known as the 'family portrait,' in its single frame it holds every body in our solar system. The Sun. Mercury. Venus. Earth. Mars. Jupiter. Saturn. Uranus. Neptune.

Everybody, and everybody. But this is not the glorious, multicoloured global selfie that William Anders shot. Earth here is no more than a minuscule dot, a speck of dust in a ray of sunlight, in no way identifiably different from any other object, its once-erotic Moon now reduced to invisibility. On the day when, far far away, Earth celebrated *Eros* and the myth of wholeness through the romantic lunacy of love, this photograph dragged Plato kicking and screaming away from his neat ideal and showed him the vast and endless blackness of space.

Carl Sagan wrote at the time:

> *Look again at that dot. That's here, that's home, that's us. On it everyone you love, everyone you know, everyone you ever heard of, every human being who ever was, lived out their lives. The aggregate of our joy and suffering, thousands of confident religions, ideologies and economic doctrines, every hunter and forager, every hero and coward, every creator and destroyer of civilization, every king and peasant, every young couple in love, every mother and father, hopeful child, inventor and explorer, every teacher of morals, every corrupt politician, every "superstar," every "supreme leader," every saint and sinner in the history of our species lived there.*[20]

Nobody handed that photo could pick out which pixel was Earth. At this vast zoom level the fallacy that our world is coherent is blown apart. We are an insignificant planet in a small solar system in one of a billion galaxies. We are in a distant corner of...mostly nothing.

The voyage to the Moon was meant to be the start of preparations for a possible evacuation of human life if the sun died. That journey had taken a few short days, and the proposed one to Mars would take about 8 months each way. But to reach our closest star would take over 10,000 years, around 300 generations of human life, living and dying on a capsule that was meant to save humanity. By then, what memories would we be saving?

—

For how many generations had my family travelled through darkness in pressurised vessels? Heading full thrust into marriage, I had had high hopes that its light would counteract the black hole within me. Instead I found myself struggling with loneliness and a profound feeling of detachment.

Voyaging further and further from the place where all this pain had begun, looking back at my own family portraits, less and less of what we'd all been through made any sense at all. The pain and suffering of that diminishing world seemed once to have had some deeper point; now it just seemed a random place of cruelty, an unfriendly body in an almost-empty universe.

As the 90s drew to a close, these memories of that time in Yorkshire were disturbed by the first of three awful *Star Wars* prequels. Sitting in a dark cinema as those unmistakeable chords stuck up in symphony, the well-worn graphics rolling up the screen again, I was thrown back to my childhood, to the soaring feelings the first films had raised in me.

Aside from the horror of Jar Jar Binks, what hit me wasn't that I'd never made it into space, never fired a laser gun nor rolled an X-wing, but that a long time ago, in a life that seemed now far, far away, I'd had higher hopes.

Back then the films had seemed to offer a story to live by. Now, in 1999, with pre-millennial tension rising, the truth that I was quietly beginning to voice was this: there was no force that could be with me. There had been no higher purpose to my sister's illness, no mechanism of redemption behind the things that had caused it, no hope that someone would—or could—explain what the whole gut-punching trip had been for.

I'd watched all the films again, and one scene from *The Empire Strikes Back* leapt out at me. Luke Skywalker has already brought about the death of the Death Star, but what power will replace it no one can be sure. He meets Yoda in the swamp of Dagobah, his X-wing fighter submerged in the filth. If he is to raise it again and fly away from this stench and shit he must redirect the anger that destroyed his father, get in touch with his higher power and train his mind.

Like a man performing a Pentecostal miracle, Luke feels the force surge through him, the wings of his ship ascending out of the stagnant, putrid water... But no, he can't do it, and it sinks down again, and like him I no longer feel strong or sure, the beginnings of concern sown that I may not be able to raise my marriage clear of the dark mire of myself by the force of thought alone.

Like Luke's, my own father has masked his wounds, covered up his failings. 'Perfection is the enemy of good,' Voltaire once wrote, and for Hitler and von Braun, just as for me and my father and back through generations, *this* had been the darth, the dark power that had captured and twisted us into anger. If only we could do the exact right things, live the exact right lives, arrange the cushions in the exact right way or be the exact right person that the Emperor demanded then we would rise above our affliction and build ourselves a new star, a sun more powerful than death itself.

This hope is extinguished by *The Family Portrait*. If the sun dies we will have nowhere to go. There is no body close enough.

Whether by powerful religion or the power of our minds, my family had been convinced of some force that would offer miraculous rescue from our pain, healing at the speed of light. Yet the further I journeyed from the burning core of this trauma, the more I understood that this force didn't exist.

—

While wars still raged and children went hungry, why did we expend such great money and energy to reach for the Moon? At the end of it all, what did Apollo mean?

For William Anders, *Earthrise* became the most valuable thing that the Apollo astronauts did. 'We had come to study the Moon,' he said, 'but what we really did was discover the Earth.'

Not in being launched to the heavens, it was in their descent back to the ground that these men found themselves most moved, returning to the only home they had in the universe.

'They have a wild look,' Dolores O'Hara said of them to Fallaci. She was chief nurse to the astronauts, and tended them carefully.

'Don't pay any attention to people who tell you that wild look is because of exhaustion or joy at having made it. It's rage at having to come back to Earth. As if up there they're not only freed from weight, from the force of gravity, but from desires, affections, passions, ambitions, from the body.'[21]

The pursuit of weightlessness. Freed from desire. In search of a new sun. Raging when it could not be reached. These men knew more than anyone that this Earth was the only hope we had, these failing bodies our only vehicle.

For Thompson, suggesting otherwise formed the core bullshit of the Catholic Church, the military-industrial complex and the Maharishi. Apollo, like acid, like ecstatic religion, was just another part of it. Facing the death of the body and the collapse of the *Ancien Régime,* the powerful turned people's necks up to heaven, averting revolution by making them yell in awe, bow in prayer or trip away on drugs.

Yet there were those brave enough to see past this, men and women who refused to look up, who refused to eat the cake of flight while there was no bread for the poor. In doing so they would be dealt with in the strongest possible terms: they would be shot down.

—

Our longing for flight, our hopes of communion with the undying light above, our anger at the brokenness and pain that had always marred life with death—since the dawn of time all of this had been born in dreams of high places, and this dramatic period of the 1960s was bracketed by the dreams of one man, representing the hopes and fears of so many who were downtrodden.

'I have a dream,' Martin Luther King had sung to a quarter of a million civil rights marchers back in the hopeful days of August 1963, just months before JFK was shot.

A dream deeply rooted in the American dream—one day this nation will rise up and live up to its creed, "We hold these truths to be self-evident: that all men are created equal." With this faith, we will be able to hew out of the mountain of despair a stone of hope. With this faith, we will be able to transform the jangling discords of our nation into a beautiful symphony of brotherhood.

Seeing, like Paine and others, that these United States were so far from unity, he had had a different vision for how people might be brought together. 'Let freedom ring,' he'd roared, listing the many high places of America, from the mighty mountains of New York to Lookout Mountain Tennessee. Not through a display of state power, but in a great song of liberty—this was how a new story would be created.

Just 5 years later, in April 1968, it didn't take Hunter Thompson to see that that hilltop dream of a coherent and unified society was as distant as ever. Wars still raged, racism was still rife and the threat of nuclear holocaust—the sun blotted out behind a radioactive sky—was still very real. And yet through all of that, King remained rooted and committed.

As he rose to speak he talked of another dream, of one where he was asked by God which age he would like to live in. He considered Mount Olympus and the glorious periods of the great Roman Empire, the Renaissance and Enlightenment, but none of that was for him.

Strangely enough, I would turn to the Almighty and say, "If you allow me to live just a few years in the second half of the twentieth century, I will be happy. Now that's a strange statement to make because the world is all messed up. The nation is sick, trouble is in the land, confusion all around. That's a strange statement. But I know, somehow, that only when it is dark enough can you see the stars.[22]

For him, the purpose of altitude was not escape, was not as a display of terrifying might. He had learned the best lessons Apollo had taught us: the reason to go up *was* to come down because, rage and dream as we might, from on high we quickly learned that this is the one and only Earth that we have.

'Down you must go then,' Plato urged in his *Republic*. Once freed from the cave and its chains, 'down you must go, each in his turn, to the habitation of the others.'[23] This was the way of King: in the face of people dying he refused to lift away to an easier world. His choice was to descend, to return to rocky pits and help those who still remained oppressed.

Like Kesey, Leary and von Braun, he'd spent the decade trying to answer the question of how his violent and warring world could be transformed into a peaceful paradise. Unlike them, he'd resisted the temptation to present taking flight—or violent displays of power—as realistic solutions. King saw through the spectacles that powerful regimes employed: as diverting as Apollo was, as amazing the inner worlds of LSD seemed to be, he would not be drawn from the reality of life on the ground that his people were suffering.

Tragically, in the anger and disarray that scarred so much of the 60s, many not only disagreed, but were so frightened by his vision of unity and desegregation that they took up arms against him. Those who they had once trodden down as slaves would not be allowed to rise as equals.

The Summer of Love was a short blast of hot air in a winter of terrible hate. The scent of lemon soap and the still-strong desire for social purity. In this chilling atmosphere of fear, King was shot down the day after his Memphis speech, killed and laid in the ground before he could walk on from that high place he had dreamed of and see the world made that tiny bit more like heaven, with races and creeds playing together in peace.

—

JFK in 1963 and MLK in 1968. Two of America's finest sons, dead.

In the dark days that followed each shooting people gathered and worried. The Potland world of LSD had been shot down by the end of '66; the excitement of Apollo kept Squareland hoping until '69. The decade was fast finishing. The explosion of hope and energy that had lit up the world after the austere 50s was waning. Nothing had delivered any genuine hope of rescue from our warring and violent selves, nor any means of outrunning the principalities and powers that exerted such control over our lives.

The highly complex feats of astro-engineering and synthetic chemistry that had given us such remarkable new wings had both become modes of flight experienced in explicitly religious terms. Apollo and LSD had both promised communion with the above, and both creeds had ended in profound disappointment for the millions who had put their faith in them. The high priests of both, narconauts and astronauts, now stumbled into the 1970s raging at their inability to lift off and float away for good.

I was racing towards the end of a millennium, the same transcendent questions looming for me: given that none of the vehicles I had commandeered had transported me to more peaceful systems, where should I now turn?

None of the great trips on high had revealed any force tending the light. So, would we simply accept our place as 'a mote of dust suspended in a sunbeam?' Would we come to terms life on Earth, making peace with the knowledge that our sun was destined to die?

No. Not yet. Having tripped with Kesey and then demanded *Earthrise*, Stewart Brand still had one more dream to come. Into the horrible vacuum that followed King's death, in reaction to the deepening disgust at the seemingly intractable violence, into this black hole he helped birth an entirely new world, one that held out fresh promise of another myth that might save us.

Just 12 short weeks after that first Moon landing, after the Summer of Love had deflated and soured, after the hope that King had presented had been cut down, in the dying light of this decade of such great heights combined with such violent lows, the 'high technology' of pure digital machines burst into our world like a brand new sun.

These weren't tools tainted with mysticism, nor ones so blunt as to search for answers in holes punched in the sky. They offered wings of an entirely different nature: not the deafening, dirty, intimidating ones of the Hells Angels, but clean and logical, and as fast as light itself.

Disillusioned with Apollo, sickened by King's assassination, abandoning the drugs and the growing social unrest of the cities and disaffected by the inability of these things to offer enlightenment, hippies fled with millions of others, trekking up into the hills of California to escape the violence and riots below.

There they found Stewart Brand already, the prophet once again marching ahead. He'd got off his back, gone on beyond the Pranksters, beyond the Trips Festival, beyond button badges and dreams of space. Here he was now taking part in the greatest demonstration of the power electronics ever witnessed.

Here the ashes of Potland and Squareland were transformed and raised, an alchemical fusion of countercultural attitude and scientific brilliance. Here—not in acids but in transistors, not in space modules but in microchips—utopian visions dared soar once more, visions that seemed outside of the control of the state and untarnished by talk of god or religion.

Here I found myself too, 30 years behind Brand as ever, so very nearly ready to be content with life on the ground before this new technology arrived, promising lift in a totally new way, a new force by which we might be elevated and enlightened.

The succulent fruit of higher knowledge was dangled right within my grasp. How could I resist?

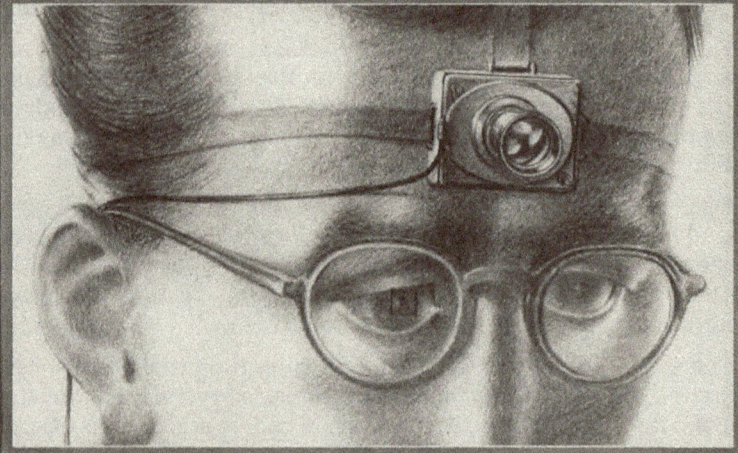

A SCIENTIST OF THE FUTURE RECORDS EXPERIMENTS WITH A TINY CAMERA FITTED WITH UNIVERSAL-FOCUS LENS. THE SMALL SQUARE IN THE EYEGLASS AT THE LEFT SIGHTS THE OBJECT

AS WE MAY THINK

A TOP U. S. SCIENTIST FORESEES A POSSIBLE FUTURE WORLD IN WHICH MAN-MADE MACHINES WILL START TO THINK

by VANNEVAR BUSH

DIRECTOR OF THE OFFICE OF SCIENTIFIC RESEARCH AND DEVELOPMENT

Condensed from the *Atlantic Monthly*, July 1945

Article by Vannevar Bush in Atlantic Magazine, July 1945

5. Transcendent Man

Having sold their drugs and made a mint, Wyatt and Billy, *Easy Rider's* hippie and Hells Angel, cruised out of the city at the beginning of the film on two roaring motorcycles, far beyond the bustle and hustle of LA, out into the long horizons of the Californian countryside.

Hopper and Fonda's film was released in the summer of '69, but filmed in the early months of 1968. Filmed or, more accurately, *shot*, the sound of gunfire peppering those months. Not only was King killed in April and Bobby Kennedy assassinated in June—but, further afield—the shock of the Viet Cong's massive Tet Offensive sent US politics reeling and tumbling as America turned *en masse* against further bloody losses. Too many sons were dying. Not even Apollo could staunch the wounds.

Before their eventual downfall at Mardi Gras, Wyatt and Billy pass through a commune in the hills. Here, a group of young people are trying to live off-grid, their 'dropping out' actually meaning flight to high ground to escape the flood of violence. They are rejecting the city, out of earshot of the riots, protests, shootings and civil unrest, aiming for a simple life, getting high and working in community. Except they are failing miserably. They might be modern Noahs, but there's no goddamn rain and the soil is hard and infertile. People are hungry and tensions are beginning to mount.

Easy Rider refuses an easy ride to anything in the counterculture. The empty chemical highs and the even more empty religious icons, all of it Hopper tracks into the crosshairs of his camera and shoots down, and the hippies who'd fled to alternative communities after the failure of Kesey's Graduation got the same treatment.

They were hardly part of a fringe movement. Estimates of the numbers who left 'normal' life for these Potland collectives range between 10 and 20 million, making it one of the largest migrations in US history. Whatever the true numbers, Hopper was spot-on: life in the hills was far harder and a lot less bucolic than the hippies had imagined.

Quick to spot a need, who should step in but Stewart Brand.

Having hung out with Kesey, organised the Trips Festival and hitchhiked his way around the country selling his WHOLE EARTH button badges, Brand now hit upon a new plan. Ever the man of action, never one for standing still, he began the *Whole Earth Truck Store*. Using a 1963 Dodge truck, Brand and his wife packed it full of books and tools and began touring round these hilltop communities, offering much-needed education on farming and building techniques and selling seed, milling equipment and virtually everything imaginable to help sustain them.

Problem was, with millions having made this shift, once you started looking, there were just so *many* of the damn things. Having driven around doing what they could and getting a sense of what people needed, Brand and his wife settled in Menlo Park, California and decided that the only way to continue was to publish a *Whole Earth Catalog*, carrying articles and a database of the things that Brand had carried on the truck, with phone numbers for people to get in direct touch with suppliers. Issue 1 went out in the autumn of 1968, the Whole Earth photograph taken from NASA's weather satellite slapped right on the front page.

Speaking at Stanford University in 2005, Apple founder Steve Jobs spoke loving of this 'Google in paperback form, idealistic and overflowing with neat tools and great notions.' If you were going to build an ark, the Whole Earth Catalog could help you source lumber and hammers. But it was more than that, as Brand explained in the first issue:

> *Personal power is developing—power of the individual to conduct his own education, find his own inspiration, shape his own environment, and share his adventure with whoever is interested. Tools that aid this process are sought and promoted by the WHOLE EARTH CATALOG.*

When the drugs can no longer lift us, when Apollo fails to save us, when the Graduation is done and the Moon is conquered and the violent oppression of the state has been unmasked, what remains still is the power of the individual to conduct their own education.

In other words, the Platonic view, the way of Simon Magus, this work of ascension and enlightenment not to be achieved via church or establishment, but through self-education and intellectual inquiry. A plane could shape wood, but what sort of tool helped a man 'shape his own environment'? Power tools were one thing, but the tools of power—which page were they on? Brand's distillation of the hippie ethic was simple: if the sun dies, if your world starts collapsing around you, and you decide to pack your tattered knapsack and shod your feet with sandals and leave the squares behind to their wars, this is the stuff you'll need to survive, both materially and intellectually.

What he knew even as the first issue went out was that helping people achieve this would need a better format than a quarterly publication put together with scissors and glue. He needed something fast and peer-led, a network of ideas where learning in one area could immediately be communicated across all these myriad, dispersed, hilltop community outposts.

As it turned out, the answer was right on his doorstep.

Still doing some work as a professional photographer, Brand was asked by Doug Engelbart—a computer scientist friend also in Menlo Park—to help him out with a demonstration he was giving at a conference in San Francisco. The title was *A Research Center for Augmenting Human Intellect,* and was scheduled for the afternoon session on Monday 9th December, 1968. It was just a fortnight before Earthrise would be shot, only weeks after the first WEC had rolled off the presses, and Brand's brain exploded in sunlight as he read Engelbart's notes in the conference handbook:

> *This session is entirely devoted to a presentation on a computer-based, interactive, multi-console display system which is being developed at the Stanford Research Institute under the sponsorship of ARPA, NASA and RADC. The system is being used as an experimental laboratory for investigating principles by which interactive computer aids can augment intellectual capacity.*

Interactive computers that could augment intellectual capacity? This was the very damned thing he'd been looking for.

Engelbart knew that Brand was handy around camera equipment, so had him controlling things at his lab in Menlo Park while, 30 miles away, Engelbart introduced delegates to his 'oNLine System.' To enable everyone in the room to see what he was doing, video feeds were mixed and projected onto a huge screen using one of NASA's Eidophor video projection systems—the cutting edge equipment normally used to display information at Mission Control. One of Kesey's old lags on the cameras at one end and NASA gadgetry at the other: it was like Engelbart was mashing the two source codes of the 60s for fun.

Standing Zeus-like, Engelbart blew the minds of everyone in the audience. It became known simply as 'The Mother of All Demos.' Some spoke later of it as like a religious experience, him 'dealing lightening with both hands,' one using the first mouse the world had ever seen while the other tapped away on a specially modified keyboard, demonstrating clickable hypertext, cloud storage, video conferencing, logical file structures, collaborative word processing and spreadsheet-style calculations all for the first time.

Which planet did this guy say he'd come from again? In fact, for those in the know, Engelbart's Augmentation Research Centre was like a digital version of Perry Lane, and only a stone's throw from it. Part of the Stanford Research Institute in Menlo Park, interesting people were always in and out—people like Al Hubbard, the shady military man and uranium dealer who'd been such a strong early proponent for LSD use among the rich and powerful. He was the reason the CIA had plugged into SRI and the experiments at the Menlo Park veterans hospital that Kesey had taken part on, and the man who had introduced Doug Engelbart to the drug too.

Engelbart had good reasons for wanting to augment human intellectual capacity. Serving in World War 2, he'd spent years dodging Japanese and German soldiers who were trying to blow him to pieces with guns, bayonets and missiles. Now the biggest brains in science had deployed a bomb that had terrorised the Japanese into surrender, which had left him stuck on a tiny island in the Pacific in 1945, waiting to get home.

Kicking back, the sand between his toes, someone had thrown a copy of July's *Atlantic* magazine at him and, with nothing else to do, he'd lit a cigarette and flicked at the pages, not realising that he was about to stumble on an article that would totally blow his mind and inform his work for the rest of his life.

Written by Vannevar Bush, head of the U.S. Office of Scientific Research and Development and a former administrator of the Manhattan Project, *As We May Think* asked the same question that every soldier had puzzled over: how the hell had the human race ended up in a World War for the second time in 40 years, and how could we avoid doing so again? Bush's view was that we needed rewiring, and the solution he proposed was a hypothetical machine he called a Memex, which would be 'an enlarged, intimate supplement to one's memory.'[1]

In short: an empathy machine. All of your photos, data records and letters would be scanned onto microfilm reels and be available for instant recall. With these links and interconnections, knowledge would be shared and understanding would increase and the scourge of war banished and a machine-led age of peace would dawn.

To a guy who'd been shot at, this machine sounded like the absolute bomb. Bush was only sketching out ideas rather than offering solid blueprints, but Engelbart made up his mind: he would commit his life to building the Memex and consign 'lest we forget' to history. What he hadn't realised was that, like the great technologist Leonardo da Vinci centuries before him, he had inadvertently swung in behind a mini-renaissance of Platonist thought.

—

In 1966, just as Kesey was trying to blow the doors off his brain and achieve unity with the Universal Mind, Francis Yates published *The Art of Memory*. In it, she shared her decades-long research into the history of the quest to augment human memory, the origins of which she traced back to a gruesome tale told by the Greek poet Simonides.

Legend had it that he had given a recital and then sat down to enjoy the feast that followed. Word was then passed that two men were outside wanting to speak to him, so he excused himself and left the building. As he stood and talked the whole structure collapsed like a cake, not only killing everyone inside but leaving their bodies so maimed that they could not be identified.

It's CSI in togas, and Simonides realised that he had a mental picture of each one of the dead. The feast had been in the round, each man in his particular place, and with this orderly seating plan imprinted on his mind he was able to recall the name of every victim. Brushing the tragedy aside, Yates gets to the eureka moment: 'Simonides realised that orderly arrangement is essential for good memory.'[2]

This was the software that Platonism ran on: the True Forms of things would be grasped and the cave left behind through the training of the mind in the art of memory. Yet, as classical civilisation collapsed and the Dark Ages took hold, the early medieval world became a black hole into which almost all this ancient learning vanished. It was only 1000 years later that Renaissance thinkers returned to these ancient Greek ideas about memory, seeking to reignite this collapsed star.

Tommaso Campanella, still convinced of his idea that Eden would be found on the Moon, imagined a fictional hilltop utopia in *The City of the Sun*, published in 1602. In beautiful dialogue between a Knight and a Genoese sea captain, he describes how the walls of this city were concentric circles onto which murals and texts were painted. This created an orderly, walk-through arrangement of ideas, a 'memory theatre' for the city's citizens, a living means by which they could learn and recall knowledge as they wandered the streets.

> *On the inside of the second circuit, that is to say of the second ring of buildings, paintings of all kinds of precious and common stones, of minerals and metals, are seen. On the outside are marked all the seas, rivers, lakes, and streams which are on the face of the Earth; as are also the wines and the oils and the different liquids.*[3]

These weren't walks that Campanella himself could take. He wrote the book from prison, having been horribly tortured for supporting Platonic ideas, suggesting that reason—not the Christ—should be the means by which humanity should rise from its fallen, violent state. The art of memory he built into the fabric of his heavenly city was an act of resistance in the face of an oppressive regime. It was an occult sacred rite, one that dared question the power of a despotic Church to effect ascension, one that celebrated the flight of Simon Magus not as a tragedy of demonic possession, but a triumph of mnemonic learning.

He wasn't the only one to suffer for these beliefs. Campanella's writing had been inspired by the plight of another heretical monk, Giordano Bruno. He was burned at the stake by the Inquisition in 1600 for proposing that the stars above were distant suns, around which there might orbit planets that could sustain life. Even as the flames were about to begin licking at the pyre, Bruno persisted in spouting these ridiculous 'scientific' views to the crowd gathered, so the authorities twisted his head to one side and nailed his tongue into the wooden post before setting him alight, a bonfire for his vanity.

Going far beyond even what Copernicus had proposed 50 years previously, Bruno's ideas on astronomy were problematic enough in a world where physical altitude was still widely held to carry spiritual consequence. Yet even more troubling than his beliefs about outer space were his Platonic opinions on the inner mind, which he taught could become divine and immortal. Touring around Europe and speaking at leading universities, secret societies and other institutions, he proposed that once a person knew all they would rise above earthly ignorance into unity with Truth, and thus defeat death itself.

Those who dared gather at his lectures would hear that each was born with a basic natural memory. In the dust illuminated by the shafts of sunlight and accompanied by the creak of wooden boards, they would then be told that if they were to ascend to The Source then their natural mind had to be augmented, an enhanced memory created through the use of mysterious mnemonics based on concentric circles of runic symbols and texts.

Despite the gruesome manner of his execution, Bruno's ideas lived on, secreted away by occult networks of non-conformist thinkers convinced that the art of memory was central to the revolutionary struggle to free society from the violent ways of monarchy and religion. They knew that whoever controlled what was remembered held the keys to power. Christianity had totally failed to bring an end to mankind's warring; with the concentric circles of their memory systems, up in their utopian hilltop communes, the Neoplatonists truly believed that they had an alternative technology that really worked.

Vannevar Bush makes no mention of Plato, Campanella or Bruno, and neither does Frances Yates mention Bush or his machine. But somehow occult ideas about memory resonated through history, pulsing onto the pages of *Atlantic* magazine in his designs for the Memex. With its microfilms and cameras set in circular arrangements, the glass panels and screens built into a round desk, it was no less than a classical memory theatre created from the limited technology of the 1940s.

—

The canopy of stars is bright and clear. Though many of them have long-since burned out, their light continues to emanate and illuminate the night. Having survived a brutal war in South East Asia, ignorant of Simonides and the torture of Campanella and the torching of Bruno, Doug Engelbart slugs a beer and takes his time over a cigarette as he reads Bush's article, thinking yes, that's what I'm going to do, and while Hofmann labours at LSD and von Braun hurriedly gathers up the technical drawings for his missiles, he steams back to the US to work for a new age of enlightened peace, not by means of ballistics or synthetic chemistry, but via the well-ordered, logical workings of a memory machine.

If Engelbart had hoped to get any further help from Bush he was sadly mistaken. In all of his extensive writing on technology and its role in promoting peaceful democracy, Bush never mentioned the Memex again.

It wasn't as if his piece in *Atlantic* had been the naïve musings of a Heath Robinson. With a colleague at MIT he had constructed the most sophisticated analogue computing machine in the world, a 'differential analyser' that could be used to find solutions to terrifically complex mathematical equations. Twelve of these had been built and used to perform flight calculations for the US aeronautics department that would eventually become NASA.

In fact, as Engelbart got home and set to work, these clockwork instruments were where his own thinking began. What he didn't know was that hidden in the history of their inner workings, among the spinning cogs and precision cams, was a powerful story about the relationship between people, machines and state power.

In the gardens of Versailles, 50 years before Etienne Montgolfier had strapped a duck to the basket of his balloon, Jacques Vaucanson had been inside the palace itself, the French court again gathered, a duck stood on a plinth in front of him. Von Braun's grandfather and Fallaci's father might both have itched to draw their hunting rifles, but at Vaucanson's command the duck flapped its wings, craned its neck and bent down to drink from a bowl of water before turning and eating some grain.

When, minutes later, it then shat out the digested food, the astonishment of the cream of French society was not that a man had dared bring a defecating duck into the presence of the king, but that the shitting and flapping and eating bird was in fact a machine.

Like Michelangelo before him, Vaucanson was an avid anatomist. Less interested in drawing what he saw on the inside of creatures, he wanted to recreate them, taking the functions of each organ and replicating them mechanically, putting these parts together inside a beautiful frame. Like Descartes, he came to the conclusion that there was no significant difference between humans and machines. His genius lay in the complex concentric circles of cams that were the memory of these mechanisms, lowering the duck's neck, turning its head and unfurling its wings.

His automata were bought by wealthy aristocrats, and gasps of amazement were the currency that Vaucanson traded in. They were the ancestors of Bush's differential analysers, and had in turn descended from the large clocks of the 14th century that rich merchants had paid for to display the time to a town's workforce. They were symbols of how they wanted society run: smoothly and regularly, with controlled, well-behaved movement.

As time went by a sort of clockwork Moore's Law took hold, mechanisms shrinking and becoming more powerful year on year, followed by additions of dazzling models of people going about their work, striking anvils, moving smoothly around in circles and doffing hats. Funded by the powerful, these performing town clocks offered a utopian vision of a robotic workforce running with minimised friction and fuss and, hanging from the highest point of the church, they had a divine weight given to the work of their hands, their orderly revolutions reminding the people that revolution would not be tolerated.

However, revolution did come to France, and Vaucanson's stunning automata were destroyed. A period of great chaos ensued until Napoleon restored order, and it was then that the great Emperor came face to face with the most famous automata of them all.

A large desk with a model of an Oriental gentleman sat atop it, 'The Turk' toured the grand salons of Europe and Prussia, playing chess with anyone who dared challenge it. Napoleon did, and was beaten, the device only exposed as an elaborate fake in the 1820s, well after he had died. A man had been hidden inside the machine, but the wide opinion that it really *did* work revealed a belief both that a human mind *could* be simulated by engineering, and that it *should* be. In post-revolutionary France, the way out of the dark chaos of war and unrest was through enlightened thought and reasonable, predictable behaviour.

The Turk was a human pretending to be a machine pretending to be a human—one hailed as perfectly rational and worthy of imitation—and it was into this culture of ideas about the mechanisation of human behaviour that Bush's Memex arrived.

The problem Engelbart faced when trying to actually make one boiled down to adaptability. Vaucanson's duck was extraordinary, but it couldn't play chess; The Turk was quite brilliant, but it couldn't learn the piano. Clockwork machines could do one thing well, but if a device was going to augment human memory it needed to be as flexible and versatile as the mind itself.

—

That the war had ended when it did—gifting Engelbart the opportunity to kick back and think about the Memex, opening the door for Hofmann's wonder-drug to escape the lab, and giving Wernher von Braun the chance to save his rocket programme—was in large part due to the work of a British mathematician, Alan Turing.

In 1936, Turing had published an academic paper proving that a series of electrical logic gates could, in theory, be programmed to adapt to *any* computational task. It was a radical idea, but Turing was proposing that all a machine needed to achieve this was ... memory.

His theory was given a chance to be put into practice with 'Colossus,' the first programmable digital computer, which was built to break the German's *Enigma* code, ending the war years earlier than it otherwise would have done.

Like the first clocks, the computers that followed quickly increased in power and shrank in size, and Engelbart soon realised that they were how the Memex would be built. Through Al Hubbard he'd experimented with LSD—tiny, charged wafers sparking through his neural networks—but he was far more impressed by the new wafers of silicon that were appearing at the same time, packing an equally amazing punch into a similarly-sized housing. Just as LSD was a marvel of chemistry, these integrated circuits were marvels of physics, finally beginning to deliver on Turing's promise of an adaptable, learning machine.

As the 60s waned, to the hippies obsessed with breaking down barriers between different worlds there seemed something almost mystical about this ability of computers to shape-shift and perform different tasks at super-human speeds. In Issue 1 of the *Whole Earth Catalog*, Brand had given systems theorist Buckminster Fuller a double-page spread where he waxed about seeing something divine in the lightning quick digital machines that were beginning to blossom, linking this to a 'vast harmonic reordering of the universe' from which there would be born a 'great natural peace' and 'infinite understanding.'

However, the Potland part of Engelbart was smart enough to see that one Memex could only aid human memory to a point. But hook them together and a brain-like *network* of machines might then be able to reach for infinite understanding. What was needed was to lift us out of the shadows of the cave, beginning this vast harmonic reordering that would usher in a digital age of world peace, was a string of digital memory theatres.

The system that Engelbart demonstrated to such dramatic effect just weeks after the Whole Earth Catalog was launched was just the stand-alone Memex—*an interactive computer aid to augment intellectual capacity'*— but he had already been working on a way of networking these machines together.

The problem he faced was cost. Like LSD, like Apollo, all this research was cutting edge and mind-blowingly expensive, so up popped the US military's Advanced Research Projects Agency to foot the bill and sponsor Engelbart's work.

ARPA had been set up by Eisenhower amidst the national panic over the launch of Sputnik 1, tasked with making sure that US military technology never fell behind again. That meant blank cheques all round, and though he was doing it to promote peace, the irony of Engelbart accepting their funding was that in his work the military saw the possibility of creating a devolved computer network that could survive a nuclear war. They paid their money and they got the naming rights: 'ARPANet' was created, beginning as a two-node network between Engelbart's lab at SRI and another computer 300 miles down the coast at UCLA.

It was an idea that stretched back through Bush and Turing and Vaucanson and the clockmakers of the early Renaissance, back through Tommaso Campanella and Giordano Bruno and Simonides. All of them were convinced that, through the augmentation of human memory, warring human society could be brought to peace. With the bright hopes of LSD and Apollo both dashed, Engelbart and his friend Stewart Brand were convinced that a global digital network would be a new light in the darkness.

Thus, on 29th of October, 1969, Charlie Kline, a computing student at UCLA, pushed through the doors of his lab and began setting up the department's Sigma 7 machine. It was late. *Easy Rider* was still burning through local cinema screens in nearby Hollywood and, though only 12 weeks had passed since Armstrong and Aldrin had walked on the Moon, people were already tiring of the spectacle. The decade was ending and wars were still raging; there was a hunger, a yearning for a new spark of hope.

At 10.30 pm ARPANet seemed to be ready to go and Kline began transmission, attempting to send the word 'LOGIN' to the SDS 940 computer in Engelbart's lab at Menlo Park. He typed, and the memory drums began to spin, and then ground to a halt.

Damn it. Something had gone wrong. After just two characters, the system had crashed.

Far away in Menlo Park, Engelbart's team were tending their equipment at SRI, Kesey's old Perry Lane shack just round the corner, Stewart Brand a few streets down putting together the next *Whole Earth Catalog*. Tension crackled through the room, the huge machines pumping out heat. One way or the other it felt like the future of mankind rested on this thing they'd built. Surviving nuclear war, or building peace? Who knew?

The tele-printer hammered briefly into life and Engelbart's team gathered in anticipation around it.

They'd been expecting more, but the first ever online message sent over a digital network turned out to be just two characters long. It would sprawl from here to become the Internet, but in dot-matrix letters they read the angelic announcement that a new saviour had been born and that we should not be afraid: *LO.*

—

The mid 80s. A family party, New Year's Eve I expect. There are cold cuts of turkey and ham, parlour games, a brisk walk along the beach in the short arc of daylight. My cousin is upstairs, and the only way I'm going to get to spend time with him is to join him in his bedroom. The door opens only a tiny way, obstructed by leads and wires and a cassette player. He's staring intently at it, watching it spool with his breath held, listening to each blip and beep, willing it to continue. He has just been given a Commodore 64, and it's the first home computer I have ever seen.

I persevered then, found a free edge of bed to sit on and joined in the mood of intercession, clueless as to what it was we were praying for. It turned out to be a game called *Elite,* and we flew our ship between different space stations, trading goods and moving quickly onto narcotics, shooting the hell out of anyone who dared cross us.

Drugs, spaceships, computers. Parents poked their head round the door and sighed. Perhaps we had finally found an outlet for our aggressive nature. When it was time to go he shouted down goodbye and we left and went home.

My family were, and remained for years to come, a zero computer household. Dad had a typewriter in his study, my brother and I our hi-fi systems; the most powerful machine in the house was probably Mum's food processor. I returned to riding my BMX and reading books, but more and more of my friends began vacating the streets and playing fields to spend time with their machines.

The Berlin Wall was crumbling, the great edifice of the Cold War was thawing, anxieties mutating from these global political events down to the invisible threat of AIDS. Fear went viral.

I stumbled into the 90s and, during an orientation session in my first week at university, I remember a bespectacled Second Year handing me a slip of paper as if he were offering me the sacraments, as if this were solely what I'd come to college for. It wasn't a flyer for a peace march, or even an invite to a happening. 'This is your JANET address!' he announced with great reverence.

My look of confusion about who the hell Janet was and why I was being given her address precipitated an excited explanation: this was my username and password to allow me to send electronic messages on the Joint Academic Network—an iteration of ARPANet that had grown up to serve British universities in the 1970s.

I laughed, scrunched up the paper and put it in my pocket, thinking the guy had a screw loose. I didn't visit the computing centre again that year. The only message boards I read were those in the Student Union building, guys scrawling notes in vain hope for that girl they wanted to see again, people wanting keyboard players, urgent requests for lifts to London.

When I went out and closed the front door of my student house behind me I became incommunicado. There were no signals that could locate me, no calls that could reach me, no messages that could wing their way to me. Apart from a pocket calculator I didn't own a digital machine and had no desire to do so. That a grey box of wires might offer a means by which my painful memory might be augmented and my fragmented sense of self made whole never crossed my mind.

The ensnaring was gradual. Pure Newton and Kepler, in my second year we were set a programming project to simulate the orbits of different planets with different masses, an on-screen solar system.

After countless hours swatting bugs, my friend and I sat in awed silence as we watched this micro-universe we had created spin and evolve, the larger planets sucking smaller ones into their orbits, some colliding and coalescing, some flying off into untold extremities. With small changes in initial conditions some galaxies immediately and violently crunched into an agitated nucleus, some dispersed off screen while others, the tiny minority, settled into stable, beautiful, hypnotically parabolic orbits. We saved these worlds.

It was the first time I had seen something about these machines that seemed to be... *living*? In a few lines of script we had created something that was flexible, adaptable, responsive in some way, something that Kepler himself could never have dreamed of, that could not have been constructed by even by the finest clockwork artisans of the 18th century. Something shifted in me, and by the end of our third year I too was crammed into the computer centre, writing my dissertation on paper totally out of the question.

One hot May afternoon that year a friend beckoned me over to a terminal bolted down to a table in the Engineering library, and offered to show me the Internet. I had heard of this thing and I approached with intrigue and trepidation, aware that I might catch something nasty or find myself inadvertently setting off missiles in a far-off country. My friend opened windows and clicked on connections and little pulses flew across from telephone graphic to telephone graphic, but when, after a number of minutes, a crude page of text appeared, terribly set in horrible type, some of it underlined, some of it not, I shrugged and pretended it was cool and went back to my books deciding that it wasn't. Disappointing. A geeky niche. In terms of the big questions in my life, unimportant.

—

Brighter minds than mine were quicker to see the potential. Present at the angelic announcement of the birth of the net was a young programmer called Bob Duvall, who'd written the part of the code that allowed Engelbart's NLS to 'talk to' ARPANet. Despite the early crash—soon fixed—he had a powerful revelation of the implications of this technology on human life and labour. Following the October launch he moved out of Menlo Park up into the rural hills of Sonoma County, taking with him a phone line, a workstation and a version of his software, becoming the world's first remote worker.

Right behind him was Steward Brand. Already resourcing the huge numbers of distributed communities living up in hills with agricultural and organisational skills, the Whole Earth Catalog became *the* source of information about the newly-birthed home-build computer movement, the best place to get yourself a modem so that you could become another node in the proto-web and join the party.

Through Engelbart, 'the vast harmonic reordering of the universe' was underway, the revolution in peace through higher consciousness back on, not powered by drugs or rocket boosters but memory chips. As the Whole Earth Catalog grew, Brand was explicit about his hopes for the future. It was no longer psychedelic, nor intergalactic. He'd been there with LSD and Apollo, and completely bought into the religious promises that both had made about delivering a new Eden. Now that they had both failed, he had a new hope, cyberdelics, and he put his chips down right on the front cover of the first issue of WEC:

We are as gods and might as well get good at it.

Via email, I pressed him about what he'd meant by this, and his answer was short and firm: *'Lowercase 'g.' Think Greek or Roman gods.'* When the riots and shootings get too much, when the Summer of Love is over, when space has failed to draw down the heavens, march up Mount Olympus and start being the god that you truly are. Like LSD, like Apollo, computers were outstanding feats of engineering that were now being spoken about in explicitly religious language.

Back in '64, Fallaci had described how the groups of American astronauts were seen as almost superhuman, were 'exalted to the level of gods.' Using technologies that NASA had pioneered, Brand now wanted to make astronauts of everyone. An online persona was weightless, and here he could augment the mind and make it divine, firing us all up into the celestial firmament.

Kesey, fresh out of jail, hooked up with his old friend from the Lane and wanted to know what was new. Brand took him up to Engelbart's lab and showed him ARPANet. He'd always been a little old to be a hippy, and now age seemed to suddenly catch up with him. He sighed deeply and commented, 'it's the next thing after acid.' Having quickly lost interest in rebooting humanity in space, Leary scrambled around for years before finally finding the new pulse that Brand had hit on. He did little more than rework his soundbite, telling everyone decades too late that 'the PC is the LSD of the 1990s—turn on, boot up, jack in.'

Far closer to the zeitgeist, as modem-connected computers began spreading across the communes of California, Kevin Kelly, a young editor at the Whole Earth Catalog, began to talk to Brand about this continuum between the ideals of the counterculture and that of the emerging cyberculture. The same people who had been excited by one were now moving on and being turned on by the other.

Kelly was a devout Christian and photographer and, like Brand, an astute observer of social trends. He could see the spiritual nature of this digital revolution. In 1993, just as I was waiting around impatiently for the internet to load, he finally took the plunge, left WEC with some other writers and became founding editor of *Wired* magazine.

Taking a lead from Brand, he put the magazine's ideology right up front of the cover of the opening issue:

We have it in our power to begin the world over again.

This was a quote from another Thomas Paine—not the head of NASA, but the English revolutionary and associate of William Blake. He'd not only become one of the Founding Fathers of the United States, but had also moved to France in the early 1790s to help secure the French revolution.

This was where Kelly placed his magazine, in continuity with the explorers and Puritans and Rebels and Jacobeans and Beatniks and Hells Angels and Pranksters and Astronauts. All of these revolutionaries had faced head-on the death of the force that had sustained them. All had launched outwards away from oppression, upwards, along whichever vector was the most radical, seeking to remake a purer world elsewhere, drawing on new spirits to help them recapture Eden.

All of them had failed, but Brand and Kelly knew that none of them had had the power to modify mass human behaviour in the way that digital culture could. Kelly was clear, the key was 'out of body experiences.' By ditching the body, the mind could be perfected.

With one foot in the counterculture and another in ecstatic religion, he was well practised in these sublime moves. What he'd experienced with LSD and charismatic worship had been temporary and ineffectual, but computers were different: 'an out-of-body experience you could have whenever you wanted,' he gushed. Using these newer and better tools they were aiming at nothing less than a wholesale transformation of society, bringing about an age of peace through the distributed power of the web.

Channelling the spirits of Leary and JFK, *Wired* co-founder Louis Rosetto carried on Kelly's theme:

> It's finally time to embrace the future with optimism again in the realization that this peaceful, inevitable revolution isn't a problem, but an opportunity to build a new and better civilisation for ourselves and our children.[4]

Where Kesey had failed, Kelly thought he could now succeed. What would permanently prop open Blake's doors of perception, augment humanity for good, achieve the true Acid Graduation and herald in a new world order? For the staff moving from the *Whole Earth Catalog* to *Wired* the answer was digital technology, and at the heart of this great hope was AI.

—

Still trying to build the Memex, this machine that would end wars by enhancing our memories, in 1962 Engelbart had been joined by MIT graduate John McCarthy. Though the two men initially got on well, things soon turned frosty. Engelbart's vision was to use machines to enable humans to surpass their limits. For McCarthy, the future of computers wasn't *enhancing* human capabilities, but moving *beyond* them, becoming separate, sentient entities. The Turk rising from the table, the duck flying the nest, automata becoming autonomous: he didn't foresee machines that imitated life, but ones that were actually alive.

This move McCarthy described as 'artificial intelligence,' and though his new colleague Engelbart was resistant, back at MIT his old friend Marv Minsky was becoming something of an AI provocateur. Echoing Descartes and Vaucanson, at an early conference he described the brain as 'nothing more than a meat machine,' and the body as 'that bloody mess of organic matter.' Analogue. Limited. Needing to be ditched. One of Minsky's most passionate PhD students was Danny Hillis, who was talking the same way. 'What's good about humans is the idea thing. It's not the animal thing.'⁵ Mind, not body. If only he could perform an act of Cartesian surgery—somehow free the brilliant mind from the dull and dying body—he could fulfil this vision that had been passed from Plato to Bruno to Bush: the perfection of our memory and the achievement of immortality.

Totally serious about this, Hillis began researching the possibility of Artificial *Life*, whereby we might upload our minds to a network and continue existing for eternity in purely digital form. Another associate, Hans Moravec, even set out the theoretical process to achieve this, a 'Moravec transfer' whereby 'a human brain could be transformed into a mechanical structure made from nanobots, without the brain in question losing consciousness.'⁶ The body gradually consumed by a machine, each part upgraded to become more reliable, until it ran perfectly... like clockwork.

Their reasoning was simple: what was the point of having a computer network that could survive a nuclear attack if human intelligence couldn't?

Von Braun had paradoxically worked on atomic missiles and simultaneously proposed that his technology could be used to help mankind escape to other planets if these missiles were ever deployed. In the same way, through the 1950s the mathematician John von Neumann had worked tirelessly on the US nuclear programme, even proposing mathematical models that showed that America's best game plan for winning the Cold War would be to wipe out Russia in a pre-emptive strike. Putting these equations and papers to one side on his desk, he would then open others, developing the foundations for modern computer architecture and the theory of digital viruses, self-replicating cells of code that could infect the memory of a machine. It was the ultimate spread-bet: pushing the world towards nuclear holocaust, while doing the groundwork for a digital escape pod: the transfer of human consciousness to viral, digital form.

None of this was hypothetical. On 9th November, 1979, the handing over of control to digital systems almost brought this apocalypse about. A computer technician mistakenly uploaded military exercise data into the North American Air Defence system, causing alerts to be sent out that Russia had launched a full-scale attack. Planes armed with warheads were scrambled and crews were screaming through their radios if they were really being asked to fire before the call finally came through that it was a false alarm.

In the fallout that followed, Strategic Air Command were criticised for not having followed through on protocol. They should, investigators concluded, have assumed that the attack was real. The very human weakness that had saved the planet was slammed for not having had the guts to pull the trigger.

A war fought by intelligent machines? None of this worries Hillis and his AI troops. A nuclear winter is a minor worry.

The goliath among these minds is Ray Kurzweil, another man who spends half of his time working to create a threat to the human race, and the other half on a means of escaping it. Kurzweil hopes to have created true artificial life within the next 20 years. Against Engelbart's wishes, this will not be an augmentation to human intellect, but a fully sentient computer. When Kurzweil has created a truly autonomous, artificially intelligent machine that is more powerful and more brilliant than us, history will have reached what he calls 'the singularity.' Able to imagine more powerful versions of themselves and possessing the ability to self-replicate, these super-clever machines will multiply exponentially and quickly colonise Earth and outer space.

For Kurzweil and Hillis the biggest danger to humanity isn't from something so benign as a nuclear war. For the men working to create the singularity, the real problem lies in how human life might survive once they succeed. Hans Moravec has been so keen to work out how to transcend the biological membrane and become a digital consciousness because he knows that it will be the only way to survive once this singularity hits. In the AI age, getting out of your head won't be a matter of hedonism, it'll be one of survival.

'We're men, not machines,' John Glenn said to Fallaci as they sat and sipped coffee in a NASA canteen in 1963, talking about the future. 'You aren't supposing that we have gasoline instead of blood and an electronic computer instead of a brain?'

She hoped not, she said, then Bill Douglas, the astronaut's physician joined her and they fell to talking about replacing human organs with more efficient, artificial ones. Vaucanson, 2.0.

'There are no limits to the changes we can make in man,' Douglas said confidently, explaining that in future we'd send cyborg versions of ourselves to scout space for a new home.

The mood shifted in the room, and he became blue at this thought. He wanted to send men into space, not monsters.

'I'd rather be Bill Douglas, mortal, than an immortal monster. I hope that it'll never come about,' he said blackly.

'Do you really believe that it won't?' she asked.

'No,' he said glumly. 'It'll come. It'll come worse luck. It's only a matter of time.'

—

As the prospect of the singularity looms darkly, Fallaci's question rings with a new urgency: if the sun does die soon, why will we have allowed men like Kurzweil to have worked so hard to kill it? When Kevin Kelly packed up his things at the *Whole Earth Catalog* and stepped out to start *Wired*, was this the 'inevitable revolution' that he hoped for?

The first issue I ever read happened to be the last UK edition. 'PUSH!' ran the cover text in March of '97, next to a photograph of a pointing hand. I'd recently started teaching and the fingers belonged to a guy I'd just met, a graphic designer who had started work at the UK branch of *Wired* a few weeks before, his digits somehow voted as most photogenic as they put together the cover.

He was gutted the magazine was closing in the UK and brought a copy to show me, and we talked about this weird coming world where data would be 'pushed' to our devices even without us requesting it. He also told me about Kevin Kelly, and we cracked open drinks and looked puzzled, wondering how this guy could be totally embedded in the world of cutting edge technology, and yet a Christian.

Born in '68, Nic was, like me, a son of the cloth. Like me, his experience of growing up in a vicarage had both burned him badly and gifted him the vectors that defined his life's path. We were two angry young men, grappling with the spirituality that had been pushed to us, raiding every resource we could to fund our mission to hack it, break it completely down and see what else could be built from the ruins.

Out of this mess of thinking about technology and religion and Kelly and *Wired* came Vaux, a collective of artists and thinkers he and I put together with the partners we'd married just months before. A hybrid vehicle we built to navigate the bombed-out and fragmented terrain that lay between us and a safe exit from belief, the excitement of the project also served to cover over the doubts I had about the vows I'd taken. Me still working full-time as a teacher, we began in November of 1998, our first event a chaotic exploration of memory and atonement on the 80th anniversary of the end of World War 1.

My day-to-day work was still all blackboard and chalk, an overhead projector if you were lucky. A computer sat on a trolley gathering dust by the kettle in our departmental office, a useful shelf for mugs. I had an old laptop at home and an AOL address that I went to check like an empty house every once in a while. Meeting Nic, this all changed quickly.

An exceptional artist as well as an avid reader of culture, he dragged me into the digital now and, with articles like those in the last UK issue of *Wired*, forced me finally to wake up to the deeper human implications of what was happening. With Vaux we now had a means of mixing up these technological revolutions with theology, philosophy, social theory, psychoanalysis and all the dirt and shit of life.

The Victorian barn of a building is naturally dark. Pillars stand to attention at regular intervals up the main body of the church, an electric heater atop each one, bathing the whole place in a blood-red glow. It's cold though. People are wearing coats and scarves. Between the pillars we've strung up screens and from a snaking nest of extension cables slide projectors, amps and video displays are plugged in. In huge letters, a heavy cut of Helvetica kerned to within a point of its life, the words GOD IS FOUND IN THE SHIT covering the beautiful brickwork at the back. Opposite, a pure white cube has been built, on top of which red wine in a cut glass and a loaf of bread sit. A DJ is mixing electronica and a piece of contemporary dance is being performed in front of an accompanying piece of video. This is Vaux, a homage to the Acid Tests that Nic and I have built.

The evening is the first of a series of explorations we are doing around the theme of dirt. 'This is my body, broken for you,' a young woman says to the crowd gathered late that Sunday night. She holds the loaf of bread above her head and then drops it, and because of the way it has been cut it smashes and breaks on the altar. She lifts the glass of wine and there's a look of horror on some faces. 'This is my blood, shed for you.' Her fingers open and, as if in slow motion, we watch the glass fall and hit and shatter, the pure white surface now a mess of broken glass and hunks of bloodied bread. We're later accused of performing a black mass, but many people are weeping, this deadened ritual of Holy Communion brought alive in all its shocking violence.

Experimental, heretical, iconoclastic and creative, Vaux was not only brilliant fun but the most spiritually enriching environment Nic or I had ever engaged in. It was hard work too though; carrying on our day jobs, we were putting evening events on every month, and with the demands of publicity came email, blog posts, the need for a mobile. We would spend hours editing video on his Mac, generating graphics and animations and trying to lay our hands on higher quality video projection systems. Whereas once I'd lived happily without and digital devices, now whole evenings began getting sucked into screens as we prepared for each event.

When Vaux began to attract attention I started to reflect and theorise a little, gathering thoughts in my first book. It was well received, and new circles opened up, and one evening in the bar of the Institute of Contemporary Art in central London a friend introduced me to a guy from Belfast who was doing similar things to Vaux with a group called Ikon, his first book not far behind. We got drunk and immediately started talking ideas, the possibilities all delicious. I convinced myself that to keep up with this dispersed community of radicals I had to join the newly-emerging social networks.

I might as well have installed a morphine drip. Every ping was a personal validation. Someone wanted me. Someone cared. Someone liked me. I found it almost impossible to resist, the reward centres of my brain lapping up the dopamine hits, becoming finely tuned to the vibrate alerts and different tones of the smartphone I'd now bought too.

What I couldn't admit was that I was pressing escape. Each virtual interaction was a click away from the chronic stress I was feeling in my relationships, knowing that there was so much in me that needed dealing with, but terrified about the fall-out of doing so. My sister had started coming along to Vaux and contributed hugely. This made me so proud—seeing how far she had come from those terrible years and what she was able to share from that journey—but it also tore at me too. Having spectacularly failed to deal with any of the trauma the time around her illness had left me with, I found her presence around Vaux stirring monsters within me whose forms and scale I was petrified of.

I'd noticed this a year or so before when Nic and I had travelled to visit a friend outside Nottingham. We'd driven up for a walk on the moors, a couple of pints of bitter after. Driving back we passed through Sheffield. I was sat in the front seat, the three of us talking art, sharing jokes, taking the piss out of this and that. Quite suddenly I was struck dumb. This road, what was it? We were heading down a hill through the city. I had no idea where I was, but my chest was in a vice, bile rising in my throat. And then I saw it coming. The Children's Hospital where my sister had been, a pin dropped into the GPS of my unconscious so long ago, suddenly awake and burning, pure psychogeography.

'You ok?'

A while to answer, brushing it off with Nic as best I could.

'I'm fine.'

It passed quickly. He didn't press it.

I became a father, and took a job in a school closer to home in order to cut down my commute. It turned out to be a huge mistake. I lost the colleagues I loved. The classroom door would shut and the chill of isolation would hit. By this time I was pretty good at what I did, but the emotional cost was immense. My own son was at home, but all day I was *in loco parentis* to scores of very needy children. Added to this, the draining tide of my changing beliefs was only exposing more clearly the hurts that had been submerged for so long. Feeling raw and confused, I blamed those closest to me.

Digital communications increased as healthy communication at home nosedived. Angry, exhausted, disappointed, lonely, and feeling unsupported and isolated, I turned to computers at school and home, venerating them as portals out of the turmoil of my classroom and the strain of home into a world where I was, in the tiny ways I over-amplified, significant and important.

I was surfing the net constantly, but in truth the net was serfing me. I was addicted, not so much updating my status as assuring myself that I had one. I was disappearing, hardly present with those I was with, glazing over in conversations until I could gaze at the screen again, willing my body to be gone, just as my sister had done, this bloody mess of organic matter no more than a means by which I could sustain a mind that yearned to be elsewhere.

Vaux had taken us a long way, but eventually had to be abandoned. Landing us safely far beyond any kind of orthodox belief, it was now time for new directions, and—along with so many other friends—Nic and his family moved out of London. It was stupid, but I felt abandoned. I was more lonely in my marriage than ever, but struck dumb, was too cowardly to confront what was going on, drowning out these thoughts by burying myself more in the virtual, where geography, history or physical chemistry were said not to matter.

I couldn't go on like this, that I knew.

'Charges of dynamite, that's what we need,' Herb Rosen said in his 1963 interview with Fallaci. He was high up in NASA's PR machine and they too had gone on from space to talking about technology. With this Florentine sat in front of him, a woman who had seen German soldiers enter her city and blow up its ancient Renaissance bridges, Rosen had launched into a tirade against Shakespeare, the Sistine Chapel and anything else that came before the great age of digital machines, demanding it all be wiped out. Yes, he confirmed as she pressed him, even Florence. Again.

You surely don't want to hang on to those narrow streets and crooked houses? New streets. New Houses. New churches. That's what we need. Charges of dynamite.[7]

My own childhood love affair with Tuscany had continued, and during one of my regular visits to friends in Lucca I somehow contrived to agree with Rosen, determining that every bridge in my life needed blowing up and tearing down. 'We have it in our power to begin the world over again,' I thought, and in the jumbled way that my mind was wired, even as I wandered the beautiful narrow streets and drank in the warm welcome of the crooked houses, I believed Kelly and threw my lot in with the bright new hope of revolution.

I returned from Italy and began the difficult conversation that ended my marriage. Whatever atmosphere it had needed to survive had been starved of many elements, but the vacuum of tender communication had been intensified in great part by the engulfing black hole of the web. Hoping technology could deliver to me the Platonic Moon I still yearned for, it had instead landed me in my own Dresden, bombed out, broken down and ruined, all light occluded by the smoke and dust.

—

What happens when the sun dies? What happens when the night comes, black as pitch? Like Antoine de Saint-Exupéry's pilot in *Night Flight*, sometimes we have to set our course and fly blindly ahead, pushing on through the choking darkness, thrown about by colliding depressions, the maps all useless as we try to pull up towards whatever chinks of starlight open momentarily through the clouds.

Like one of von Neumann's viruses, Vaux had been expertly coded for deconstruction. It had brilliantly torn into theology and art and philosophy, but once I'd got it running it had got out of control, burrowed, worm-like into my system and run rampant through my drives, unzipping the archives of my anger and sending me crashing.

I moved out and of our house into a tiny studio. One small window, two skylights through which I lay on my bed and watched the shifting moods of the night. When a system is under threat, you pull the plug, take it off-line, isolate it. No network. Reboot in safe mode.

It was alone in this small space I had cleared that I found myself late one night watching a documentary about Ray Kurzweil. In a nearby garden two foxes were screaming, while onscreen Hugo de Garis, a leader in the field of AI, was calmly setting out the future rolling towards us.

'We swat pests like ants and flies and don't give a damn because we are so much greater in intellect than they are. So who's to say that an 'artillect'—an artificial intellect—won't do the same to us?'

I was flung back to that Yorkshire vicarage, the pig farm next door, fly papers hanging from the ceiling, all of us on guard with swatters, not caring a damn for the tiny, stupid life forms that licked up food from our table, food that they had dissolved in their own vomit.

Tears came. Indiscriminately, blinded by hurt, I'd never stopped hitting out, robotically, reflexively pushing everyone away until I found myself here, no one left within reach.

Faced with this impending apocalypse, humankind's only option for escaping extinction will be to upload itself.

Auto-apocalypse. One entirely of our own making, Kurzweil arguing that—like Sputnik and nuclear proliferation—it would be remiss not to be keeping up with your enemies. But the Cold War will have nothing on this. De Garis predicts a great battle in the late 21st century between one group of humans and another, the one side fighting to stop these AI machines ever being built, and the other fighting to ensure that they are, *'because for them it will be like a religion—these machines to them will be godlike.'*[8]

Stripped bare, drowning in memories and guilt, I watch talking heads in the film express profound theological discomfort at wholesale digital augmentation of human life. But Kurzweil is unabashed and comes back at them, seeing his mission in Biblical terms, reading on camera the very same verses from the book of Revelation that I had grown up with: *there will be no more death or mourning or crying or pain.*

Bringing about the singularity will be a fulfilment of Scripture, mankind changed and perfected, Plato's True Form finally realised as we leave the dim cave of the physical body and lift ourselves into the bright new sun of the immortal virtual.

As we merge with machines we will transform into something new. Anyone resisting this will be resisting evolution, and eventually they will die out.

I hadn't resisted. Here I was transformed and mutated, my humanity diminished. I'd merged gladly with my machines, so why did I feel as if I was the one dying out?

'I don't accept death,' Kurzweil says defiantly. A spark of German comes back to me: his name translates as 'a short, diverting entertainment,' but I can see in his eyes that he's not joking and the film cuts to his daily routine, chugging his way through a mixture of over 200 pills and supplements, doing all he can to give himself time to invent eternity.

The one death he definitely hasn't accepted is that of his father, his obvious grief stirring up more tears of my own, unsure if my Dad even knows my address any more. Kurzweil hopes he'll be able to resurrect his father in digital form, both of them uploaded into a higher, distributed consciousness—*popping out of the time warp into the silver haze of...The Universal Mind...*

'It will be the universe waking up,' he says of the self-replicating nano-machines spreading through every element and atom as the film closes. 'People say "does God exist?" and I say, *not yet.*'

Not yet. As the credits roll and silence falls in my flat, another evening alone with my devices, I feel something turn in me. I lie back and see the faint stars above. A great storm has now passed, landing me here, buffeted and bruised, in my crib. Perhaps the reawakening of the soul can now begin. With a spark of understanding a great sadness begins to burn, the title of the biopic summing up all that I had spent the past 30 years striving for: *Transcendent Man.*

—

Leonardo was 'Renaissance Man'—man reborn, depicted in *The Creation of Adam* as almost divine, within touching distance of God. The dialectic that drove the Renaissance project was how that tiny gap between humanity and divinity might be closed.

Before painting it, Michelangelo had attended a Neoplatonist Medici Academy. There he had been exposed to and heavily influenced by the works of contemporary thinkers there such as Giovanni Pico della Mirandola. His vast *900 Theses* was at the time considered the sum of all knowledge, the complete works that would need to be memorised to lift oneself out of the shadows of ignorance and up the chain of being towards the immortal Truth.

It was 'occult' hidden teachings such as these that forged Michelangelo's artistic vision. Like Da Vinci, Descartes and Vaucanson he was a keen anatomist, and recent research by doctors on the shadowy forms that he painted around the figure of God in *The Creation of Adam* has revealed that they are almost perfect representations of the different parts that make up the human brain: the stem, the cerebrum, the pituitary gland and the paths of the optic nerves.[9] Viewed in this way, God's hand stretches out to Adam through the prefrontal cortex, the part of the brain most closely associated with personality and conscience, the part sent into ecstasy by entheogens.

Extraordinarily, on the ceiling of the most hallowed hall of the Catholic Church, 'il divino' left a heretical coded message: the locus of divinity was within the mind itself. According to Michelangelo, the tiny gap that remained between ourselves and deity could be bridged by the augmentation of the intellect: to reach out and touch the divine, all we had to do was perfect the Neoplatonic art of memory.

All attempts to do this have failed. Now, a half a millennium later, Kurzweil looks at the outstretched hand of Adam and the possibility of grasping the divine mind and declares that the only way to become Transcendent Man, the final means to traverse this finger-wide gap is... *digitally.*

His coming AI future is no more than an ancient past: from Simonides and Plato's cave right through Giordano Bruno's memory theatre and on to the Memex—all of it is the same hope of redeeming our failing flesh, driving to perfect our minds, spring them from their bloody Bastilles so that they might rise up and become transcendent.

Nic had recently lent me David Noble's book *The Religion of Technology*, but I'd never got round to it. His argument was that the Christian idea of the trinity had pushed a form of polytheism into Jewish monotheism, opening up the possibility of humans returning to Eden and taking their place among the gods. Thus, around the time of the Middle Ages, monks began connecting technological advance with this spiritual goal of redemption. As the 11th century Saxon theologian Hugh St. Victor put it, '*the mechanical arts supply all the remedies for our weakness.*'[10] They are how we will restore our pre-Fall nature, and the strength and supply of these remedies has exploded as technology has progressed.

Though traditional religious practice may have faded, our deep-felt need for restoration has not, and Noble argues that we have simply shifted our hope for redemption. The technology of religion has morphed seamlessly into the religion of technology:

> *We routinely expect far more from our artificial contrivances than mere convenience, comfort, or even survival. We demand deliverance.*[11]

Hadn't I ached for this deliverance all my life? 'O wretched man that I am!' Paul railed in Romans. 'Who shall deliver me from the body of this death?' In weaker hand, hadn't my sister scratched the same desperate plea into her diary? We had all begged Jesus to perform an act of deliverance on her, not seeing that we were each straining to be delivered from our bodies in different ways. Drugs, higher knowledge, religious ecstasy and digital technology—I'd been through them all, but each had failed me, each left me more broken.

Dreaming of human flight, Da Vinci had sketched artificial contrivances, longing to be delivered from the deadened corpus of orthodox dogma. Then Michelangelo sided with Simon Magus too, believing that through the memory arts we could leave our bodies behind and overcome our fallen imperfection.

Hadn't Hunter Thompson come to the same conclusion? 'I find myself an appendage,' he said in his suicide note, 'I'm no longer necessary,' his anger and depression grounded in the failure of LSD or religion or any other technology to deliver him from a body that was now crumbling and failing.

He'd taken matters into his own hands, leaving the floor clear for Kurzweil, Hillis and the other A-Life evangelists, their litany of promises recorded by Noble:

> 'On the other side of our data gloves we become creatures of coloured light in motion, pulsing with golden particles. We will all become angels, and for eternity. Cyberspace will feel like Paradise, a space for collective restoration of the habit of perfection.'

> 'Cyberspace is the dimension where floats the image of a Heavenly City, the New Jerusalem of the Book of Revelation. Like a bejewelled, weightless palace it comes out of heaven itself, a place where we might re-enter God's graces.'

> 'The gradual transition from carnal existence to embodiment into electronic hardware would guarantee the continuity of an individual's subjective experience beyond death.'

> 'The body in cyberspace is immortal.'

> 'Technology will soon enable human beings to change into something else altogether and thereby escape the human condition.'[12]

To become angels! Weightless astronauts! To fight our way further up the evolutionary scale and join the celestial hierarchy! Like Apollo, like LSD, with AI our ancient drives are being alloyed to a once-benign work of engineering, elevating it to the level of transcendent revelation, a religious imperative whose narrative we must follow.

—

It's a few months since I'd laid those charges of dynamite. As the dust has settled I've begun writing again, trying to put form to these thoughts about family, future and the human quest for flight. I've laughed at Harvey Kling and then fallen silent, seeing in his own irate bewilderment how little I understand of my own world. I can't write to the President, but I can get away for a while, back to California to try to get some much-needed perspective.

'We didn't stay in the cave,' another writer on AI gushes. I'm in the departure lounge at Heathrow, reading, Kurzweil's ideas now seemingly everywhere I look. 'We haven't stayed on the planet, and soon with the biotech revolution, we won't stay within the limitations of biology. And why do we do this? To defy mortality.'

Sunglasses. Perfumes. Anti-ageing creams. Electronic gadgets. Self-help books. Readying ourselves for lift-off, airports are a bridgehead into this coming world, so much so that as my gate it announced it hardly seems odd to read the conclusion of the article:

Being transhuman is actually what makes us human.

Is that true? Is struggling to escape the human condition the most human thing that we can do? It feels like double-speak from Orwell's *1984*, twisted propaganda from Huxley's *Brave New World*.

Thrust back in my seat again as we take off, my plane cuts its way between open space above and the jagged peaks of the Canadian Rockies below, my body twisting and turning uncomfortably in the cramped seat, held between Earth and heaven by these alloy wings alone, trying to order my thoughts.

'The AI enterprise is a god-like one,' Noble writes. His book is open on the seat-back tray in front of me, my thoughts reaching right back to Stewart Brand and Issue 1 of the *Whole Earth Catalog*: 'we are all as gods and we had better get used to it.'

Is this the final encapsulation of all that the Renaissance tried to capture? The god within is the restless mind, a revolutionary organ fighting for liberation from its bloody coop.

'The body is always a hindrance to the mind in its thinking,' Descartes wrote, and now Transcendent Man wants to finish what Renaissance Man began, what the Pranksters attempted and the Brotherhood of the Right Stuff shot for. LSD and ecstatic religion and space travel took us 'as high as any fucker could go,' but all of them failed because the carnal self remained.

Our bodies are colonies, playing host to more bacterial cells than there are human ones. Like the suits and spaceships NASA worked so hard to sterilise, so much of our lifetime is spent trying shake off this dirt, to separate it out so that only the pure parts of us remain, us convinced that we won't be able to escape the grave until we can escape our impure bodies. With AI, Kurzweil wants to finish the job. Pull open the ribcage and release our inner god for flight.

Squashed in my seat, I'm irritated at my own body constantly reminding me of its bloody physicality, brooding on my own parallel failures to leave the brutal, painful reality of my past behind. With our journey through dirt, Vaux had been onto something, but it feels like we didn't finish the job. It's not that god is found in the shit, but that what we discard as shit reveals, in what remains, what it is we want to worship.

Half into a dream a thought then comes, a dawning realisation about what I hadn't earlier been comfortable reading. Being transhuman isn't what makes us *human*. The hungry pursuit of augmentation, the ancient striving to lift ourselves out of the cave, off the bacterial surface of the Earth and up into the crystal clear sky, uncovers something far more profound.

This is why, among all my exploration into the means of flight that came to define the 60s, these powerful digital technologies that were born in the closing weeks of this decade now pose questions that cannot be left unexamined.

As ARPANet has evolved into the Internet and threatens to mutate into AI, these tools have roots as deeply religious as the counterculture and the Moon landings, and rose from the very same troubled ground. I wasn't lucky enough to be around for the 60s, but I've been fortunate enough to have been in my 20s when the digital waves first broke and the world began to surf. Stretching forward from that decade now so romanticised, the web has become *our* trip, *our* counterculture, *our* pioneering exploration of a vast new galaxy. Outstripping the powers of LSD or Apollo, Kurzweil's fantasy that has sprung from it is an exceptional psychedelic, peeling back the body and revealing the truth dug deep into our souls.

That truth is this: since the dawn of creation, since the awakening of the soul, we have always looked up to the light, always been anxious about the short time we have before we are extinguished. Terrified of the sun dying, we've never really wanted to be human at all. Our hopes are higher than that, and this is what advanced digital machines reach out and promise to deliver: what we've longed for all this time is to be done with our bodies, and become gods.

*Woodcut from 1620 printing of Christopher Marlowe's
Doctor Faustus, showing Faustus conjuring the demon
Mephistopheles whilst standing in a
circle of magical symbols.*

6. Let Down

In 1969 an ex-Hollywood stunt man called Jim Baker opened The Source, a vegetarian restaurant that he used to promote his healthy life regimen. After all the shit of the past decade, this was a symbol of cleansing. Sat in a prime spot on LA's Sunset Boulevard it attracted everyone from John Lennon to Marlon Brando.

A martial arts expert and decorated Marine from World War II, Baker had a history of physical violence and had been jailed for killing his lover's husband with a karate chop to the neck. Claiming self-defence, when Baker was released in early 60s he'd turned to eastern mysticism and, like The Beatles, spent time under the tutelage of a yogic guru. Though he was born in the 20s and was thus a lot older than most hippies, he'd thrown himself into LSD culture.

When that fell apart after the Summer of Love, like Frisbee, like Manson, he gathered a group of around 140 disillusioned and disappointed young people under his charismatic wing and offered them a new hope. Changing his name to Father Yod, taking to wearing flowing white robes and growing out his long white hair and beard, he founded The Source Family. Bruised and lost hippies would turn up and he'd offer them work in the kitchen or waiting tables, and when the day was done they'd gather and listen to his teachings.

By the early 70s, with the restaurant pulling in around $10,000 each day, the Family were living in a mansion in the Hollywood Hills and Father Yod wasn't just *looking* exactly like a Sunday School caricature of The Almighty, but had given himself 13 wives was actually calling himself God.

It turned out that God was as anxious as anyone else about Armageddon though and, predicting a nuclear apocalypse would hit in the mid 70s, Yod sold the restaurant and moved the entire cult out to Hawaii. There they ran into trouble with the local residents and island authorities, who were nervous that they were another Manson Family in the making. This wasn't the case, but Yod was exerting extreme psychological influence over his own Family, instructing young women whom they should take for partners and insisting that no one received medical attention or proper treatment when ill.

Under his gracious wing, things were hardly Edenic. Struggling to eek out a living there, like all the other communes Hopper had depicted in *Easy Rider*, the Family found that growing your own food and being self-sufficient was a lot harder work than it looked.

The strain began to tell, and Yod became more and more disturbed. With the community having no income and no proper direction, he took a dark turn. On the morning of August 25th, 1975, with no training or experience, Yod launched himself in a hang-glider from the top of 400m cliffs on the island of Oahu. 'God,' it became immediately apparent, could not fly. He spiralled uncontrollably, crashed to the beach far below and died of his injuries late that afternoon.

—

Between thumping beats and the splashing and laughing of beautiful bodies at play, the tale of Yod is being recounted to me at a swish Hollywood pool party, close to where The Source restaurant was. I'm still teaching full-time, but it's the holidays and I've been invited out here to speak on one of my books. A fellow Brit who's done very well in the music business has read some of my work, and smuggled me and a friend in past the queues of people trying to catch the eyes of the men on the door. Looking up at the warm sky and thinking about Yod, the hills and lights lifting above us into the night, this vision of the self-made god falling to Earth, his robes billowing out behind him, seems the perfect LA story.

There are no hang-gliders in sight, but everyone has their own means of flight to hand: entheogens, therapy regimes, digital solutions. As the party gets higher there seems nothing we cannot know, no person we cannot immediately conjure into our midst. Through the almost Eucharistic, wafer-thin medium of phones and the donning of totemic wearables we become omniscient and omnipresent. One heavily augmented specimen hands me his pearl-white card—in case I need an attorney, he says—and for a moment I'm tempted to ask him if he fancies a manic drive out to Vegas. I resist; he probably drives a Prius.

They are all tanned here, though no one sunbathes. That might wrinkle the skin, accelerate ageing. This is Kurzweil country, through and through, something of Yod in everyone, a desperate craving for divinity apparent in every direction I look.

That said, it's great to be here. Getting out of London for a while, enjoying some space, flying like Kling to get some fresh perspective, I'm visiting friends and doing a couple of talks, but also doing some research, dowsing the ground between here and San Francisco, the highways Kesey hurtled along, the campuses he and Leary and Engelbart set alight, the places I'd visited as a young man, so many years ago. It's almost as many years between then and now as it had been between then and the 60s. Man, I'm getting old.

All this runs through my mind as we're driving back from Hollywood in the early hours, windows down, the stars hardly visible above the canopy of streetlights, head still spinning from stories and other things. In preparation for the trip I'd sent a speculative email to Stewart Brand, hoping he'd agree to an interview. He was away from California but generous in correspondence, relaying stories of the links between Stanford Research Institute and the *Whole Earth Catalog*, and working the cameras at The Mother of All Demos.

'When it was over I asked if it went okay, and they said yeah it went okay, and I wandered home.'

Simple as that. He comes across as a genuinely nice guy. With the Trips Festival, the Earthrise button-badges and the Whole Earth Catalog, his has already been such a rich life and yet still he pushes onto the next thing, just as he had done with the Pranksters.

'LSD,' he went on, 'was the opposite of consciousness expanding, even though we were pleased with our coinage.' Like Huxley focusing on his trousers, he'd seen people spend hours and hours tripping, obsessing some detail of their hands but doing nothing with them.

'It was consciousness-contracting. The attraction, I suppose, was to fuck around with your mind and society's mind. Leary I had little use for. He came late and half-witted to digital tech. Drugs proved to be self-limiting, but computers and bio-tech proved to be infinitely self-enhancing. That's where I'm working now.'[1]

The complete trajectory in one life. Drugs, ecstatic experience, the great hopes of space, the shift to digital culture and bio-augmentation, all of it taking aim at the same heights of heaven itself, casting off all limits, expanding consciousness in infinite self-enhancement, not for mere convenience, but demanding full deliverance from the human condition.

We blast along through the LA night, all warm air, palm fronds and sodium-orange light, spirits soaring. To become young gods. This is what California yearns for, what it picks up in all of us, and after a tough few months it's so damned tempting, and I close my eyes and lean my head back and say fuck it all, bring it all on, and open my arms to all of it.

—

I feel a lot less than divine the next morning, definitely very mortal as I drag myself out of bed. I'm jet-lagged and hungover but have an urge to get up and out. I need coffee.

As I hit the morning sunlight my head is swimming with drugs, Apollo and ecstatic religion. Each promising a powerful means to deliver a better society, the hopes placed in them had been so strong that they had lifted a whole decade. Lifted, and then let down: by the end of the 60s, when none of them had delivered, in the midst of the continuing war and anxiety and social conflict a void opened up.

'Human beings cannot endure emptiness and desolation,' Karen Armstrong concludes in A History of God. 'They will fill the vacuum by creating a new focus of meaning.' As the 60s closed, into this new vacuum of meaning rushed digital technology.

LSD, ecstatic spiritualities and the space-race had ended up as explicitly religious enterprises. Opening the doors of perception, rockets with which we could now talk to God, each had offered communion with the divine above, and promised Eden in return. They were technologies to aid our reconnection with the Higher Power but, having failed to deliver, rather than questioning this drive to repeatedly theologise our tools, following Armstrong's pattern we again elevated the latest high-tech innovation and looked to it to elevate us to divinity.

We are all born flightless. Every one. We turn to the gods to lift us. Only later do we understand that if we are going to fly we will have to forge our wings for ourselves...

The technology of religion, and the religion of technology: in the long stretch of history, one and the same thing. The religion bit I know so well—I've worn those vestments all my life. Sunglasses on and notebook packed, to get to the bottom of this quest to get high it's to the deeper meaning of our relationship to the tools that we craft that I know I must apply myself.

I'm slightly unnerved by the pattern, but it's to another tainted German that I turn to for help. Like von Braun, Martin Heidegger had shown far more than a passive enthusiasm for Hitler's project. Apologists for both men have argued that their Nazi allegiances were a means of self-preservation, the only way which they could continue to pursue the work that was the absolute core of their being. I'm not so sure.

Grabbing a table at a coffee shop — *Deus Ex Machina* it's appropriately called — I find myself wishing that I was Oriana Fallaci. She was the stylish Italian jewel-thief of journalists, charming her interviewees over drinks, making them drop their guard, allowing her to saunter up and take their most precious pearls. My subjects are either dead or out of town (though in LA this amounts to pretty much the same thing) and all I have is a battered copy of Heidegger's notoriously tricky *The Question Concerning Technology*. Nevertheless, I order a large dose of caffeine and ready my weapons.

'Between my finger and my thumb / the squat pen rests / I'll dig with it.' Lines of Heaney's percolated up from somewhere. It could be a long day's mining.

—

At the party last night there'd been a lot of chatter about new devices, who was going to get which smart watch, accusations that I was a Luddite thrown with some venom, any question about whether an upgrade was really worth having taken as a personal slight. The first gem from Heidegger is that he won't hear of this.

'Everywhere we remain unfree and chained to technology, whether we passionately affirm or deny it.'[2]

Luddism isn't an option. Our tools cannot be disentangled from our culture, the times we live in, nor the people that we are. Necessity might be the mother of invention, but our inventions are the arms that cradle us, the clothes that cover us, the wheels that move us and the means by which we are fed, watered, kept warm and able to communicate. None of our tools—religions, drugs, rocket ships or computers—are intrinsically bad or harmful. They are a part of what it means to be us and, whatever we might want to claim, there is no human world without them.

The long history of humankind is the long history of our tools and what we have achieved with them. Technology is a fusion of *techne*— of craft and making—and *poiesis*—a 'bringing forth' (from which we get the word poetry.) In our creative transformation of raw materials our world is brought into blossom, a beautiful metaphor for what happened in the Renaissance and the latter half of the 60s. During both periods there was a flowering of humankind's long-gestating desires to get high. In the Renaissance it was art and Neoplatonic thought and architectural soaring, while in the 60s the *techne-poiesis* of drugs and space-flight and digital computing all burst forth together.

In other words, all this fuss about wearables is a sideshow because all technology is—and always has been—deeply connected to the human body. We're all transformers, all robots in disguise, all people from whom craft blossoms.

I don't feel all that floral, truth be told, and what's not helping my pounding headache is a guy smacking nails into a wall, prepping for an exhibition. He's looking over his work and I'm reminded of Neal Cassady, Wolfe meeting him as he set up for the Graduation, 'in a kinetic trance, flipping a small sledge hammer up in the air over and over, always managing to catch the handle of the way down.'[3]

To use Leary's language: all tools are psychedelic. The smooth wooden handle of the hammer gets under the skin of the guy's hand and reaches right back into his soul, revealing in his inner being something of his desires. Namely: does he want to put up a picture or break open my face?

Perhaps I should stop staring.

The true power of the hammer comes in combining this ability to reach back into the heart with the power to extend forward and amplify the actions we can take in the world. Setting to work to prepare for the Acid Graduation, Cassady couldn't push nails in with his bare hands, nor break down doors, but grasped tight, this tool became a powerful amplifier that could act out his desires with greater strength than his own.

From Cassady via Kesey to the Hells Angels: in the thundering roar of their Harley Davidsons this idea of technological amplification was turned up to 11. Leather-gloved hands on the throttle, these machines broadcasted the inner lives of their riders, amplifying and thrusting them forward at frightening, threatening speeds and deafening volumes.

Up at Altamont, over in Watts, down in Memphis, anxiety comes to the boil in racist anger and the hand moves from motorcycle to shotgun. The trigger is enfolded by the hand of King's assassin, becoming part of it, reaching back into the darkness of his heart. The amplification is so large now and the forward movement has devastatingly bigger consequences. The very slightest squeeze of his finger, and King's body drops lifeless to the floor 100 yards away.

Frightened by the killing, the hippies escape to the hills. There they find Doug Engelbart, 'dealing lightening with both hands,' his fingers now given digital amplification and—LO!—using these tools, nuclear warheads are almost unleashed by mistake on a country thousands of miles away. Decades later, gripped in the hands of a troll, a smartphone unloads tweets like bullets, firing out threats of violence or rape to uncountable, unseen victims on the other side of the world, or, in gentler hands, held aloft at a protest march, exposing injustice and shining light on malpractice.

Now, my own question concerning technology is how the strength of this psychedelic amplification has changed as our tools have evolved. Cassady could only hit one thing at one time with his sledgehammer. It might have exerted great force, but even in the hands of the Angel-headed Hipster, its reach had been limited.

At the party last night some Apple bore rolled out the line that there was more computing power in his new iPhone than in the entire systems that took Armstrong and Aldrin to the Moon. I stifled a yawn then, but now realise there's something interesting lurking under the surface.

Norman Mailer had hailed that Saturn V rocket as something with which we could finally speak to God. 40 years later, Steve Jobs held the first iPhone aloft and dialled a number live on stage. So, if the guy last night was right, if this densely packed sliver of silicon *is* more mighty than Apollo, does that mean that each of us now has the power to speak with divine thunder? If so, hasn't the power of the smartphone begun to take on a transcendent, religious dimension? An instant messenger, words and pictures arriving from nowhere out of the air, is the iPhone not an angel for the modern man?

LSD had been for Potland what Apollo's rockets had been for Squareland, a tool venerated as a breakthrough in communication with the above. When both had failed, Lonnie Frisbee had stepped in with his ecstatic Christianity, making the exact same claim. Tongues of fire! A direct line to God!

Now, after Earthrise, after the *Whole Earth Catalog* and ARPANet and *Wired*, here comes Kurzweil and Artificial Life, striding into the black hole of disappointment left by all these other technologies, offering a completely new level of amplification, one that extends beyond the hammer, beyond the motorcycle, beyond guns and drugs and tablets, right up to the promise of immortality and omniscience in the here and now.

'Ultimately,' says Google chief Sergey Brin, 'you want to have the entire world's knowledge connected directly to your mind.' To know all, instantly, without moving a muscle.

LSD peeled back the world to reveal a new layer underneath; Apollo afforded us the chance to see Earth from space. All technologies contribute to revelation, and the more powerful our tools, the more our eyes can see. With AI, Kurzweil is promising nothing less than our full blossoming as a species. But he is adamant: achieving Brin's goal of full revelation will require the disposal of the physical bodies that holds our minds back.

This, we are told, will be the final book in the human scriptures, what we have worked for since our Genesis: the great Revelation of AI will not be that god has come down to us, but that we have risen up and become gods. The promise that it punches forward into the world is deification itself, but it is one that, reaching backwards through the long arc of history, is drawn out of the desperate desire for divinity that lies deep within our very human hearts.

—

I take a sip of coffee and push Heidegger's book away for a moment. My sister wanted to be rid of her body, wanted to penetrate minds and know exactly what people thought about her. The memory of her withering makes me anxious about this gradual digital blossoming, this shedding of our biological limits, bodies discarded like spent rocket stages. If Brin and Kurzweil are right, the real question concerning this very religious hope for technology is this: can it deliver on the promises it is making?

In Southern California the answer is always yes. This was what I'd always loved about the place. In the sunshine, the space, the brilliance of the light and the bikinied valleys of silicone, for a Yorkshire lad it sang so seductively: here I could be free, here I could be healed, here I could be whole. On the corner of Haight-Ashbury, stood in Wimber's church, speaking at conferences or drawing up at parties, whatever ecstasy I was into at the time, if I asked LA if it could heal me it would roar back that it definitely would.

This time it is different. The sun still shines as brightly and the water still glistens like cut glass, but so many years after their first impact, the bruises of my life are finally beginning to surface, and not even Los Angeles can stop them. Over the years I've been through the whole carousel of technologies, each promising a revelation of perfection and wholeness. None of them has delivered, and the sober truth is that the siren call of the city of Angels is beginning to sound hollow.

Flicking back through Stewart Brand's emails, it's like he's been round and round so many times too. *Drugs proved to be self-limiting, but computers proved to be infinitely self-enhancing and biotech has the same quality.* I can't help feel a twinge of sadness. His has already

159

been such a long and rich life, dissatisfaction driving him always onto the next thing. Academia wasn't it. Drugs weren't it. Space wasn't it. Communal living wasn't it. All acts of human blossoming, offering wonderful and varied revelations of the world, all of them were eventually exposed as self-limiting.

Returning to the text, 'enframing' is how Heidegger puts it, each technology offering a revelation but, as it does so, 'driving out every other possibility of revealing.'[4]

Not this time! Brand believes, unable to see a pattern. *Not with computers! Not with biotechnology!* But he is wrong. No matter how great its revelations, every technology will, in some way, enframe us. When high on acid, the world unfurled itself in new and extraordinary ways, but what the Pranksters found harder to see were the ways in which acid blinkered too, life concealing its other dimensions while this one, singular perspective shone so brightly.

Here is Kesey straining to glimpse the Universal Mind while his own child is crying; here is Huxley incapable of tearing his focus away from his trousers. Their decade become known as the psychedelic age, extraordinary new technologies revealing the soul in ways never seen before, nobody wanting to admit that it was equally *psyche-lethaic—* performing acts of mass psychological concealment.[5]

So when Kurzweil and his A-Life disciples talk about AI making us limitless, I hear the old German philosopher sigh in resignation, mumbling that what they have missed is that *precisely* what technology does is establish limits on our experience.

I close my eyes and imagine for a moment Kurzweil achieving his goal, one final physical click of finger on mouse as he uploads himself as a digital consciousness. His body slumps to the floor, discarded, his mind now immortal, undying, housed inside minuscule electronic components, the first horrified realisation of his light-speed brain being that he no longer has a body that can be held by another, no eyes able to shed tears nor a belly to curl up in laughter. As viruses begin to attack and hackers inevitably begin their assaults, he sees that this heaven he exists in might well be a prison not so very far from hell itself.

'But if that door is the last door,' Fallaci's father warned, 'it will take you headlong into the void.' As he walked away from his daughter, he was glad that his coffin would be closed before he saw that door open. 'They tell me that on the Moon there are no seas, no rivers, no fish, no woods, no fields, no birds.' Will Kurzweil have to explain to his own father that the new world he has brought him to offers no hunting or fishing, no birds or cool breezes?

On the plane over to California I watched Spike Jonze's film *Her.* A lonely and heart-broken Theodore begins using a fabulous new personal Operating System called Samantha, who talks and laughs and jokes and reminds him to sign his divorce papers. Yet her advanced

AI code begins to prompt existential questions within herself. She becomes depressed, lusting after a physical body, wanting Theodore to describe in intimate detail the physical world, as well as graphic physical acts.

Kurzweil knows too well: any machine would be insane to want to become flesh and blood. We decay and die, and virtual machines do not, but his problem is that he has become blind to the enframing the other way. He is Theodore longing to be Samantha, a human who wants to become a digital machine, limitless, immortal and omniscient. Every day he chugs down his vitamins and works towards the moment when an artificially intelligent machine will be smarter than us and powerful enough to replicate itself.

He has dubbed this moment 'the singularity.' In doing so, he is borrowing from astrophysics. A singularity occurs in a black hole, after a sun dies. It becomes a system from which nothing can escape, not even light itself. In its possession of all things, in its swallowing of all information into itself, an event horizon is formed, a boundary beyond which the traveller could no longer communicate with the world on other side.

This is the place Transcendent Man is straining to reach: a system with infinite information density—where all things can be known simultaneously—but one with no possible connection to the world it leaves behind. It is a place of extraordinary cerebral revelation, but one which achieves it by the total enframing of the mind, collapsing the complex analogues of embodied human experience into binary arrays of 1's and 0's.

—

I don't know. Maybe I've had too much caffeine, too little sleep. This fully-fledged AI is so fantastical, such a mind-storm to think about, it's no surprise it shares its roots with LSD and Apollo. It's pure psychedelia, a whole new orbit of experience, yet people still bustle around me, going to church, going to the Apple store, apparently caring less about the possibility of an apocalyptic future at the hands of viral nanobots than the time it's taking the barista to knock up a decent flat white.

I want to care as little as they seem to, to rip up all my notes and walk away. 'Relax, it won't hurt,' Thompson whispers, and I feel like I did with my sister again, wanting things to be normal, and frustrated at my seeming inability just to let them be.

Let it go, let it go, Disney sings at me. But I can't. I try to for a while, but the ideas refuse to melt away, and I think that it's perhaps because I keep seeing messages about AI and this limitless digital future drip-fed into our consciousness. An email from a huge telecoms company offering 'Infinity Broadband.' A website promoting 'infinite storage online.' A mobile operator calling itself 'Everything, Everywhere.' A flyer for a Christian group promising 'A Life Without Limits.'

It happens so often that it feels like society is being softened up for something.

I drain the dregs of my coffee and take a walk in the shade of some trees, waiting for my lift. Snake-oil salesmen, they used to be known as: slippery preachers and smooth talking ad-men, trying to pull a fast one with an amazing offer we couldn't refuse, a miracle remedy that would cure all our ills. It's an ancient scam, stretching back to another garden with another snake asking us to question what we knew, a sweet thing sat plump in our digits, one that made the ultimate promise:

God knows, the serpent says, *that the day you eat of it your eyes will be opened, and you will be like God...*

Here it is in the ancient text, our ultimate fantasy, to know all, to become divine.

Perhaps, the couple are told, you were commanded not to eat the apple because God didn't want you threatening his position. *You will not surely die!* the serpent says. *Quite the opposite!* As Plato and Bruno believed, in possession of all knowledge death is conquered.

The snake was lying. The promise could not be kept. Way back at our genesis we ate and we fell, but still we didn't learn.

Thousands of years after this 'fall,' in *The Creation of Adam* Michelangelo depicts us as having climbed so far up again, Renaissance man's finely sculpted human body nearly reaching the level of God. Yet those gazing up at the chapel ceiling know that another has been here before, so close, so hungry to be divine, desperate to take the highest place. One finger-breadth from divinity, they recall the Genesis myth and tremble, knowing that great caution is needed.

This was the dramatic tension behind Michelangelo's masterpiece that left the congregation on the edge of their seats, muttering prayers under their breath: in the push to raise ourselves to the heights of gods, do we not risk repeating Lucifer's ancient hubris, and ending up as devils?

The threat is very real and, in the end, the reason why I cannot let it go is because some of the world's leading thinkers are convinced that it would be foolish and dangerous to do so.

—

In October 2014, MIT held the 'Aero-Astro Centennial Symposium,' and Elon Musk was the star guest. Just a year older than me, he is a fearsomely impressive individual. Having made a fortune from PayPal, he founded the electric car and home power company Tesla, as well as SpaceX, whom NASA now contracts to resupply the International Space Station. His vision goes way beyond that though and, public in his disappointment that things didn't progress from the conquest of the Moon, he's determined to find a way to build a base on Mars.

I think humanity needs to be on the path to becoming a multi-planet species, and to establishing life as we know it in more than one place.[6]

The apparent inspiration for the latest *Iron Man* film franchise, Musk is no Luddite. Yet when at MIT he was asked about AI, his answer was careful, considered, and dramatic.

'We should be very careful about Artificial Intelligence. If I were to guess at what our biggest existential threat is… it's probably that. I'm increasingly inclined to think that there should be some regulatory oversight at the national and international level, just to make sure that we don't do something very foolish.

'With Artificial Intelligence we are summoning the demon. You know all those stories where there's the guy with the pentagram and the holy water and he's like yeah, he's sure he can control the demon… well it didn't work out.'[7]

Watching the video of this exchange, Musk isn't jokey or flippant. He speaks slowly and thoughtfully and ends up so deep in reflection on his own answer that he completely misses what the next questioner says, has to apologise and ask her to repeat it.

This is why I don't tear up my notes.

Playing the clip over and over, the line that keeps grabbing me is 'the guy with the pentagram.' Musk was perhaps thinking of some trashy horror flick, but all I can picture is the godfather of them all, Christopher Marlowe's play *The Tragical History of the Life and Death of Doctor Faustus*.

Like a 16th century Kurzweil, Faustus is a brilliant academic, but he is bored. Having reaching the limits of human knowledge, he wants to push further, and is taken by the promise of magic. Delighted at his ability not only to summon a demon but make him change form, Faustus believes that he has everything under control.

How pliant is this Mephistopheles,
Full of obedience and humility.
Such is the force of magic and my spells!

But he is already in deeper than he thinks. He demands that Mephistopheles obey his every command, but the demon refuses, saying he is already sworn to serve another:

M.: I am a servant to great Lucifer, and may not follow thee without his leave. […]

F.: Was not that Lucifer an angel once?

M.: Yes, Faustus, and most dearly loved of God

F.: How comes it then that he is prince of devils?

M.: O, by aspiring pride and insolence, for which God threw him from the face of heaven.

In some versions of this long-told story Faustus is given a chance to burn his occult books and repent. Marlowe will have none of it. The temptation of omniscience is too much, and he can only plunge onwards, not now towards angelic levels of knowledge but, as demons rise from hell below to take him down, eternal damnation.

A man who rises up using the power of the mind, only to be damned and cast down? The ancient legend of Faust was in fact inspired by the apocryphal stories about another man who dabbled in magic: Simon Magus. But Marlowe fills in the faint outline of this mythical Gnostic with a colourful contemporary of his own. The man he bases his Faustus on had taught in Oxford and London in the 1580s. Marlowe himself had met him through the circle of radical thinkers that included William Shakespeare.

In his fiery lectures this man had vehemently condemned Oxford University for paying too much attention to Aristotle when it should have been focusing on Plato. A subversive Neoplatonist, a heretic teaching an occult system of higher knowledge—that visiting monk who had so impressed Marlowe was none other than the father of the memory theatre, Giordano Bruno.

'When all is done,' Marlowe has Faustus declare, lifting directly from one of Bruno's lectures, 'divinity is best.'

Like Faustus, like Simon Magus, Bruno was fed up with the human limits of knowledge, with the 'natural memory' that we were born with. He saw the orthodox religious teachings and practices of the day as preventing the full blossoming of human potential. Like Faustus, he wanted to push beyond, to augment his faculties by other, occult means.

The memory system that Bruno preached, this mental theatre that would allow all knowledge to be grasped, he represented on paper in a series of concentric wheels. Each contained arrays of mnemonic symbols, but the central disc was reserved for a set of astral devices that Bruno had derived from Egyptian astrology and star-magic. Frances Yates' 1968 reproduction of it in *The Art of Memory* is remarkable for its similarity to a computer's spinning hard drive, but she makes it clear that Bruno's wheels are designed for one purpose only: 'conjuring the demons, or angels, beyond the stars.'[8]

Through astronomic sorcery Bruno will perfect his memory. By summoning the demon he will gain access to a revelation of all things, but in doing so he will damn himself to hell.

—

Can we risk falling for the same temptation? When Elon Musk worries that AI is the greatest risk to our continued existence, when Professor Stephen Hawking adds that, 'the development of full artificial intelligence could spell the end of the human race,' we should sit bolt upright and listen. We might imagine that there should be moral panic, damning AI as a manifesting evil arriving from the future. That there is none is because the demon already possesses us, and it always has.

'Western man is Faust,' Time Magazine wrote at beginning of 1969, awarding its 'person of the year' for 1968 to the three astronauts who had orbited the Moon. 'He knows how to challenge nature, how to dare against dangerous odds and even against reason.'

AI is not from the future. It is like any other technology, a tool that reaches back into our souls and is charged by ancient anxieties about death, both our own and that of our world. Its potential is highly dangerous, but it is no more than another device promising to amplify our human strength, to thrust us upwards, to fulfil our goal of storming heaven and being transformed into gods.

As such, it fits perfectly with the story the ancients told about the birth of craft, one that transports us back to the discomforting might of Apollo.

The first US astronauts were launched into the heavens aboard the *Mercury* missions. The Roman god of trickery and commerce, Mercury's Greek name was Hermes, the lowborn younger half-brother of the aristocratic Apollo.

Sharing Zeus as a father, Hermes' mother was the nymph Maia. As soon as he was born, Hermes became dissatisfied with his place in the world. He was living in poverty in a cave, and so he slipped away. He came across a turtle that he turned into a lyre, then wove a pair of sandals from reed, going on to cunningly steal 50 of Apollo's cows, walking them away backwards, covering his tracks.

Discovering the theft, Apollo was furious and, suspecting his cunning young half-brother, descended to his cave and confronted him. Hermes pleaded that he was just a baby, and soiled himself on Apollo to prove his point. Taking the matter before their father, Zeus laughed it off and told Apollo not to have his high status so offended by this scrap of a child. The arguments continued until Hermes was forced to concede. The cows were returned and Apollo's status restored.

What the Greeks took from this ancient myth was that craft had been born amidst an act of theft from the gods. The lyre and the sandals were the first works of technology, and the stealing of the cattle that followed from them was Hermes' way of demanding equality, of achieving ascension to his rightful place on high with the mighty gods of Olympus.

Since these ancient depths of time, technology and religion have been inseparable. One material, one spiritual, both are about the human struggle to lift ourselves above our fallen state.

Now, in AI we have the final alloying of the two: the technology of religion has become the religion of technology, the lyre and sandals finally perfected to lead us up Olympus where we can become the gods that we truly are.

But wait, the story is not done!

For Plato, writing down this tale, this tale of equality gained simply would not do. Within his philosophy of higher, True Forms above, deities like Apollo were undying, unimpeachable. They could not be subjected to the low cunning of inferior beings. Thus, Plato closes his version of the myth with the divine order restored. Apollo's cows are returned, and the little shit Hermes is put back in his place.

Promised transformation into mighty Apollo, at the close of things we're still Hermes, our brilliant tools no more effective than Catholicism or Leary's acid, another dimension of Thompson's cruel and paradoxically benevolent bullshit.

—

This is what is bugging me: over and again, by gurus and governments and technology giants, we are sold the idea of flight. But who is it that is really taking off?

I'm scooped into a car and, heading to the local Apple Store, it's an endless parade of billboards and churches and churches with billboards. Having a very deep and ancient longing for divinity, it's this myth of higher power that I know is being used to sell me newer and better machines, each of which promises to raise me to ever-more perfect states of revelation.

Just like Father Yod, like Kesey, Leary, von Braun and Jobs, long lines of gods have taken to Silicon Valley pulpits—all white, all men— and preached the good news that *this* time, *this* phone, *this* will be perfection.

The truly beautiful advertisements, the viral marketing campaigns: like the serpent in the garden all of it deliberately over-reaches, promising very big but delivering something less than that. It is not *so* much less to generate too much complaint, but just enough to ensure that, as I open the box and the screen lights up, one of the first things that my newly purchased iPad wirelessly delivers is a tiny pang of disappointment.

I know that this immaculately designed let-down will sit quietly, waiting to be activated after a few months, then growing and mutating and whispering and jeering, insisting that I can't possibly live with apps running this slow, with this paltry number of pixels per inch and this minuscule screen on this dead-weight, slab-thick *piece of shit*.

Priests once made it clear that last week's confession wouldn't deal with this week's sins; now the cult of upgrade insists we return to the cathedral-sized malls and walk the aisles often. So we despise our low states and string our lyres and make our sandals and go out again, believing their messages again that this time, with these tools, Father Zeus will make us equals, going back to the store and opening another door, and another and another, hoping that this time it won't be the void.

And so it goes on, not just in the constant switching of handsets, but in our constant dissatisfaction with everything. We upgrade to a more lively church, we upgrade to a nicer community, further up the hill, out of the city, away from the chaos, all of these moves 'up' attempts to obey the message we are fed from birth that we are gods-in-the-making, that the most human thing that we can do is to constantly augment our humanity, that we should channel our anger and slip from our low cave and thieve from Olympus in order that we might fulfil our destiny and become Apollo himself.

Promised equality with god, is the truth behind the benevolent bullshit that we are destined ever to be Hermes? Is the promise that we can be more just an illusion to keep us at our labours?

Before Plato's time, in an even more ancient version of the story, the action ends with Hermes achieving his goal, Apollo forced to share his power and wealth with his brother. Cows are earthly creatures so, Zeus' reasoning goes, Apollo must have stolen them from the Earth in the first place.

In this earliest telling, Hermes is no thief; he is simply restoring to himself what the powerful gods had previously stolen from him. Unfortunately, this original ending was unpalatable to the powerful, and it still is.

—

It was Steward Brand who splashed across the Whole Earth Catalog that we were all gods, and had better get used to it. Thinking back over his life, I can't help but feel sorry for him, this Hermes from who so much has been robbed. LSD was co-opted by both Leary and the CIA, his Whole Earth vision given a brutal political twist by NASA. Then, having done so much to resource the beginnings of the Internet, a distributed network of countercultural idealists, in May 2013, it was revealed that Apollo had stolen from him again.

Edward Snowden, a highly skilled CIA operative with access to the most secret government surveillance programmes, revealed to journalists the extent to which the NSA and GCHQ had been covertly monitoring every aspect of our lives. Snowden's theft handed to us a taxonomy of what the powerful had been stealing, exposing the extent to which the digital dream has perfectly played out Plato's version of the myth of technology.

For a while, Hermes had the cows and the gods were fooled. Steve Jobs was a hippie through and through. Google *was* like the Whole Earth Catalog, its mission statement clear: Don't Be Evil.

But then comes Plato. Then comes the retelling of the tale. Then come Apollo's accusations of theft, levelled against powerless Hermes by one who has so much power. The cows are returned; Apollo ascends and Hermes is thrown down.

I want to grab Brand by the lapels and force him to answer: if we are as gods, who is it who is *really* approaching deity? The story we are fed is that we are becoming more knowledgeable, more powerful and more able to be present in more places but, as we upload more and more of our personal and private information into 'the cloud,' abdicate more and more responsibility for remembering to the web and sit in shrugged silence while the NSA and GCHQ freely and constantly monitor every digital action we make, it is the technology companies and government security services who are now functionally divine. The more we bind their devices to our wrists and give them permission to know our locations, the more they know the number of our days, the beats of our hearts, the most intimate details of our relationships.

Critics of Kurzweil's vision talk of a possible future where we will be farmed by higher-intelligence machines, but in the worst excesses of my own over-dependence on technology I know that this is already happening. Logging on to the servers of Facebook, Google and Twitter is free, but I am the one who has been genuflecting, my communications harvested for information that can be used to target products at me with laser-guided accuracy, happy to have my every move tracked in return for the repeated message that it is me who is benefiting, me who is achieving lift. I am told that I am winning my freedom through ever-more-human gadgets, even as they turn me into a well-behaved automata, running like clockwork, obeying pings and reminders, advised to walk more, given updates on how I'm sleeping.

With serpentine smoothness, sophisticated advertisements convince us that, with each newly purchased device, with each new aspect of our lives that we move online, it is we who are becoming more powerful, we who are climbing Mount Olympus, we who are storming heaven. But, while all along we are being robbed, it is Plato who gets to write the ending. While the rich steal from the poor, the powerful remain in power by offering the illusion of power to the powerless.

In the heat of the sun, signs on the Interstate pointing to Vegas, I find myself missing Hunter. This was just the kind of grand larceny he loved exposing. To the bullshit of the Maharishi and the bullshit of the Generals he could equally have added the bullshit of the digital evangelists, their promise of a force tending the light no more than a means of sucking wealth from the poor to sustain the status of the wealthy. 62 people in the world own for themselves as much as 3.6 billion of the world's poor can pool together. Forget the 1%. This is the high and mighty 0.0000017% of the population having as much as the lowest 50%, yet still selling them the dream that their ascension is possible.

It's the bullshit of Plato too, and the creed of all his disciples—from Michelangelo and Da Vinci and Bruno and Faustus, through to Huxley, Leary, Yod and onto Bush and Engelbart and Minsky and Hillis and

Kurzweil—has been that there exists some True Form of things, some perfect Apollonian ideal that we can only reach through the sacrifice of our bodies in pursuit of the radical augmentation of our minds. If we could achieve this—through technologies of drugs, religious practice or digital transfer of consciousness—we would grasp such a unified vision of all things that we would be returned to our rightful place back among the gods, omniscient, omnipresent and immortal.

Can low Hermes become high Apollo? For a while Plato eggs us on and holds out this hope, but then, as Heidegger returns to the room, this narrative begins to stink.

The huge companies don't want to admit it, but as much as they perform wonderful acts of revelation, their dazzling technologies *always* enframe and conceal. In granting us a vision of the world in one way, they hide something in another. Though we do have it in our power to begin the world again, Heidegger insists that the worlds we are able to create are, even as we conquer the Moon, inexorably destined to be very like the one we have now: imperfect, limited and failing.

—

In their ancient intertwining, it suddenly strikes me that if this is true for the religion of technology, then it must hold for the technology of religion. I'm in the passenger seat, windows down, layers of me being stripped by the beating desert-dry wind, raw thoughts exposed beneath. Mental roadblocks are being smashed through, forbidden paths trespassed onto.

In our desperate drive to get high, technology and religion are one and the same. 'Be perfect,' the gospel says, 'just as your father in heaven is perfect.' Yet, in asking the question concerning technology, Heidegger also answers that, even in religion, there can be no perfection, no place free from enframing.

Jesus had refused food for 40 days and nights, wrestling with his demons. Twisted into a story about pleasing Daddy and the pursuit of the perfect through the refusal of food, it was spiritualised anorexia, an inherited, unachievable myth striking down my sister and sending me flying with it.

I'd prayed and prayed to purify my mind, just as she'd scrubbed and scrubbed to disinfect kitchen surfaces. We'd believed in a Most High, put our faith in an infallible revelation, been promised the great power of Apollo, ascension to a place where there would be no more dirt or crying or pain. Thinking we were storing up riches in heaven, we'd allowed our lives on Earth to be robbed.

The engine is loud, the sun hot. I feel a little bit Hunter, somewhat empty and fucked up, but surprisingly clear headed too, as if waking from a very, very long trip.

In the yearning to get high, the 60s damaged so many, leaving people like Thompson struggling for mental equilibrium. Pounding through the city I look back over my own life, counting the numbers of people damaged by the quest for spiritual highs, hurt by the fall-out of others doing so. Me, my family, so many others in the Christian world have lived stricken with depression—*anger turned inwards*—as we've fallen short of Our Father's perfection, beating ourselves up for being fallen angels. I can't think of a vicar's family who've not been similarly afflicted, and the numbers are so large that I begin to wonder if Christianity *is* a theologised depression: the divine anger of God turned on himself on the cross, a model of our own ascent-through-immolation.

We pull into the drive. I won't do it anymore. In a low-roofed house in a two-bit suburb of Los Angeles, I finally come to the end of the road. I put my phone down and sit and close my eyes. I put my hands together, and with a few whispered words take back the life I'd stood on a football field in 1984 and given to Jesus.

It goes far deeper than that, and wider. Beyond reclaiming what the church has stolen, in turn I go back through the ledgers of my past and take back all of the parts of myself I've offered to all the technologies that had promised to transport me to an Eden above, all these forces that had claimed to tend the light.

—

In amongst my things is a postcard copy of Gozzoli's painting. I've prayed the prayers and felt the nudge of demons, sought great knowledge and experienced ecstasy and fallen flat on my bloody face. But now, looking at the image again, I see that the true villain is the one who remains quietly seated throughout. The real menace is Nero himself, the powerful, wealthy emperor who demanded that—by whatever means anyone might offer—flight must be achieved.

It's in the state-sponsored religion of his Empire that the story of the existence of Apollo and Zeus is sustained. Priests and magi and financiers in the temple courts are employed to keep the myth of an Almighty God and a divine salvation going. The pomp around temple rites is done in the name of the Most High, but is, in reality, performed to sustain the status of his Royal Highness.

Fundamentalist and extremist versions of this model continue to blight lives across the globe, but even where traditional religious belief has waned, Nero remains strong. With acid and Apollo done, the big technology companies continue his game, shoring up their stock valuations by assuring us that we are slowly being lifted up to powerful godhood, that death will soon be put to the sword, that even if the sun dies a new utopia is coming.

It is not. The inhabitants of Mount Olympus are playing us for sport. Religious factions, the drug lords, the over-bearing state, the sprawling web of technology companies—all of them call down, bid us to get high and join them, luring us with promises of wonderful visions and Elysian Fields. The psychedelic technologies that they offer open up our souls and allow them to rob us when we are most vulnerable.

Huxley's letter to Orwell comes back to me: 'Within the next generation I believe that the world's rulers will discover that infant conditioning and narco-hypnosis are more efficient, as instruments of government, than clubs and prisons...' Far better than all of them is the luxurious panopticon of smartphones and Big Data that we willingly lock ourselves into. The first people to sport wearables were prisoners, released on parole and tagged. Now we all queue to have our movements tagged by multinationals and the state too, flouting our glimmering shackles, choosing to ignore the question of whether it is us who are glancing at our watches, or our watches who are now watching us.

We upgrade and upgrade again, praying that we too will become improved as a result. But the finger-wide gap between us and perfection will not—*cannot*—be bridged. Avoiding this truth is a multi-billion pound business that blows hot air under us to offer the illusion of flight.

LSD, Apollo, digital culture, ecstatic religion—all of it promises that we can be angels, purified, bacteria-free winged gods of instant communication, bright-shining and perfect. It breathes through LED screens and social networks and space tourism. It gusts through anti-bacterial sprays, anti-depressants, anti-ageing creams and gravity-defying surgery. It rushes through drinks that 'give you wings,' all of it an act of permanent sublimation to keep us high at all times. Yet it is a trick of misdirection, the new flying carpet, the updated Indian rope. It masquerades as divine revelation, sustaining the perception of altitude while actually hiding the reality of the approaching ground beneath us, until it is too late.

When Jim Baker mutated into divinity it wasn't as the cunning child Hermes. Flowing robes, long white hair, working at The Source, Father Yod was a strong and muscular god in the mould of Zeus or Apollo, standing tall atop Olympus, boldly gripping his hang-glider and launching himself into the air. But to the brutal shock of his devoted, this fucked-up god fell like a stone and died. It's a tragic story I heard only yesterday, but one I can't now help but stand and cheer, a descent back to honest ground, Apollo exposed as another bilious Wizard of Oz.

'Religion,' Karl Marx wrote, 'is the sigh of the oppressed creature, the heart of a heartless world, and the soul of soulless conditions. It is the opium of the people.' In the long and intimate entanglement of religion and technology that exploded in the 60s, it would perhaps be more accurate to say that it is opium all the way down. Marx's core concern about the alienation of people from their labour is really one about the ways in which capital has conspired, through the alchemy of protestant religion and growing mechanisation, to lift one class away from another. The rich got high, abandoning the poor, then selling back to them means of escaping their condition for a while.

The digital revolution is no more than an upgrade to this same problem: the opiate become virtual. John Gray once wrote that 'we are forced to live as if we were free.' In the same way, in this high-pressure, high tech world, too often we are forced to live as if we are flying. Marx urges us to come down from our trips and admit that we are not. Beneath the blurring clouds of ecstatic worship and the bedazzling fantasies of AI and interstellar travel, we need to see that the reality for so many is hard ground.

I'm so tired. I pull myself into bed and try to sleep. I want to call my sister. I'll try her later.

When he had spoken these things, while they watched, He was taken up, and a cloud received him. On the road out to Bethany, this man so perfect that even death couldn't touch him, blessed them and was uploaded to the cloud, and they went back to Jerusalem with great joy. I close my eyes, hoping he'll never come back, knowing that real happiness lies in living as if he won't.

The people who hide themselves behind a wall of illusion, George Harrison sang on 'Within You, Without You,' the mysterious 1967 song that expanded my world so many years ago. *Never glimpse the truth, then it's far too late, when they pass away.*

Religion, and technology. Born flightless, we first turn to the gods to lift us, and then try to forge wings for ourselves, and then the illusion is broken.

As we finally exhale, as the hang-glider plummets, it's only then that we get to see the grim meat-hook reality of our plight. Just as the sun rose on Kesey's failed Graduation and blew away the Pranksters' dreams, so the parallel fantasies of our own counterculture, our own yearning to escape to Eden via web, will be rudely awakened.

As the vultures circle above and the flies begin to land, just before we are lowered into the ground does this ultimate let down hit us: that we are human after all, that body and mind are the same, that even if the sun dies there will be no final upgrade, no angelic transformation, no closing revelation of coherence; that we were dust once and are now returning to it, that we have been robbed blind by those dressed up as gods, sold consciousness expansion, peace and understanding for £30 a month and unlimited text messages.

Too late to take our lives back to the Advertising Standards Authority, like Father Yod, like Simon Magus, it all comes crashing down, falling to the ground around us as we borrow Kesey's chorus and cry out in sad lament,

WE BLEW IT,

WE BLEW IT,

WE BLEW IT.

C. R. E. WULFF.

MEANS AND APPARATUS FOR PROPELLING AND GUIDING BALLOONS.

No. 363,037.   Patented May 17, 1887.

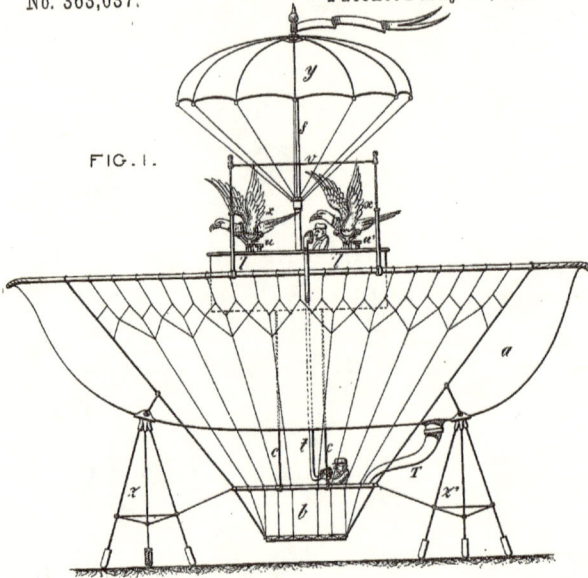

FIG. 1.

FIG. 2.

Witnesses: Inventor:

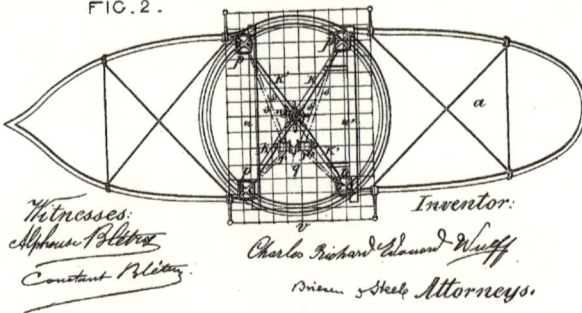

*Patented Design for Steering a Passenger
Balloon using tethered Eagles*

174

7. Returning to Earth

I don't want to blow it.

It's time for me to leave California and return to London. It's an overnight flight; the falling darkness will be accelerated by our trajectory east. The ads all announce great comfort and service, but the reality for those of us flying coach is that you're never closer to being treated as cattle than crammed into the back of an Airbus. Flying thinks it's Harrods. In reality it's Wal-Mart.

'Journeys are the midwives of thought,' Alan de Botton says in *The Art of Travel*, a time where we might imagine that we too might one day surge above much that now looms over us. For the precious moments before the clouds occlude our view we are able to see our world, our lives, from this commanding new perspective, 'the way we must appear to the hawk and to the gods.'

Thrown back in my seat, the airliner thrusts forward and leans into the sky, the crowded urban patchwork of roads and stadia, freeways and scrubland falling into neat order below me as we gain altitude. Above the flies, above the trees, above the skyscrapers, above the birds, above the hills and drones and light aircraft, so many thoughts coming into labour, all the things in my life that have loomed, hawk-like, for so long.

In 1969 Ken Loach released *Kes*, a film based on Barry Hines' 1968 book, *A Kestrel for a Knave*. Set in Yorkshire, not so many miles from where I spent my childhood, it follows the story of Billy, a boy who suffers constant bullying at the hands of his brother and his school, and is both neglected and set upon at home. Billy is terrified of ending up being sent, like all the others, down the pit, underground, mining coal.

Into this impoverished life comes Kes, a kestrel chick that Billy steals from a nearby farm. In training this bird of prey his perspective on life gradually changes, the penetration of the above giving the boy hope that he too might, one day, soar.

Kes: what my sister has always called me. Because of my unusual name people have often made connections with the film and my own Yorkshire roots. An original poster hangs in my lounge. 'They beat him, they deprived him, they ridiculed him,' the strap-line goes in bold black letters across the middle. 'They broke his heart, but they couldn't break his spirit.'

It's me and it's not me. Billy was beaten down and found hope when Kes flew up above him. I was a happy enough boy until the shadow of a terrible hawk darkened my childhood. We both went to the above for help, looking to the sky for solutions to our problems. As de Botton suggests, I turned to flight in the hope of surging above this thing that loomed over me, this hawk that threatened to order my life. Like the ads for transatlantic travel, each technology I put my faith in was a tantalising prospect that turned out to be bullshit.

The plane cuts a smooth incision through the thin air above Canada. So many years ago, that very first flight I'd taken had been thrown around like a paper bag. In that, at least, I'd been in good company: when Montgolfier and Tournachon had risen above Paris they'd been entirely at the mercy of the prevailing winds, unable to steer their craft at all.

If flight was ever to be useful, that was a problem that urgently needed solving. In 1887 a patent was granted to one C.R.E. Wulff for 'a means and apparatus for propelling and guiding balloons.'[1] Steerage would be provided by large birds tethered to a platform above the balloon, the pilot pulling on reins as if guiding a horse. Wulff provided a drawing to accompany his application, optimistically showing two eagles steering a cumbersome blimp against the blowing winds.

'Cybernetics' comes from the Greek word *kubernētēs*, meaning the helmsman or pilot of a ship. It was adopted by digital pioneers thrilled at the tools they were developing that could control the flows of everything from industrial processes to hurricanes of information.

If all technologies are angelic and psychedelic, they are also cybernetic too, attempts to seize the reins and provide steerage through life's strong currents. Struggling to make headway through the fog I'd called upon so many different pilots, *kubernētēs* of religion, knowledge and digital technology all summoned to help me hold some kind of course.

Whatever winds I faced, they were nothing compared to the tempests that raged through the 20th century as a whole. From Titanic to the rotting corpses on the Somme, to the rubble of Guernica and the feather-light remains of Hiroshima and Auschwitz, these years from the first half of the 1900s were hit by extraordinarily powerful storms. Struggling to stay aloft, technologies of religion, drugs and digital augmentation were strapped to the great blimp of Western society, everyone praying that they would help us steer a path through these tragedies and perhaps even help reveal a purpose behind them.

Despite the powerful innovations in each of these areas in the 1960s, each turned out to be as naive as Wulff's tethered eagles. The turbulent, chaotic winds proved too strong, refusing our attempts to tame them. We stood boldly on our tiny blue ship in an unspeakably vast and dark sea proclaiming ourselves helmsmen of the universe, Hunter Thompson the mad stowaway, laughing manically as each *kubernētēs* we put our faith in gave up and failed.

What if there is no final shore to which we are heading? At 30,000 feet the Canadian tundra seems an orderly and straightforward place. Flying higher still, *Earthrise* suggested that Earth was a beautiful and coherent ecosystem, keeping itself in agreeable homeostasis. My plane slams into the night, the sky melts into darkness; I look up, the next landfall some millions of light years above. It took the commanding new perspective of the *Voyager* probes to show that all our dreams of coherence were an illusion, a comfort blanket to protect us from the chilling truth.

A friend in California has given me some Freud to read. I said I'd try not to take too much offence, wondering if I came across as that messed up. He'd laughed and flipped me the bird and the truth is, he's smart and knew what he was doing. After my day at *Deus Ex Machina*, he and I had talked about the illusion of coherence, and here in this book he'd sent was Freud addressing the issue head on.

Aristotle, to use Freud's example, had believed that vermin had evolved from cow shit. This was simply an error, but when Columbus landed in America and believed that he had found a new sea-route to India, he hadn't just been wrong, he'd been under an *illusion*. His mistake had been driven by wish-fulfilment.

That the universe will, in the end, offer up some ultimate purpose is not just an error, but an illusion. It is driven by our great and passionate wish for our lives and deaths to have lasting meaning.

Sustaining this illusion of a perfect being above, a force tending the light, is a major religious, socio-political and cultural project, one that Freud knew consumed huge amounts of time and energy.

You have to defend the [...] illusion with all your might; if it were discredited then your world would collapse, there would be nothing left for you but to despair of everything.[2]

Perhaps we fear that whatever sun warms our world is going to die, but to avoid facing up to this horror we generate illusion upon illusion, defending the collapse of meaning with angelic beings that bring messages of our divine destiny and technologies that will make us immortal. Exploiting our fear of this sense of coherence being discredited, companies and brands and political parties throw up wings that we gladly shelter under, paying them to keep the illusion aloft.

Martin Luther King discredited the illusion of racial and economic harmony and paid for it with his life. Those who feared the collapse of their comfortable world defended it with all their hateful might.

Then there was Hunter, refusing to do so, shooting holes in this bullshit as often as he could, tearing through American culture, pulling back the curtain, turning on the lights, ending the dream. Yet, just as Freud predicted, having uncovered the deep fear and loathing at the heart of his nation, he descended into a deep and angry depression, despairing of everything.

There are tough choices I have to make. In suspended animation for a few precious hours I need to decide which way to fall. Behind me are the tantalising illusions, the delicious ecstasies I have shut my eyes and enjoyed, all of them calling me to turn around and forget what I know and rejoin the throng. The crowd in the club, the swaying congregation, the theology hipsters and their gleaming new devices. *Put your hands in the air* they each call, their melodic insistence masking a thumping bass-line of menace. Ahead, someplace else, a shifting landscape not easy to describe, one for which few maps have yet been made.

Deep down, I already know the answer. Once your world is unmasked as mere flickering shadow, there is no choice. We cannot undo our enlightenment. Painful as it might be, the illusion—once identified as such—is already broken. If journeys are the midwives of thoughts it's perhaps because here—gifted a chance to stop and reflect even as we hurtle forward—the tumbling, nose-diving illusion unblocks the womb of new truth.

Freud knew this; he didn't live to see it in Hunter Thompson, but had observed the process in an equally celebrated writer as they had walked together in 1913, the devastating storm clouds of a vast war gathering darkly on the horizon.

—

I know which way I have to turn, and I know that it won't be easy. Landing in London from California I take a train across the channel and down through northern France, off to meet my brother and some friends for a week's camping on the coast.

It's 50 years since the beginning of those extraordinary years in the latter 1960s. 50 years earlier still, the sound of gunfire and heavy shelling pounded the fields I now pass through as Europe tore itself to bloody shreds in the trenches of Flanders and beyond.

It's the precise centenary of the outbreak of that war and the newspapers I've spread out on my table are full of reflection and memorial, asking how we managed to do such a god-awful thing, turning great innovations in chemistry, mechanical engineering and aeronautics into ever-more efficient ways to maim and kill. It was here that floating mustard gas was used to such deadly effect, here that simple aircraft and tethered blimps were used to spy out enemy lines—Tournachon's aerial photography employed to reap devastation—and here too that Zeppelin airships propelled themselves slowly across Paris, London and other British cities in aerial bombing raids. If technology has the power to transform us into gods then, for these 5 years, we became some of the most cruel and savage deities in all mythology.

With his sharp eye, Freud observed the trauma and loss of illusion precipitated by this awful war, in another short paper titled *On Transience*. It begins with his description of a summer walk in the countryside with the poet Rainer Maria Rilke, a man who, like Thompson 50 years later, like me later still, was experiencing the disintegration of all that he had felt sure of.

The poet admired the beauty of the scene around us, but felt no joy in it. He was disturbed by the thought that all this beauty was fated to extinction, that it would vanish when winter came, like all human beauty. All that he would otherwise have loved and admired seemed to him to be shorn of its worth by the transience which was its doom.

The walk Freud describes was likely taken in 1913, the piece written as a commission in November of 1915 for the Goethe Society of Berlin. Rilke had got to know Freud through his lover Lou Andreas-Salomé—a student of Freud's—and with tensions high throughout Europe, he was in a state of high anxiety at the possibility of being called up for military service. His fears turned out to be true, and when war did break out Rilke found himself marooned in Germany, his property in Paris confiscated, himself then conscripted. With fortune and privilege so many didn't enjoy, influential friends managed to get him out of front-line duties, but these war years nonetheless inflicted terrible mental trauma on him. He produced no poetry at all.

Others managed to. 'Things fall apart; the centre cannot hold,' Yeats wrote in 1919. Instead of the long-expected Second Coming, 'anarchy is loosed upon the world.' The illusion of a benevolent transcendent force guiding the universe lies battered, broken and rotting in the trenches that run like open wounds through Northern Europe.

World War 1 'robbed us of very much that we had loved,' Freud believed, tearing through Rilke's belief that the world he had grown up in was changeless. It wasn't. Despite its apparent solidity it was ephemeral and transient, but it had taken a terrible tragedy to unmask it as such.

Europe, Russia and Asia suffered so much in that war, and the one that followed in 1939. Von Braun and his V2 team surrendered to the Americans because they knew that mainland America hadn't witnessed firsthand the trauma of either of them. Looking out of the train window at the ruined churches and abandoned monasteries, I wonder if this explains why religion is still so popular in the States. The same national trauma, the feeling of violent robbery and shattered illusions only came decades later, two almighty towers that seemed immovable suddenly reduced to fog and dust.

—

In December of 1968, as the Apollo 8 crew looked down from cosmic space and William Anders opened the shutter to take the *Earthrise* photo, what they wouldn't quite have been able to pick out was the scene of ground being broken in downtown Manhattan as construction began on the twin towers of the World Trade Centre. The buildings—at the time the highest ever constructed—would take until the early 1970s to top out at nearly 1400 feet, some 110 floors of glass and steel.

For thirty years they stood until, in September of 2001, two aeroplanes were hijacked and turned into weapons. This was America's blitz, her Leningrad, Dresden or Nagasaki. This was her Babel. People from all around the world had come together and built a tower that reached to the heavens. God, some said, had again smitten those who'd dared challenge him.

I had drunk cocktails in the Windows on the World bar with my wife a few months before 9/11. I returned without her a few years later, shocked by the absence, the vacuum of unfilled space, these two strong towers broken, ruined, gone.

The First World War had sent Rilke into a state of psychic paralysis. One of the books I've brought with me is Eugene Thacker's *The Horror of Philosophy*, his own attempt to get to grips with what traumas like Rilke's do to us. Where Freud calls it the shattering of illusion, Thacker explains it as 'the paradoxical thought of the unthinkable.' Far beyond film or fantasy, war and terrorism open up places of true horror, forcing us to confront our very deepest fears.

He doesn't mention it himself, but as I'm reading—half of me still in America, half racing through old battlefields—one image in particular from 9/11 brings this home for me more than anything else. Shot by the Associated Press photographer Richard Drew, it is the picture of the 'falling man,' plummeting in his white shirt and dark trousers from the very highest floors of the North Tower.

Here is a man in free-fall, without doubt heading to his death. Here is a man who must have looked at his options and taken the decision to jump. His descent would have taken him around 10 seconds, during which the thousands of people who had gathered in shock to see the events unfolding would have watched, then heard the grim thump of him hitting the ground.

He wasn't the only one, by far. Hundreds were caught in the buildings above where the planes had hit, and had no way down. Fire was raging at extraordinary temperatures and smoke was overcoming them. Other pictures show people climbing one on another and another at windows they'd smashed, desperate for air, waving for help. There was only one outcome: they were going to die.

When, on 12th September, Drew's picture spread around the world, there was shock and outrage. Few wanted to face the terrible fact of the jumpers. Many said it wasn't the Christian thing to do, but others saw things differently. One, Jack Gentul, spoke to his wife as she was stranded high up in the South Tower and is sure that she jumped soon after. For him, this wasn't a lack of courage, but the highest expression of it:

'It might have been the last element of control that you have. Everything around you is chaos and you can't stop it. But this is something that you can do.'

Rather than wait longer for her inevitable fate to come, she did the only thing she could to stand up to those who had put her into this impossible predicament. She told her husband how much she loved him, and took her own life.

'To be out of the smoke and the heat, to be out in the air, it must have felt like flying.'

In the image of the falling man, in the extraordinary bravery of one woman's flight, I found myself confronted with the essential horror of existence, forced to face up to unthinkable, unconscionable thoughts.

Though it is hard, the inevitability of my own descent, my own death, is something I can just about grasp. Like the phone on the table in front of me, one day I am going to slow down, shut down and be lowered into the Earth. All my years involved in religion have gone some way to helping me to accept this.

Far more difficult, far more terrifying, is the realisation that behind my death there is no majestic story, no *kubernētēs*, no great force that will finally lift me again. Ironically, it was in believing otherwise that religion prospered in my life for quite as long as it did.

As Freud understood, we defend this illusion with all of our might, worried that without it we might despair of everything. I'd armed myself with any technology that might sustain it, just as, throughout the 60s, people at all levels of society defended themselves against the horror of alienation and the fear of nuclear annihilation by grabbing onto whatever tools might offer them the appearance of flight.

Speeding past the myriad graveyards and war memorials, I know that if I'm really going to make a go of this new direction it's not going to be about facing up to death. It's deeper than that. The reflexes so long exercised within me have been to generate a new illusion whenever the old one is under threat. Church. Club. Books. Devices. For Freud and Jung the process of 'decreation' isn't just about stripping back our anxiety at dying, but going on to dismantle the technology of religion, this psychedelic machine that keeps firing off new stories about the above, promising us that this will make sense of the universe and load our lives with meaning.

If I'm going to refuse to defer to the above, how can I begin to make peace with the ground? My only hunch is that part of the answer will lie in doing what—fatefully—Hunter Thompson appeared to find too hard.

On reaching the heart of the matter and facing the death of meaning, he'd averted his eyes from the horror and fallen to spectacular excess. Following the breakdown of my marriage I'd had some sessions with a therapist and I can picture her now, looking at Gonzo across her bamboo table, him tapping his knee furiously, his jumping eyes hidden behind his shades. Everything about him reads deflection, but she tries to pin him with her gaze, just as she had done with me, equally jittery, trying to wisecrack my way through the sessions.

'What you desperately need,' she says quietly and firmly, 'is to allow yourself to go through a proper period of mourning.'

—

For years after World War 1, Rilke produced nothing. When he finally did it was in a savage, creative storm precipitated by the death of a playmate of his daughter's, the words coming out of this tempest so different to the love poems to God he had written in his pre-war *Book of Hours*.

Opening his *Duino Elegies* in 1922 was this burning question of human horror:

Who, if I cried, would hear me among the angelic orders?...
Alas, who is there will come to help us? Not angels...
Do you not know yet? Fling the emptiness from your arms
Into the spaces where we breathe-, the birds, perhaps,
Will feel the expanded air in quickened flight.

There are no angels in Rilke's post-war world, no transcendent wings to fly down to our aid. The young poet never fully recovered from the war, never spoke again in the sweet, unbroken poetic voice of his youth.

'What spoilt his enjoyment of beauty,' Freud noted, 'must have been a revolt in his mind against mourning.' The inability to fully process death.

I know that sometimes the revolt can take the form of depression. In the face of trauma, we push down into a grief that seems endless. There can be no more beauty. Ever.

At other times we fall the other way into denial, refusing to accept our loss. It was from this ground that Spiritualism exploded after the war: the dead had simply passed onto another place, and here was a religion that had opened up a communication technology with it.

He didn't live to witness the 1960s, but I wonder if Freud would have looked around and concluded that his theory was being played out quite perfectly. Still smarting at a Second World War—thought by many impossible after the first one—young adults born around this time undertook a revolution against mourning.

While the Beat poets and parents of the hippies had descended into a sort of love-less existential depression, the next generation reacted to this bloody wound, to this trauma that had again exposed our underlying transience, with an escape into denial. The deafening roar of motorcycles and rocket engines, the blinding visions of drugs and ecstatic religion, from Hells Angels to spiritual tongues, from LSD to the 'LO' of the birth of the internet—all of it was an increasingly vigorous rebellion against death, the spectre of which haunted more powerfully than ever before in overseas wars, internal racial conflicts and the very real threats of nuclear annihilation.

It's there in the 'Beatlemania' that swept the US in 1964. Landing just 11 weeks after the shocking assassination of JFK, an event that paralysed the nation with confusion and sadness, the band catalysed a mass revolt by teenagers against this national mood of sorrow.

I'd seen it on the plane the day before. In the opening scenes of the film *Gravity*, Sandra Bullock's character turns from grief. Dr Ryan Stone has reached the summit; working aboard the Space Shuttle she is at the pinnacle of her career. Yet all of this—her work, her spaceship, her sealed spacesuit, her breathing apparatus, her high-tech tools—all of it is there to insulate her from mourning the death of her daughter. When tragedy hits the mission, all of these layers of insulation are, one by one, stripped away. The true horror she experiences is not simply that she is hurtling towards Earth, but that she is plummeting naked into a confrontation with the grief she has shielded herself from for so long.

Kurzweil and his Artificial Life movement are no more than the digital upgrade of this revolt. In the face of the death of his father, his own coming death and the death of God, Kurzweil doesn't blink: not only will he *not* die, he will become a god himself—and thus remain permanently insulated from grief.

We keep generating illusions to stop us having to do the hard work of mourning, and gurus and politicians and brands do all they can to help us in this. I know it too well myself: the price we are paying for the constant and intense socio-economic pressure to remain high is in the widespread problem of depression and mental illness. Drip-fed messages about how ecstatic we should feel about modern life, and the awesome heights we can achieve, our subconscious demands balance, dragging us under, acting as ballast against this culture of lift.

Time and again though, through the bright-coloured veil of drugs, through spiritual revivals and the gleaming screens of our devices come more terrible events that pierce and tear and send us scrambling. A death in the family, an illness, a war, an act of terror: momentarily stripped of all of our contrivances, we are horrified to realise that we are not flying, that no one is lifting us, that we are falling and will inevitably, unavoidably, hit the ground and be taken back into it.

—

A book slides off my table and lands with a crack on the floor next to me, one of the snoozing passengers nearby starting awake at the sound.

Hurtling through this rather drab swathe of French countryside, rain spatters on the carriage window where I'd been hoping for glorious sunshine. Is this what life becomes once the illusion is broken, a long horizontal trip through perpetual grey until we finally reach our terminus?

Freud is adamant that it does not.

I dispute the pessimistic poet's view that the transience of what is beautiful involves any loss in its worth.

What Rilke had seen was quite true: nothing was going to last, everything would, at some point, fall and die. But, Freud counters, why should this transience lead us to believe that life is worth any less, that it is any less beautiful?

Rilke had been paralysed by the destructive power of World War 1, but a few hundred miles away, another young writer couldn't *stop* the flow of words.

Exiled in Zürich from 1915 to 1918, James Joyce worked tirelessly on *Ulysses*. He didn't allow the monstrous violence to silence his artistic voice, but channelled its energy through his work, detonating a huge explosion under the norms of traditional fiction, his modernist stream of consciousness gushing from the wounds like a river of fresh blood, smarting and vital.

While Rilke became mired in depression, silenced by the loss of so much beauty, Joyce became invigorated. For him, stasis was death. In the war's tearing down of the pre-modern world of aloof empires and aristocratic elites, in the smashing of old ideas about what could count as high art, Joyce saw only new life.

Jung described the book as 'cold as the Moon looking on from cosmic space, allowing the drama of growth, being and decay to pursue its course.' For Joyce, the shining light of optimism in the face of a transient, non-transcendent world was found in accepting the dramatic cycle of birth and death.

In Homer's original *Odyssey* his hero is prevented from returning home from the Trojan wars by the god Poseidon. Oddly though, after years of searching, when his son Telemachus finds him, Odysseus is not bound in a divine prison, but hiding in a pig-sty, already back on his home island of Ithaca, for some reason unable to take the few steps necessary for his epic journey to be done.

To *be* home, it seemed, would too traumatic. To be home would mean admitting that it wasn't the gods that were enframing him, but his own actions. To be home would mean putting down the tools he had wielded to such deadly effect. To be home would mean becoming an ordinary man, a husband, a father. It would be to relinquish the mantle of the undying hero, to re-enter time and the inevitable journey to ageing, decay and death.

The most courageous thing that Odysseus does is not found in the sexual drama of the Sirens nor in the violence of the battles, but in the act of laying down the illusion that the gods held sway over his life.

Leopold Bloom is Joyce's modern Odysseus, an ordinary man ravaged by everyday battles, but one who refuses to blame the above, nor hanker after immortality. He is a rude iconoclast, youthful and irreverent, finally returning home, the single life-day shown in the book completely transient, but all the more beautiful for being so. 'Yes,' his wife says, opening herself to everything, putting her arms around him, drawing him into her, enjoying all of life while it lasts.

—

Finally arriving in Bordeaux, I catch a bus down to the coast. It's late evening; everyone else has already set up camp and are a good way into a few bottles of wine. Would I like a glass? Yes, I say, yes, and I quickly dump my stuff in the tent my brother has put up. This is home for the next week or so, sleeping on a thin foam mat lain on a nylon groundsheet. Hours ago I was 30,000 feet up, held aloft on steel wings, enclosed in a pressurised cabin; now returned to Earth, camping is life lived as close to the ground as possible, and it's wonderful.

I go and join the others and we laugh and eat and drink, but these are people I've mourned with too, because one of us is missing. Nic, one of my greatest friends, the man I began Vaux with, died of cancer a few months ago.

The diagnosis had been sudden, and definitive. I'd raced up to see him the moment I'd heard and it had seemed impossible. He was funny and alert, and we embraced and talked. But under the surface his body was destroying itself, and there was nothing that anyone could do to stop it. 6 months to a year. He lasted 10.

Sat at my desk in my box-like flat, bullets strafing my wings, fire tearing through my fuselage, it was this that had finally broken me, finally torn apart my flimsy repairs, exposing the true extent of the damage. My own ruptured marriage, the spluttering dysfunction of a family engine, Nic slowly descending, then gone. I'd flown to California to get away for a while. I'd crashed. I'd burned. And now I am here.

His wife is with us, his children are playing. For all of us friends here, mourning has not been an abstract concept, nor an interesting intellectual exercise. We have lived it, and it is with enormous pride that I look around the table at the bar and see these people who have refused to revolt, who have faced the horror of Nic's early death and, somehow, begun to see beauty again.

Cooking on gas stoves, minimal refrigeration, tables and chairs arrayed in the sand under the pine canopy of each pitch... camping takes us off our raised platforms and screed floors and puts us back among the rich cycle of decay. The food that drops to the ground is marched away by ants and beetles, and wasps sniff out the sweetness in opened beer bottles or jars of jam. Nothing lasts long if left out.

Nic understood this. He'd rejected the metaphor of 'battling' his disease and, with no current cure, a terminal diagnosis from the off, had decided to accept and assimilate what his body was doing to him.

In a sense, this was the terrible and unwelcome zenith of all that Vaux had worked towards. In better times we had joked that, amongst all the other deconstructions we were doing, we should write the text of a radical funeral service. Now we were going to have to.

We cannot sustain the illusion of our self-sufficiency. We are all subject to decay, old age and death, to disappointment, loss and disease. We are all engaged in a futile struggle to maintain ourselves in our own image.[3]

Writing on his blog, Nic's refusal to sustain the illusion was extraordinarily brave. Surrounded by those who believed in prayer for healing, in resurrection and eternal life, in 'God's plan in all this somewhere,' to quietly decline the lift these things promised was powerful, and moving, to witness.

Hard as it seems, we have to acknowledge that each one of us at the table will eventually become part of the meal.[4]

Whatever high table we have raised ourselves to, whatever *haute cuisine* we enjoy there, the molecules that make us will one day be lifted on the fork of another to provide sustenance for them. No transcendent meaning in our ending; just the rich, ongoing cycle of life, death, and decay.

In the months after his diagnosis, as we sat and talked and—while he still could—walked along the estuary banks near his home, he reflected on how this acknowledgement might best happen.

It seemed absurd. I was going to live and he was going to die, yet it was he who was ministering to me, helping me to begin to come to terms with the ruins of my own situation.

We spoke of our fathers, of our anger, of the damage the constant reach for the above had wreaked in our relationships.

We spoke and we grieved, and mourned for the passing of these illusions that we watched fall from the sky, burn to ash and die.

—

'Each one of us at the table...' Whenever I hear this I think back to the vicarage kitchen, to the table that had become a battlefield, all of us shell-shocked, all of us looking to higher authorities to offer some reason why we were suffering this war, each of us employing means of being airlifted away. Drugs, religion, starvation: decades spent honing techniques to heightened the illusion that our wounds made sense.

At the end of *Kes*, Billy takes money his brother had given him to place a bet, and spends it instead on a pack of chips, and food for his kestrel. Furious, while Billy is out, his brother wrings the bird's neck and throws the lifeless body into a dustbin. Billy is overcome with grief and rage, but all he can do is perform an act of burial, thankful that, at least for a time, the sky opened up to him and life looked different.

Our wounds do not make sense. Slowly, in the hours I spent with Nic as his body turned on itself, I was able to let go of the hope that they might, and mourn this loss. In his embrace of the Sputnik trajectory of life and death—of rising from the Earth and falling to it again—Nic embodied what Rilke hadn't managed, finding some spark of beauty beyond the horror, however flickering, however transient.

One of the founding thinkers of the Renaissance was the 16th century French writer Michel de Montaigne, who declared that 'to philosophise is to learn how to die.' Far from this being a recipe for some dour life of introspective depression, Montaigne understood it as fantastic liberation. Here was a man who, in his great essays, reminded the world that even 'on the highest throne of the world, we are seated, still, upon our arses,' and that 'Kings and philosophers shit, and so do ladies.'

He would, I think with a smile, have got on rather well with the irrepressibly scatological Nic.

The greatest calling of philosophy is to arm us against illusion, and to quell the revolt against mourning. It counsels us to stop wasting time building our arks and planning our escapes. Then, having revealed to us the illusion of our own ascension, it shows us how to live full lives with our feet planted firmly in the ground and our backsides planted firmly on the wooden seat.

The campsite toilets are a constant reminder of this. It has not been an easy journey for any of us sat round our tents, and each of us has mourned in different ways.

I know some would explain my rejection of high heaven as anger at God over the death of a loved one, but they couldn't be more wrong. If I come across as disillusioned, it is because I am: the illusion has been destroyed. The falling of this one precious man was the very personal horror that allowed the unthinkable thought to come, that let me tear away the final vestiges of my life-long pursuit of height.

I have mourned Nic's life so deeply, yet there is no anger in my loss of the above, only relief and gratitude. 'Grief,' Rilke was finally able to write long after the war had finished, 'is so often the source of blessed progress.'

Out of the city smog, since coming back from LA, since getting up off my knees and refusing to be robbed of life any more, it feels as if I have escaped the smoke and heat. I'm out in the air. I know I am falling, know I'll hit the ground—as we all must—but the days I have now truly feel like flying.

—

Are we allowed a celebration of sorts? Joy could feel a betrayal of grief if Nic hadn't so firmly encouraged it. There is enough rum being served to sink a ship.

In the months before he died it became apparent that his insurance company were going to refuse to pay-out on his critical illness cover, likely forcing his family out of their home. They were claiming that he'd not told them about an episode of pins and needles he'd suffered, and thus they weren't technically liable to honour the policy. Intransigent, doing all they could to maximise profits, the company wriggled out of their financial obligations, and Nic died feeling that he was leaving his family in a financially precarious state.

Aghast at their brutal insensitivity, my friends and I began an online campaign to force them to change their minds. More than 60,000 signatures later—with support via Twitter from Stephen Fry, Russell Brand and Margaret Atwood backing up a rather brilliant legal case built by two other friends of Nic's—the company were forced to climb down and pay the family in full.

The entire campaign was run from a smartphone. Sat at the bar in France, if we are raising our glasses to justice and to a family able to remain in their home, we are doing so because of the extraordinary power of the digital tools that allowed us to square up to a corporate Goliath, one that had no idea what had hit it.

Destroying the illusion isn't about tearing society down, rejecting technology and running to live naked in the woods. (We might be a little drunk, but it's a respectable campsite and there are rules about that sort of thing.) It's more often about reorienting the tools that we have, asking if we are using them to lift away from life and escape, or employing them to haul Apollonian corporate fat-cats back down to Earth. 'The continual questioning from below of any attempt to establish order from above,' is how Simon Critchley puts it in a book I've become very fond of.

Flight is wonderful. Getting high offers us a taste of great liberation. Our journeys into space are dazzling and brilliant, and our moments of ecstasy must not be frowned upon. The danger comes when we mythologise our ascent and use it to narrate our leaving behind of a hurting, unjust world.

Martin Luther King gladly went to the mountaintop, but he did so to see more clearly the patterns of injustice in the world, not to escape them. Just as in his time, those in power over us will still try to deflect anger about injustice away from themselves. The feelings of alienation and atomisation that grew as post-war America moved towards greater industrialisation haven't gone away. If anything, the bruises they inflict on us have simply become so common that, even as rates of depression continue to rise, even as corporations like Nic's insurance company act in more and more demeaning ways, we can't remember life being any different.

Growing up in the 70s and 80s, religion was presented to me as the panacea for all of these ills. Jesus had won victory over the grave. He was the one who would calm my anger, cure my depression, give my life direction and fill up the fissures that had broken through my family. Then came the ultimate get-out clause: if he couldn't quite manage to do these things while I was alive, he was up in heaven preparing a perfect place for when I died.

Why did it take Nic and I so long to realise that religion was not only unable to heal our hurts, but was responsible for causing many of them in the first place? It had taught us to turn our anger upwards and inwards, ecstasy and depression two sides of the same veil that stopped us seeing what really needed to change.

Attendance at church and the numbers of those professing strong religious beliefs have fallen dramatically, but I worry that the problem isn't going to go away anytime soon because we have simply changed the focus of our worship, replacing one angelic hope with another. Glowing instant communications and omniscient servers now offer themselves as the new way to heal our hurts, but—just as with religion—it is the alienating and atomising effects of so much time gazing at icons that is adding to our brokenness. Viral videos turn our necks toward spectacle, social networks digitise our depression, algorithms push our loneliness straight back through our eyeballs. The pews may be empty, but our time spent in head-bowed worship is growing.

If Leary was right, if the PC was the LSD of the 90s, the smartphone has turned us all into John Lennons, permanently tripping in a psychedelic haze, thinking our souls are being wonderfully revealed, but in truth tied up in such tiny worlds of ourselves that we barely make any sense at all. Religion, drugs, microchips: the medication may have changed but the disease hasn't.

It's late now and we're back at someone's tent, talking about all this, wondering if we should all delete Facebook right there and then. Problem is, we'd still have cars and still use washing machines. We could abandon all electrical goods, set up camp permanently, live off-grid... but we'd still need knives, cups, flints to make fire. Falling back through history, tumbling back through evolution, throwing off each tool as we strip life back down to its naked essence... even as cave-men we'd be left with this complex technology of our own consciousness, our very own iOS, encoded in the root language that begins to be written upon our birth.

Becoming conscious of what consciousness does, what miracles it performs and what mirages it generates: this is where the awakening of the soul can begin. Technology companies pursue miniaturisation, desperate to get wearables to disappear into our flesh, but William Blake knew that we already wear the human dress, already have deep within us the lightest, most embedded, most integrated wearable technology imaginable.

It is the recalibration of this most ancient tool that we must work on. Wired for so long to seek confirmation of some higher meaning than itself, it is our remarkable consciousness that bangs on the lid of our skull and demands escape from its cells. In doing so it has driven us to extraordinary invention, but simultaneously mired us in a painful and oppressive illusion. The task we have now is to mourn this dream of our eventual spiritual ascent, and then to rework the root code of our being to prevent the constant regeneration of new illusions that turn our minds away from one another and up to some perfect heavenly above.

Unfortunately, there are those who are working to do otherwise. In pursuit of a flawless, ordered eternity, Kurzweil wants consciousness stripped down and digitised, driven only by logic, enframing the idea of human liberty inside a silicon automata.

One of his disciples, Jaron Lanier, has since turned seer of caution. 'Using digital technology to seek perfection in human affairs is a perfect way to destroy them,' he wrote, echoing Voltaire's maxim that 'perfection is the enemy of good.'

Tragically, it took far too long for my family to find this out.

—

My dear fellow, we must do better than this from now on. It means starting now. We had such high hopes for you in the past. Don't disappoint us all now.

Having researched and written so much, only weeks ago I discovered that this was how the 60s had begun for my dad.

He'd been on holiday in France when he received three letters, each dated 3rd July, 1960, one from his father, one from his mother and one from his brother. It was a parcel of shame for him to unpack, his first year results from Cambridge just published. Lost for decades and never mentioned, though they recently turned up in a box again, their hard words seem always to have papered the rooms within which we grew up.

My father's earliest memory is of his mother's horrified face as he told her he had—for the first and only time in his school life—come second in a test. He had been entered for *everything* early, and always succeeded. On and on this went, until, when he got to Cambridge, he had had enough.

My grandmother to my father: *'We could hardly believe our eyes when we saw it in The Telegraph. It was a terrible let-down... the results in the paper for all to read. An atmosphere of gloom and sorrow has descended on us... We had to explain it to all sorts of people in the town.'* This was Knaresborough, Yorkshire.

Dad had scraped a 3rd, spent the year, as my grandfather disparagingly put it, 'reading novels, listening to the gramophone and playing the piano.' These were the records that were my first music; these, the same orange-spined Penguins that I had later devoured as he had done, his own little ecstasies, his own escape from the pressures of family. But this would have to stop.

'I thought it was only people who got into Cambridge by the back door who got 3's,' his younger brother, still at school, put sniffily in his letter. *'You know that a first in anything is only acceptable in our family. Don't let Daddy down.'*

But Daddy was let down.

My grandfather was the Headmaster of King James' Grammar School, 'The Tiger,' as they called him, who now roared with unconcealed wrath about what needed to be done. My father must work, work and work some more. The letter is peppered with timetables for the mathematics he needed to correct, the histories of the subject he must also read and the philosophy 'which leads to the link between mathematical study and religion.' As he ends, my grandfather is reminded of a prayer which hails, 'O God, how great a geometrician Thou art...'

The prison of trigonometric perfection, the faultless Father in heaven, for whom we must make sacrifices.

A workaholic Headmaster, my father's father had worked himself to the bone. He had done this so as not let his own parents down. Back one generation further: *his* father—my great grandfather—had left school at 12, fought in the first world war then worked in a factory all his life, my great grandmother going into domestic service in 'the big house' aged 12.

Their two precociously bright boys plucked from similar fates by the grammar school system, it had been made clear to them that only hard work would stop the family falling back into impoverished obscurity. My penniless grandfather and his brother had both climbed to the very top, both gaining places at Cambridge to read mathematics.

And then tragedy.

The older child, my grandfather had been prevented from active service in World War 2 because of his eyesight. His brother Ronald, 8 years younger, signed up and served. In 1944, news arrived home that he had been killed during the battle to recapture Dunkirk.

'The Tiger' had just begun his first teaching job. He was now the only remaining son. The responsibility to prevent the family's descent was now his alone. His grief had to be locked down and not discussed, turned inwards as fuel to drive him to lift the family high and clear. In 1944 my dad was 3 years old. It was made very clear from his earliest moments: there could be no room for mistakes or missteps.

In fact, my grandfather's anger at my father's first year performance at Cambridge stemmed from his own feeling of failure. In happier times, back in the early 30s, he'd received his own results from his own first year: top marks across the board. The entire town could be proud, their boy had done good.

Confidence high, my grandfather had been convinced to change course. The real cutting edge was in mathematical physics. Paul Dirac was the Lucasian Professor at the time—the same post Newton had held—and was doing absolutely foundational work on the mathematics governing quantum theory. The leading lights of this dazzling new field came and lectured that summer, and my grandfather leapt onto their tailcoats, switching to a new degree for his final two years.

He couldn't do it. It was too hard. A first in his first year, and he graduated with a pass only. Without a good degree he was barred from applying for the Headmasterships of the top schools. His hubris had been inexcusable; this error now had to be constantly atoned for in unrelenting labour. Crushed by the gravity of quantum theory, he countered it a creed of hard work.

Those who have written about him remember him as a saintly man. A demanding father, he was nonetheless a loving man and a wonderful teacher and headteacher. He never stopped though, and collapsed just as he was about to retire.

Carried out of his study with a fatal brain haemorrhage, he demands that he be allowed to address the school for the last time. 'Stop, I must do prayers!' are the last words he speaks. My father receives a sudden phone call. He rushes to the hospital, but he is too late.

I see it now. With this very sudden death in 1975, the Tiger became the hawk. My father had later returned to Cambridge to study for ordination, a second shot at coming first. In this, his father had desperately hoped, he might find great success. Become a bishop, or at least vicar of a large church.

In pursuit of this hope, Dad works incredibly hard as a young curate in Sheffield. He has an extraordinary and innovative ministry with young people in the city. He is an inspirational teacher and leader, but the constant demands take their toll at home.

He mustn't let Daddy down, but nor must he let God down. By 1973 he is exhausted. He has three young children. Close to burn-out he asks his youth group to pray for him and has a powerful, ecstatic experience, one that Mum struggles to understand, one that affects him for the rest of his life.

If he is to progress he must get his own parish, and as 1975 begins it is all arranged: we will move to the village of South Anston that summer. But, before we do, before he becomes a 'real' vicar, before he can show Daddy that he has not let him down, this terrible phone call comes, and now he must let Daddy down, down on straps into the ground.

In the throes of mourning we have to move. Mum is uprooted from her best friends and we land in a house so large, so cold, that all us siblings demand to sleep in the same room. The work is hard. The seam is not easy to mine. Dad is in charge on his own, and is often absent.

The grief, the lack of closure, all of it unfurls long-folded shadows, the pressure preying on all of us from above. After his own experiences of his own family, my Dad had sought to tame it, to keep it away from his own young, but in the unexpected claws of sorrow the past rips open again and begins to live again in our present. The sight of another coffin being lowered into the earth resurrects the generations-old feeling that lack of work is to blame. He had not been perfect enough.

The flies buzzing above the graveside, the mourners walking away, resistance begins immediately. We turn to whichever angels are closest, open our arms to whatever bright ecstasy is within reach, longing to thrust away from the earth that has taken another loved one, committing to storm the heavenly places above, where there will be no more dying or pain.

Be perfect, as your father in heaven is perfect.

Almost immediately, my sister starts to become ill.

—

Nic and I had talked about this. About fatherhood, about anger, about death and loss and its aftermath.

So many fatherless souls who lit up the 60s—Lennon, Cassady and Thompson—and so many who stepped into the breach, who gathered lost sheep and became fathers to the fatherless: Kesey, Leary, Yod, Manson, Frisbee and Wimber. Fallaci writes her book on space to her father who hated space, this thread running through the decade: what happens when the father dies, or turns out to be less than perfect? When war has taken so many fathers away, and damaged so many more, where does the path lead? Too often it is to the above, to hope of an undying Father in heaven, to an eternal place of childhood purity, a strong man to protect and rule.

Shame, depression and grief: striving to be perfect to please our fathers above us has wrought enough destruction. I am done with it. 'Now that you don't have to be perfect,' Steinbeck writes at the close of *East of Eden*, 'you can be good.'

I wish I could go back in time, back through the line of my fathers and help them to accept this. Pure mathematics and an even purer religion sent us slaving and grasping after a Protestant God that demanded perfection, casting us down into depression at the impossibility of ever achieving it. Steinbeck goes on:

> The gods are fallen and all safety gone. And there is one sure thing about the fall of gods: they do not fall a little; they crash and shatter or sink deeply into green muck.[5]

If only I could have helped them mourn the falling of these gods, helped them face the unthinkable thought, the horror of a world with no angels, the delight of one where children play with them in the mud. Perhaps I would have failed. For the many outside of my family I have been able to speak to, giving up god just seems too hard to do.

The ground of Steinbeck's work was the Great Depression, but a couple of years back a new banking crisis threw the system of global capitalism into the greatest period of doubt it had perhaps ever had to endure. I think it was Slavoj Žižek who said that people found it easier to imagine the end of the world than the end of capitalism, but here we were, global warming vs. global financial meltdown, and only one clear winner. Certain institutions were dubbed 'too big to fail.' Confidence in them had to be preserved at any cost, good money thrown after bad, not so much to pay off debt as pay off doubt. The illusion had to be defended with the might of the political high priesthood. The world, they said, would otherwise collapse.

For so many I've met along all the religious roads I've been down, the idea of a God above has similarly become too big to fail. Belief—or impoverishment of it—has become irrelevant. So long into paths of theological study, so tied into jobs in churches and the homes and insurance plans that come with them, despite their private horror, the public illusion of belief has to be defended to prevent financial meltdown.

The unthinkable thought is not allowed to be thought; bad theology is thrown after good, angels are made to dance on pins, convoluted doctrines are constructed, positions created on futures that they hope will pay off. In theory: God is dead; in practice: He is Risen. A kind of champagne atheism.

If doubt is the wolf at the door, depression is the black dog that this philosophy keeps at home. God must not be allowed to fall even a little. Doing so would land them in deep shit. And over hushed drinks, in quiet corners at conferences, all I've been able to say is this: I've seen the sun die and been through the black hole, and though life is hard there is light on the other side; a light that is transient yes, but one that allows me to look into the faces of my children with an honesty that was not there before, one that is unconcerned about being perfect, one that can celebrate simply doing good.

—

The book Nic gave to me has sat on my desk, *The Religion of Technology*, well-thumbed for its history. I've not wanted to finish it, this last literary gift, but, back from France, I pick it up, something in me ready to move forward, wanting to work out how to live in a future beholden neither to high gods nor high-tech tools.

The French Revolution was the political bleeding edge of the Enlightenment that had sprung from the Renaissance. Liberty, equality, fraternity: the people wanted freedom from a monarchy that claimed to have their best interests at heart but left them starving while they feasted, a monarchy that tried to deflect their anger with the spectacle of flight. They guillotined the king and thought they were done; before long Napoleon had risen in his place.

'So long as men worship the Caesars and Napoleons,' Huxley wrote in 1937, 'Caesars and Napoleons will duly rise and make them miserable.'[6] This is the way of Nero, and there can be no true liberty or equality until we are done with the divinity he represents. The revolutionaries butchered innocent aristocrats and massacred the king but ultimately lacked the courage to put God's neck under the blade.

Fire the laser, destroy the Death Star, kill the Emperor. I know that, for those of us brought up on obedience and duty, this is a frightening prospect. But it must be done because, as Noble says, it is about 'defiance of the divine pretensions of the few in the interest of securing the mortal necessities of the many.' Being done with the myth of cake so that all may eat bread. Or, as Kennedy said about Apollo: for all mankind.

In a fluid dream late one night, I find myself at Rice stadium in 1962, seeing the President rising to his feet. He's meant to talk of the Moon, but he tears up this speech and announces instead a great programme to help Martin Luther King in the elimination of racism and poverty. The same familiar phrases ring out:

We do these things not because it is easy, but because it is hard... because that challenge is one that we are willing accept, one we are unwilling to postpone... To be sure, all this costs us all a good deal of money... but to do all this, and do it right, and do it first before this decade is out—then we must be bold.

What would have happened if, alongside the glories of Apollo we had worked *that* hard to eliminate poverty and inequality?

50 years later I'm worried that we risk making the same choices, opting to fund the divine pretensions of the few rather than securing the mortal necessities of the many. The elite nature of religion—God's chosen people—has given way to the elite nature of consumerism. Choice is god, and we tell ourselves that we deserve that latest upgrade far more than the hungry families down the road deserve to eat.

I'm coming to understand that, in a world like this, talk of atheism or the 'death of God' is absurd. Take one look in an Apple Store, or one peek into a fashion magazine, and there are gods and angelic beings everywhere, objects of our worship promising purity and perfection.

With religion in the past and technology now, the idea that we won't die is the idea that won't die. My forefathers shared so many hopes with men who fill the stages of Silicon Valley: not only are gods alive and well, but we are on a path to becoming one of them. We might find ourselves disappointed with one means of ascent, but we quickly switch to another, and my own life is testament to this fact: the problem of God is that God keeps on being resurrected.

Because of the way our consciousness OS has evolved, the figure of Apollo has become the undying zombie-deity that we struggle to be rid of, a spectre that haunts us with a fantasy about our own enduring spirit. This haunting can become so acute that violence appears to be the only way to be rid of it. I think of Hunter raising a gun to his own head, this the only way to kill off the Duke myth that stalked him and refused to let him live in peace. Then there is Jesus turning to Jerusalem, knowing that to do so would mean death, but this the only way to be done with the Christ figure. We witness these deaths, but then insist on resurrection, summoning their Holy-Gonzo spirits to fund our own narratives of ascension.

I can't do this any more. I refuse this telling of the tale.

Some have heard me say this and beckoned me towards the radical atheism of Dawkins or Dennett, but in the coming world of AI the denial of gods will be a supine abdication focusing on wet curates and parish hymnals.

No, in a world where the illusion of god keeps on being resurrected, we need a set of practices that keep on putting the illusion to death. It's in the face of this that I've found myself wending my way back to Christianity, albeit a form of that is done with any transcendent God, a faint thread I find there of just this kind of process: the story of a perfect god put to death, no angels descending to his aid.

In this retelling, crucifixion is a technology that seeks out and destroys the religious virus that has hacked and taken over our drives, hiding away in the unconscious.

In this re-narration, the Mass is a celebration of the dismantling of these gods who've wounded us. We break bread and drink wine, Apollo torn apart into something perishable, the god we once worshipped at this table now become part of the meal, the sacred art of memory performed as we 'do this in remembrance' of the god who descended and died.

The cry goes up, he breathes his last, the sky goes black. The sun has died.

—

What then of the resurrection? Sitting with friends in France this was the question immediately fired back. I had wrestled for so long with it, then, some time after Nic's death, I found myself interviewing Professor Simon Critchley for a programme I was presenting for BBC radio, a commission squeezed into my continuing work teaching mathematics. I'd been wanting to talk about Montaigne, and his idea that to philosophise was to learn how to die. Then, more in hope than expectation I threw the question of resurrection at him.

'I believe in the after-life,' he said, 'in so far as I believe in the life of those that come after.'

I was stunned. The producer was leaning in, holding the microphone close, me sat in a chair, Critchley stretched out on the bed in his hotel room, black leather boots on crisp white linen. I was trying to formulate my next question but my mind was full of Nic, his widow and his twins. 'Kids, those you love or have been close to,' he went on, filling my silence, 'you want them to go on.'

This was a resurrection I could live with: not that when we die we are raised again, but that those who live on are able to be lifted, can get up from the grave-side and find life once we are gone. The most important task we have is not to achieve our own ascension, but to live well enough that those who come after can, once they have grieved, rise again.

Once we have mourned, once we have grieved for the loss of an above that never was, we rise again and move on and focus on the after-life that is around us, celebrating the time that we have, and striving to build a just and peaceful and sustainable Earth for those who are now and those who will come.

To her great sorrow, Fallaci never had children, never had anyone who came after. Based on her own painful experience, in 1975 she wrote *Letter To A Child Never Born*, a fictional letter to the foetus that a young mother carries...and finally miscarries.

Her life an often tragic one, she was living in New York on 11th of September, 2001. Two planes felling two strong towers, another act of terror carried out by forces of hate against a city that she loved.

She was a lonely woman, one who had struggled to sustain strong relationships. She dedicated *If The Sun Dies* to Theodore Freeman, a man she had loved dearly, killed in '64 as a goose got caught in his engine, the first NASA astronaut to die. She later wrote *A Man* about Alexandros Panagoulis, a member of the Greek resistance whom she'd interviewed and fallen madly in love with. He been killed in suspicious circumstances in a road accident in 1976. For a few months she had been pregnant with his child, a son who died.

Florence had been bombed, and now New York. Were all the Germans she interviewed guilty of Nazi crimes by association? 9/11 seemed to rupture a long-building sac of toxic hate, all Muslims apparently co-conspirators with Al Qaeda, the poor migrants who stood on street corners in Florence as equally culpable as the fundamentalists who followed Bin Laden. Giving no time for the dust to settle, even as the sun was still blotted out by debris, she published a number of vitriolic diatribes against Arab culture.

She died in Florence in 2006, celebrated but tainted, a court case looming for defaming Islam, others hailing her bravery, her lung cancer blamed not on her life-long heavy smoking but on the acrid fumes she'd been exposed to as she'd reported on Saddam Hussain's burning of Kuwait's oil wells.

Her father had been right, perhaps her grandfather too. The men who had taken planes and weaponised them? In Florence or New York—bastards, yes, they were bastards. We were as evil up there as we were down here.

For the love of God, Father, if a door is closed don't you have the urge to open it and see what's behind it? Isn't the story of man a story of closed and open doors? Father, answer me.

For the love of which God had men opened cockpit doors and steered so many innocent lives into the void? For the quest of what love had Fallaci opened her notebook, spent her life interrogating powerful men, trying to process the horror of being attacked from above, trying to understand the pain of death, trying to comprehend the injustice of miscarriage?

The story of man is perhaps this: if we force open doors in pursuit of the love of God, too often we end up closed to the suffering of other people.

'God is love' was one of the central tenets of the faith I was born into. I now wonder, what sort of love is it that seeks to get high, to disappear into a gated paradise and consign those left below to the void of hell?

For me, the only god I can speak of now is one who chose to descend and die, being broken up and consumed in the act. In the upside down Christianity I've been fumbling towards, resurrection is the life that comes after this divine death, this breaking of the illusion that we will become gods.

We get up and walk away, liberated from the looming presence of the Most High, able to work to secure the mortal necessities of the many *because* we continually defy any divine pretension.

This is love: living to fund the life of those who will come after, gifting them to best chance to take from our lives and be able to go on, refusing to knock on heaven's door, committing instead to staying in the room and making peace together.

—

The Moon is full, weakly pushing back the darkness, carrying on its illusion of light. *Illudere,* the Latin verb to mock. So many illusions I have had to break, so many ways I've been mocked by the above, believing the myth of its illumination.

We have been to the Moon, divined a complex astrology of the distant stars. We have explored inner worlds and conjured angelic devices that will fit in our pockets. 'Peace be upon you,' the angels say, but peace will not emanate from the cloud.

I know that real salvation lies in accepting that we will not be saved. I know that life cannot be about the promise of riches in heaven. It must instead be about facing the abyss, shrugging at the mystery of the lack of planetary meaning, but lifting our heads and deciding to look out for one another regardless.

In the days I have ahead of me I know that there will continue to be pain as well as joy. I'm realistic; things won't ever make perfect sense. The galaxies tend towards entropic greyness. The universe doesn't care; only we can do that.

This is the *creatio ex nihilo:* the compassionate something that emerges in the face of the acceptance that there is nothing. True love is not in the magnificent ecstasy, not in the spiritual heights, nor in the technological paradises we construct. It is in the tough choice to return from these high places to be grounded in the earth. It is in withdrawing the hand Michelangelo painted stretching out to touch God, and reaching instead for those around us.

My son grabs my hand as we arrive at an Indian restaurant in Euston. The food is so-so, the service a little lacking, but it's still one of the best meals I've had in a long time. Mum and Dad are here and next to me sits my sister, full of stories as ever, my brother slugging beer as he laughs, his boys either side of him. She's come up from the West Country to do one of her yoga retreats. London, Greece, Kent, her work is about the body and our healthy relationship to it. She's a great teacher. Things are often hard, but she's doing well.

'I've kept pushing at doors,' she said to me on the phone the other day. 'I need to learn to be happy in the room I'm in.' We've been talking a lot more recently, about life, about the past, about everything, and I'm so grateful for her support. She's no idea I've read Fallaci, but here we are, gathered around a table, making room, staying here, not launching away into the void.

A little while back, some of the friends from France gathered up on the estuary where Nic and I walked, straining and laughing and spluttering as we edged a 400kg memorial half a mile down a sandy track and settled it into the shore. It's been made by a old friend of ours, another Vaux co-pilot, a stunning cube of concrete, a place to go and sit, to look out on the water, to feel the heavy gravity of its mass, and remember. Over the past few months this immovable monolith, inseparable from the ground, has helped me enormously as I've made peace with my wounds.

Each of us in the family has our scars, but we are here round this table, our imperfect love for each other casting out the fear that once ate with us. Life won't be easy. For some it is a struggle to talk about what has happened, but my sister and I know that doing so has only helped. Therapeutic conversation is the opposite of flight, has its own anti-gravity: what's been pushed down will inevitably come back up. The art of flying is in gentle descent; that of healing relationships bringing things up to the surface without them causing rupture.

Between mouthfuls of curry, I'm talking to my brother about *Bitter Lake*, Adam Curtis' documentary about Afghanistan. That war and its aftermath, like Vietnam in the 60s, seems a mirror of our own troubled times. Alongside news about the rise of Islamic State and new terrors that threaten our existence, come daily stories of the invention of hoverboards, rideable drones and a fresh push to Mars. History repeats, and as anxiety rises so, inevitably, we seem to be placing our hopes in flight again. There's a new tranche of Star Wars films coming, but as my son talks excitedly about *The Force Awakens*

I'm hoping that, despite such strong historic cycles, there are forces that won't be reawoken in my family.

'What we need,' Curtis concludes at the close of his film, 'is a new story, one that we can believe in again.'

He's right. We need a new myth to take us forward. So many hidden stories have been uncovered. So many emails, letters and diaries of past years have been opened to the light; their words are free to go. In letting them, perhaps my brother and sister and I have begun to find a new story to live by. If we have, I hope it's not too high-minded to suggest that it might be connected to exorcising the fantasy of our ascension, rooting ourselves instead in a love for one another that refuses to look to any greater force to enact it.

Perhaps, in the music Dad and I both loved, we already knew this. In June 1962, before LSD, before America, before Elvis, before Leary, before the Maharishi and the Tibetan Book of the Dead, four lads from Liverpool stepped into Abbey Road studios to record their first ever original song, *Love Me Do*, a record Dad bought in France having pulled his socks up and gained his degree.

14 times in the course of 26 lines and 5 verses that call came: 'love me.' It was a love that catapulted The Beatles to astronomical heights of fame, fortune and influence.

In July, 1969, just 3 days after Armstrong and Aldrin landed on the Moon, the band returned to Abbey Road together for the last time. Harvey Kling was already making plans to visit Osaka, unaware of how much this journey would change him, ignorant of how much his nation had transformed itself under him. LSD had come and gone, Epstein had died, the Maharishi had impressed them and then pissed them off. They had argued and fought and written some of the finest music ever heard. But this was it. They were done.

This was *The End*, part of the final track on their final album, *Abbey Road* the place where it began and would finish, immortalised in the photo of them walking, feet firmly on the ground, across a zebra crossing outside the studio.

In this decade-spanning journey, The Beatles followed almost perfectly the trajectory of an entire counterculture. Over their short life they, more than any other influence, perhaps modelled the path I would take too—taking off, tripping high and then landing again—their transformation perhaps best encapsulated in the lyrical differences between these two opening and closing recordings.

In stark contrast to *Love Me Do*, *The End* comprises just 7 fractured lines, 28 words in total, the summation of what they had learned while getting high distilled down to this, their stark accounting of the after-life:

> *And in the end*
> *The love you take*
> *Is equal to the love*
> *You make.*

Perhaps in the after-life the equation can be even more generous, giving more love than we take. I look at my sister, looking so well, my brother, Mum and Dad, each of us walking towards our end, the next generation following on behind. I hope for clear skies for them, nothing to cast shadows.

The pain of these past few years has been in the hunting of the hawk. I know that in my obsession to track it down I've wreaked havoc in many lives and caused great damage. But in everything I've done I've been determined not to let it prey on my children like it did on me. I hope I have done the right thing. *Twenty years of fast living... Don't do what I have done* — Neal Cassady's words haunt me, all these years of uncontrolled deconstruction, but I hope my children will grow up to understand. It's cost untold amounts, and my life has been something of a wreck, but everything in this emptying has been in hope of funding a better life for them in the future we are now building. A new story, one we can believe in again.

Perhaps Montaigne was only half right: to philosophise is not to learn how to die, it is to learn how to love. We transcend our mortality not when we pop pills and soar into sparkling inner worlds, nor when we climb aboard rocket ships and hurtle above the masses into space. We truly transcend ourselves when we commit ourselves to being equals, to caring for one another here on Earth.

As Felix Tournachon glided across Paris in his balloon, he noted that 'altitude reduces all things to their relative proportions, and to the Truth.' He was right. Flying is glorious, but since taking off 250 years ago, what we have learned from our flights is the final truth that every pilot, every astronaut, every bird eventually falls. The Renaissance and Enlightenment myths that promised otherwise are done; a new one must now be written.

We remember what Karen Armstrong wrote:

The most powerful myths are about extremity; they force us to go beyond our experience. There are moments when we all, in one way or another, have to go to a place that we have never seen, and do what we have never done before.

I have been to many extremes, gone to places I did not want to see and done things I wish I hadn't done. After all these highs, I know that our task cannot be to try to escape our descent, but to find a way of being reconciled to it. For myself, I know that the skies will never be totally clear, that my sister and I are far from fully sorted. Yet distance in time and space brings perspective; anger does cool, seep away, gradually degrade and become more inert.

One thing for sure: the process of reflection and writing has helped enormously. The careful ordering of thoughts and words is not a craft that can forge flawless meaning from life's raw materials, but it does prevent our past becoming an unchartable, sinking mire.

Wherever it is we find ourselves, the gravity of our situation demands that we act, yet the most human response is not flight to some distant hoped-for Eden above, nor to fall to the ground in hopeless despair. Whether by writing or otherwise, we need a different story to live by, one that isn't about abandoning this world, but committing to it.

To transition into such a myth—one that pushes us beyond our ache for transcendence—we will need to go to new places and do new things. The first step towards this will surely be about learning to love, looking outwards from the self, upwards from the ground even though we know that it will—at some unknown time—take us.

My family are walking now to the train, saying our goodbyes, going our separate ways.

We are all born flightless, dropping into this world smooth-skinned and wingless. *Kes* was killed, but I want to believe that a feather remained lodged in Billy, a belief that love could be found, not in the mines or in the air, but in the people around him.

'Some things cannot be stolen,' Nic wrote in bold strokes of paint on one of the last pieces of art he created, and I remember this as I hug my sister.

Our bodies are taken, our looks and sharp minds are looted, our friends, our parents—sometimes even our children too. But as all of this is wrenched away and inevitably falls to the ground, one thing cannot be taken from us, not by gravity nor any other force in the universe.

We rise from it for a while before sinking again, but against the dust of the planet this commitment to love each other endures into the after-life, still takes the wing and lifts us, perhaps even beyond death.

Perhaps.

London—Los Angeles—Lacanau, January 2016

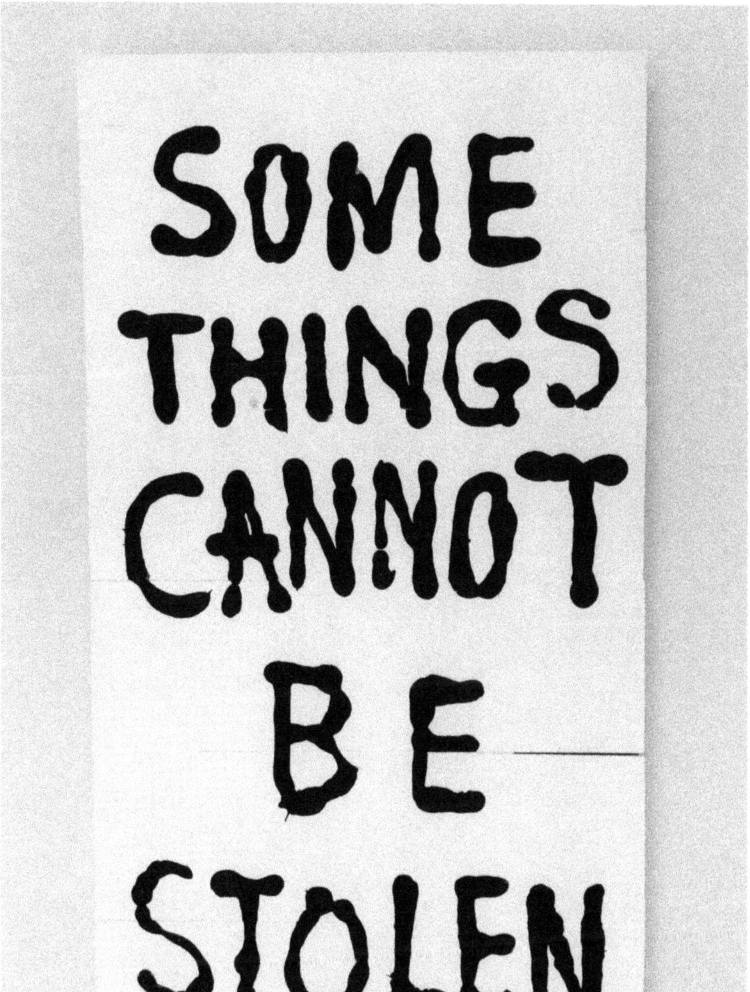
SOME
THINGS
CANNOT
BE
STOLEN

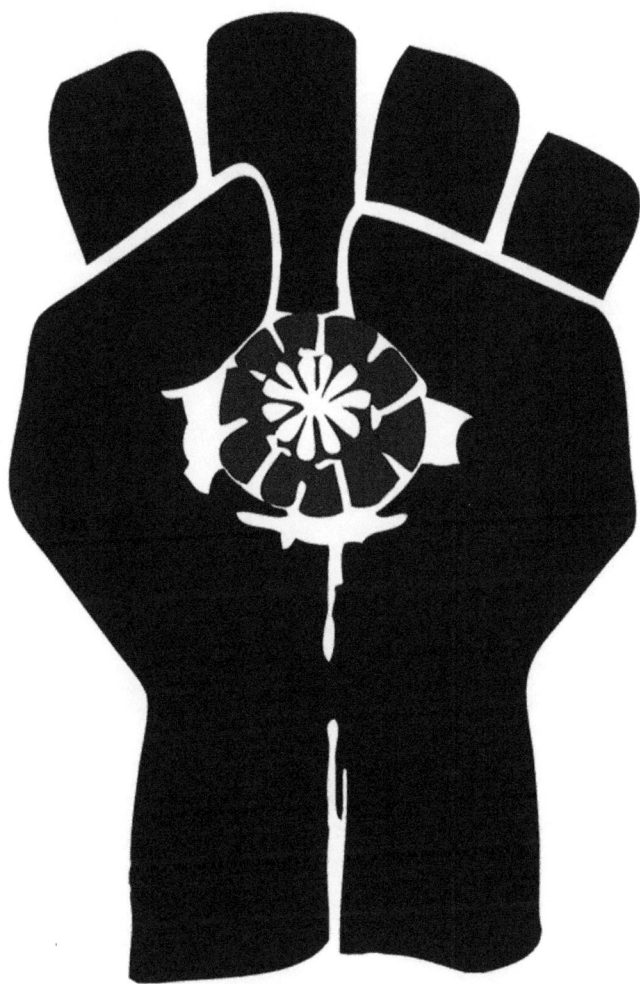

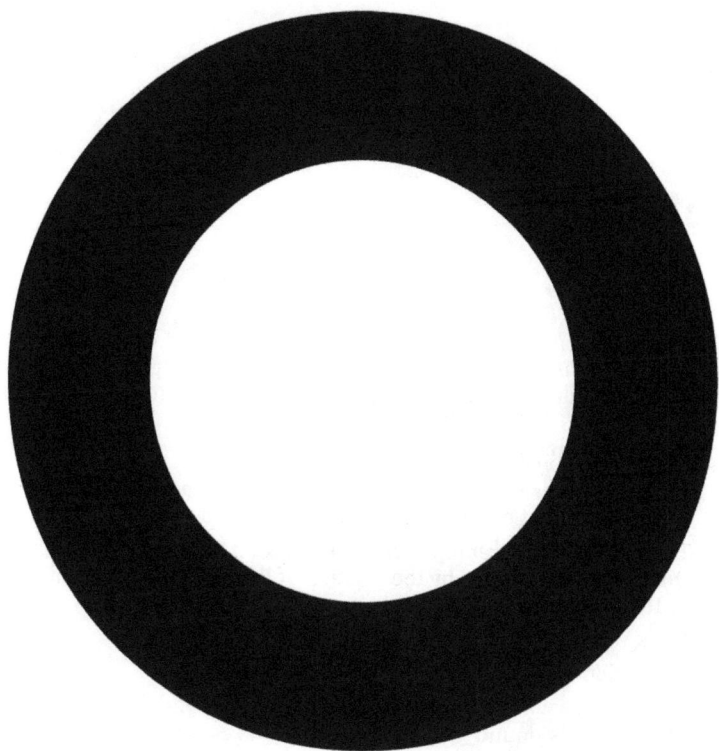

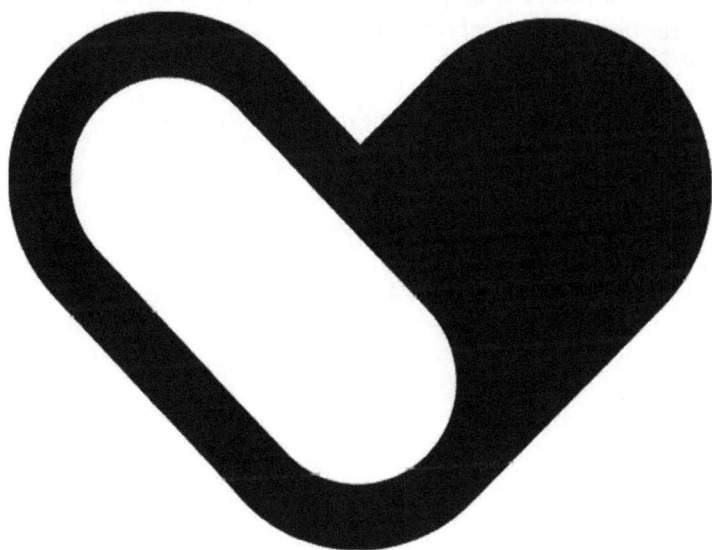

Notes

Chapter 1 - Lift Off

1. Tribbe. M, *The Rocket and the Tarot: The Apollo Moon Landings and American Culture at the Dawn of the Seventies*. https://repositories.lib.utexas.edu/bitstream/handle/2152/ETD-UT-2010-08-1584/TRIBBE-DISSERTATION.pdf?sequence=1 p. 194ff.

2. Macfarlane, R., *Mountains of the Mind*, p. 145

3. Thankfully, this was the wrong gift to the wrong girl, though my sister is convinced that others on the ward were not so lucky.

4. Tufail, I., *The Awakening of the Soul*, Second Septenary: 'Hayy Discovers Fire Kindled by the Friction of Reeds.' Project Gutenberg, 2010, translation by Paul Brönnle

5. Mark 10:29

6. Revelation 21:4

7. See: http://www.gutenberg.org/files/34572/34572-h/34572-h.htm#Hayy_is_found_by_a_Roe_which_takes_care_of_him Accessed 28th March 2015

8. Barnes, J., *Levels of Life*, Jonathan Cape, London 2013, p. 11/12

9. Armstrong, K., *A Short History of Myth*, Canongate, Edinburgh 2005, p. 2.

10. ibid. 3.

11. Gillispie, C., *The Montgolfier Brothers and the Invention of Aviation, Princeton*, 2014, p. 43.

12. *Levels of Life*, 12.

13. *Levels of Life*, 13

Chapter 2 - Getting High

1   *Rig Veda*, Book 9, Hymn CXIII. See: http://www.sacred-texts.com/hin/rigveda/rvo9113.htm

2   As described in Chapter 1 of his book, *LSD: My Problem Child*. Online version: http://www.maps.org/books/mpc/chapter1.html

3   See Stevens, J., *Storming Heaven - LSD and the American Dream*, Harper & Row, New York, 1987, p. 72.

4   Huxley, A., *Moksha*, p. 9

5   Interestingly, new research has suggested that the Nazi invasion of France was powered by German soldiers all soaring on Pervitin, a drug very like Crystal Meth. See http://www.independent.co.uk/news/world/europe/hitlers-allconquering-stormtroopers-felt-invincible-because-of-crystal-methstyle-drug-pervitin-10499087.html

6   Supreme Court report on the MK Ultra program, quoted in http://en.wikipedia.org/wiki/Project_MKUltra. Accessed 2nd Dec 2015.

7   Kesey, K., *One Flew Over the Cuckoo's Nest*, Methuen, London 1962. This edition: Picador, London, 1962, p. 254

8   Macdonald, I., *Revolution in the Head - The Beatles' Records and the Sixties*, Pimlico, London, 1998, p 169.

9   Shapiro, N., *An Encyclopedia of Quotations about Music,* London, 1981, p. 303

10 *Storming Heaven*, p. 146

11 A mission that some still pursue. Writing about LSD evangelist Amanda Feilding, Countess of Wemyss and March, Ed Cumming writes how she believes psychedelic drugs 'dangle the possibility that there is a way to measure the unconscious, to go beneath the operating system and see what's really wrong with the computer.' See: http://gu.com/p/47m7j Accessed 27th April 2015.

12 William Blake, *The Marriage of Heaven and Hell*, from 'Proverbs of Hell.'

13 *Storming Heaven*, 206.

14 Wolfe. T, *The Electric Kool Aid Acid Test*, Black Swan, London, 1990, p. 155.

15 *Storming Heaven*, p. 243.

16 ibid. 173.

17 *The Electric Kool Aid Acid Test*, p. 174.

18 Quoted in Oppenheimer, M., *Knocking on Heaven's Door: American Religion in the Age of Counterculture*, New York, Yale, 2003, p. 23.

19 *Storming Heaven*, p. 247.

20 *The Electric Kool Aid Acid Test*, p. 323

21 Aldous Huxley, *The Doors of Perception / Heaven and Hell*, London, Grafton, 1977, p. 81

22 From *The Village Voice* archives: http://blogs.villagevoice.com/runninscared/2010/01/clip_job_kesey_1.php

23 Sequence of quotes from *The Electric Kool Aid Acid Test*, p. 343ff.

Chapter 3 - Altitude Sickness

1. Wenner, J. & Seymour, C., *Gonzo: The Life of Hunter S. Thompson*, p. 99.
2. Thompson, H., *Fear and Loathing in Las Vegas*, Paladin, London, 1972, p. 202.
3. ibid., 60.
4. Fisher, M., *Capitalist Realism*, Zero Books, Winchester, 2009, p. 21.
5. *Gonzo*, p.11
6. ibid., 178.
7. ibid., 190
8. http://www.maps.org/books/mpc/chapter5.html
9. In a remarkable coincidence, Huxley called this drug 'Soma,' a name he'd lifted from the Hindu hymns praising the drug in the Rigveda - 10 years before Hofmann began synthesising LSD from ergot, a fungus that is a likely candidate as key ingredient in the ancient soma drink.
10. *Fear and Loathing*, p. 178/9
11. See: http://www.beatlesbible.com/1967/08/26/the-beatles-renounce-the-use-of-drugs/
12. See: http://www.yogicflyingclubs.org/yogic_flying.html
13. Acts 2:1 – 4
14. John 10:30
15. Quoted in http://en.wikipedia.org/wiki/The_Times_They_Are_a-Changin%27_(song) (Accessed 15th February, 2015)
16. *The Doors of Perception / Heaven and Hell*, p. 34
17. ibid. 110.
18. See: https://www.youtube.com/watch?v=laamYjSwcHI (Accessed 27th April 2015)
19. *Gonzo*, p. 433

Chapter 4 - Into Orbit

1. Fallaci, O., *If The Sun Dies*, London, Collins, 1967, p. 14. First published in Italy as *Si il Sole Muore* in 1965.

2. ibid. 15.

3. ibid. 17.

4. Quoted in Wolfe, T., *The Right Stuff*, Macmillan, London, 1990, p. 71

5. A hilariously glossed-over view of this can be heard in the commentary of the incident here: https://www.youtube.com/watch?v=zVeFkakURXM

6. Tribbe, 202.

7. *If The Sun Dies*, p. 127

8. *The Right Stuff*, p. 24

9. *If The Sun Dies*, p. 96

10. Tribbe, p. 145

11. Orlando Furioso - Canto XXXVI, vs 47. See: http://sacred-texts.com/neu/orl/orl34.htm

12. Tribbe, p. 219

13. Quoted in Noble, D., *The Religion of Technology*, p. 119.

14. Mailer, N., *Fire on the Moon*. p. 4.

15. Tribbe, p. 150

16. *The Religion of Technology* 126/7

17. *If The Sun Dies*, p. 222

18. Wenner and Seymour, *Gonzo - The Life of Hunter S Thompson*, p. 3

19. Aristophanes speech in Plato's *Symposium*. See: http://www.anselm.edu/homepage/dbanach/sym.htm

20. Sagan, C., *Pale Blue Dot - A Vision of the Human Future in Space*, 1994.

21. *If The Sun Dies*, p. 75

22. See http://mlk-kpp01.stanford.edu/index.php/encyclopedia/documentsentry/ive_been_to_the_mountaintop/

23. In full, from Book VII, 520c: 'Down you must go then, each in his turn, to the habitation of the others and accustom yourselves to the observation of the obscure things there. For once habituated you will discern them infinitely better than the dwellers there, and you will know what each of the 'idols' is and whereof it is a semblance, because you have seen the reality of the beautiful, the just and the good.' See http://www.perseus.tufts.edu/hopper/text?doc=Perseus%3Atext%3A1999.01.0168%3Abook%3D7%3Asection%3D520c

Chapter 5 - Transcendent Man

1. See http://web.mit.edu/STS.035/www/PDFs/think.pdf
2. Yates, F., *The Art of Memory*, London, Bodley Head, 2014, p. 17.
3. See: http://www.gutenberg.org/files/2816/2816-h/2816-h.htm Accessed 17th Oct 2015.
4. Quoted in Tomlinson, J., *Globalisation and Culture*, Wiley 2013, p. 99
5. Noble, D., *The Religion of Technology*, p. 163
6. See http://everything2.com/title/Moravec+Transfer
7. Tribbe., p. 162
8. 53 minutes into the film, which you can find online here: https://www.youtube.com/watch?v=tsg-___K_IAI
9. See: http://www.wellcorps.com/files/TheCreation.pdf
10. Quoted in *The Religion of Technology*, p. 19
11. ibid, p. 6
12. All quotes from ibid..

Chapter 6 - Let Down

1. From private email correspondence with Brand.
2. Heidegger, M., *The Question Concerning Technology*, (trans. W. Lovitt), New York, Harper, 1977, p.4
3. *The Electric Kool Aid Acid Test*, p. 18
4. *Question Concerning Technology*, p.27
5. I'm conscripting Heidegger here too, who used αλήθεια / aletheia — the state of not being hidden — to mean factuality or disclosure.
6. See: http://www.telegraph.co.uk/technology/news/10544247/Meet-tech-billionaire-and-real-life-Iron-Man-Elon-Musk.html
7. See report here: http://techcrunch.com/2014/10/26/elon-musk-compares-building-artificial-intelligence-to-summoning-the-demon/
8. *The Art of Memory*, p. 208.

Chapter 7 - Returning to Earth

1. http://totallyabsurd.com/birdpoweredblimp.htm
2. Freud, S., *The Future of Illusion*, p95.
3. See 'Cancer' post at: http://hauntedgeographies.typepad.com
4. He was quoting from Gary Snyder's book *The Practice of the Wild*
5. Steinbeck, J., *East of Eden*, p. 22
6. Huxley, A., *Ends and Means*, p. 99

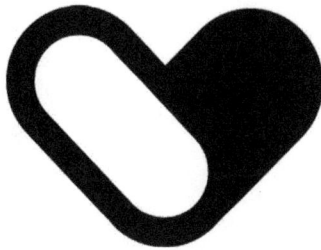

Vaux was formed in 1998 as a collective of artists and practitioners exploring the intersection of theology and contemporary thought through the medium of design, text, performance and ritual.

For 10 years Vaux put on events in and around Vauxhall, London, and became known for highly original, experimental and bleeding-edge approaches to their work.

In 2008, Vaux members took the decision to stop.
The monster must serve, never be served.

In 2011, Vaux created *Apple*, a series of talks and investigations into the much-ignored implications of the spread of digital technology on theology and sociology.

In 2016, in an attempt to fund the still-fledgling project of radical theology and post-theistic thought, Vaux has now begun a small independent publishing imprint.

The aim is to give voice to writers and creatives working on radical theological ideas. Too often, this work lies outside what mainstream religious imprints are willing to publish, or is taken on by academic presses who charge very high prices.

Vaux wants to bridge this gap, and give people space to express their ideas without thought of censure. If you are an artist or writer with high aesthetic ideals who cares about your craft, pitch your idea us at info@vaux.net.

@vaux | vaux.net

haunting theology since 1998

www.ingramcontent.com/pod-product-compliance
Lightning Source LLC
Chambersburg PA
CBHW021843090426
42811CB00033B/2126/J

* 9 7 8 0 9 9 3 5 6 2 8 0 8 *